Early Praise

"*Show Me All Your Scars* shreds the curtain of stigma and indifference that causes us to see the 'mentally ill' as 'them' and 'those people.' In these deeply personal essays, we see 'us' and understand there should be no shame in having a mental illness, only shame in our refusal to offer a hand and listen to those whose scars are badges of courage, resilience and recovery."
—Pete Earley author of *CRAZY: A Father's Search Through America's Mental Health Madness*

"Will shatter your stereotypes of mental illness and its treatment. At once gripping, chilling, compelling, and inspiring."
—Stephen P. Hinshaw, Ph.D., author of *The Mark of Shame: Stigma of Mental Illness and an Agenda for Change*

"When you live with mental illness, you learn to swallow your voice, and keep your stories to yourself. This collection stands as protest against that silence. These writers gather to tell a complex and difficult tale of powerful struggle, triumphant survival, and wisdom hard-won. Writing from multiple points of view—survivor, family member, professional, friend—the authors navigate their subject matter with nuance, insight, and skill. This collection asks us to bring our full attention to the realities of mental illness, and challenges us to create a culture that fosters true mental health."
—Marya Hornbacher, author of *Madness: A BiPolar Life*

"Heartbreaking and soaring. This sensitive and carefully cultivated anthology stands as a testament to the private battle millions of families are waging."
—Sheila Hamilton, author of *All the Things We Never Knew: Chasing the Chaos of Mental Illness*

"An intensely human exploration of the lived experience of mental illness. Harrowing, illuminating, and often surprising."
—Danielle Ofri, MD, PhD, author of *What Doctors Feel: How Emotions Affect the Practice of Medicine*

"Courageous and redemptive, *Show Me All Your Scars* displays the most poignant and stabilizing force in psychiatry and life in general: hope."

—David Fitzpatrick, author of *Sharp: My Story of Madness, Cutting, and How I Reclaimed My Life*

"Beautifully written.... A remarkable gathering of human beings who have dared to tell their stories."

—Robert Whitaker, author of *Anatomy of an Epidemic: Magic Bullets, Psychiatric Drugs, and the Astonishing Rise of Mental Illness in America*

SHOW ME ALL YOUR SCARS:
True Stories of Living with Mental Illness

SHOW ME ALL YOUR SCARS:
True Stories of Living with Mental Illness

Introduction by Patrick J. Kennedy
Edited by Lee Gutkind
Foreword by Karen Wolk Feinstein

Beth Wiles, "Sequelae: The Inner War" originally appeared
in *Creative Nonfiction*, Issue 43, Fall/Winter 2011.

Cover design by Michael Artman
Text design by Zuleikha Erbeldinger-Bjork

Contents

Foreword

Karen Wolk Feinstein

I should warn you that this collection is not a quick or easy read. I could only make it through two or three stories a day. These stories are so intimate, so intense, that I found myself lingering over each writer's fascinating encounter with madness.

With each essay, I met a new acquaintance who quickly felt like a good friend. So compelling and revealing were the narratives that I felt I wasn't just reading the contributors' words on paper; I was sitting in a coffee shop or bar with them as they told me their stories. How many times a day can one do this?

Not that this volume isn't what I had hoped for when I called on Lee Gutkind, the editor of this collection and a frequent collaborator, to activate a network of writers to dispel the common linkage of severe mental illness with *persistent* mental illness. I wanted to read stories of recovery and successful coping; I wanted confirmation—in the form of powerful, first-person narratives—that bouts of psychotic behavior are not life sentences.

After receiving the manuscript for this book, every night I lay in bed and reviewed what I'd read that day. There is so much insight and wisdom in this volume. Even the titles of many of the stories stuck in my head for days: "Make It a Daisy." "Thief of Souls." "Another Trail of Breadcrumbs."

Over the course of the couple weeks it took me to read the essays, I began to understand how those suffering from severe mental illness create and use their stories to explain, minimize, or cope with their pain. Perhaps Jennifer Metsker describes it best when she says that she is both "endlessly sympathetic and impressed," thinking "of all the creative energy that goes into the stories of those who are subject to madness."

Indeed, such stories represent the war going on in the mind as the self desperately tries to make sense of what's happening. Metsker reminds the reader of Dr. Michael Musalek's suggestion that "psychotic symptoms reflect the core existential dilemmas experienced by ordinary people," and concludes that although the world is distorted for those with psychosis, "they still want to take part in the story... They are not just trapped inside a story created by their illness; they are trying to save their own lives." And probably correctly, Susie Meserve observes, "We are all at least a little bit crazy."

Certainly, we are all living inside narratives about ourselves, of which we are the main author. Perhaps we are the good sister—always achieving, always pleasing, studying our Latin while our sisters play. Or the mischievous, rebellious baby of the family, who can push the limits because she is adored and entitled, or because competition with the perfect big sister isn't an option. Often, unless these narratives stop working for us, they carry into adulthood. If we are fortunate, our stories not only reflect reality but also help us develop a useful sense of self. If so, they tilt toward sanity.

I have been stunned by the intelligence that these writers bring in their attempt to understand and control their mental illness without being didactic. Alison Townsend gave me an understanding of the neurochemistry that trumps reason, and what happens when parts of the brain are in conflict. Several of these stories awakened me to the intergenerational nature of suicidal behavior and to how, within a family, self-destruction can seem to be an acceptable method of escaping from psychic pain. Annita Sawyer, Andy Smart, and Optimism One give hope that the cycle can be broken; Ella Wilson, Madeline Strong Diehl, and Yvette Frock Gottshall escape self-destruction, seeking and accepting help in order to protect their children.

And how could I race through the beautiful narratives of family members—their near poetic descriptions of the emotional roller coaster they experience; the curse of beloved relatives who can't love back; the absurd moments of humor that provide relief. As Joyce O'Connor realizes of her autistic son, "I could lose my own sanity trying to make Henry into who I wanted him to be, or I could take a look at my own needs and accept him for who he was." Or Peg Quinn, who describes her "gratitude for the intense experience of trying to stay balanced, though shaking, on the tightrope of life." in the wake of her college-aged daughter's psychotic break.

I grew up with my own family narrative—as, I suppose, we all do, though some more than others. My mother's mother was diagnosed as bipolar schizophrenic. At eleven, my mom watched as the police forcibly took her mother to Bellevue in a straightjacket. My grandmother was angry and violent, and my mother was frequently forced to visit her in the mental hospital at the height of her madness, with traumatic results, until my grandfather moved the children to Iowa. Many years and a lobotomy later, my grandmother was returned to society. I met her only a few times, and not until I was a teenager. Although she seemed sedate and surprisingly alert, her presence terrified my mother, and Mom protected her own family instinctively.

But what if my grandmother had captured her illness on paper? What if she had left a legacy of explanation, describing her journey into hell and her victory over madness, as so many of these authors have done. Would that have helped my mother and the rest of my family overcome our fears? Could it have created a different bond, a kind of acceptance that comes from understanding? Of course, I'll never know. But I do know that the authors here have courageously described their own journeys, and that is an invaluable gift—not only to those who love them, but also to you who are about to enter their stories.

Karen Wolk Feinstein, PhD, *is president and chief executive officer of the Jewish Healthcare Foundation (JHF) and its two supporting organizations, the Pittsburgh Regional Health Initiative (PRHI) and Health Careers Futures (HCF). Appointed as the Foundation's first president, Dr. Feinstein has become widely regarded as the national leader in healthcare quality improvement and often presents at national and international* *conferences. She is the author of numerous regional and national publications on quality and safety; she was the editor of the* Urban & Social Change Review, *and she is the editor of the book* Moving Beyond Repair: Perfecting Health Care. *Additionally, she has served on the faculties of Boston College and Carnegie Mellon University, and taught at the University of Pittsburgh.*

Introduction

Patrick J. Kennedy

Inside these pages, you will meet 20 people who are living with mental illness. Be prepared to recognize yourself. Expect to meet someone just like a person you love. Through the stories that follow, you will reach new levels of empathy and understanding for the full range of human experience.

With exceptionally beautiful prose, the writers who have contributed their stories to *Show Me All Your Scars* bring us inside their daily lives with unprecedented intimacy and clarity. Their stories—and yours—must be told.

For far too long, silence, shame, and stigma has surrounded mental illness in this country. Everything in our culture has told us to clam up and suck it up.

The only way for this to change is for people to share their truth. Total honesty is essential not only for recovery, but also for changing societal attitudes and enacting public policies.

We are transforming how we talk about mental illness in this country. We are moving away from seeing mental illness as a personal or moral failing. We are moving toward a more useful and forward-looking discussion about proper diagnosis and care.

In these pages, you will find hope. With appropriate diagnosis, treatment, and monitoring, up to 80 percent of people with mental illness improve, according to the World Health Organization. It is possible for people, even with serious mental illnesses, to create lives they love, ones of contribution and connection.

It is time for us to stand together and demand an end to discrimination against people with mental illness. Many people do not realize that they have a *right* to care and treatment. My father, Senator Ted Kennedy, and I were the primary sponsors of the Mental Health Parity and Addiction Equity Act of 2008, which was signed into law by President George W. Bush. The Parity Act requires insurance companies to cover illnesses in the brain, like bipolar disorder or alcoholism, on par with diseases in the body, like cancer and heart disease. It has been a slow start, and we have much work left to do, but the Parity Act is beginning to get implemented and recognized as the law of the land.

In speaking out, we find each other. We are not simply breaking free from fear and isolation, as important as that is. We are building a national movement to press insurers, employers, doctors, policymakers, and all segments of society to help every person get the support and care they need.

Show Me All Your Scars is being published in an election year. It is incumbent on all of us to ask the candidates for detailed and actionable plans for improving diagnosis, treatment, and prevention of brain diseases. Once in office, we must hold elected officials accountable for enforcing the laws that can save the lives of our brothers and sisters struggling with mental illness.

Most important of all, we must avoid passing on the stigma surrounding mental illness or addiction to next generation. As parents, we have a duty to create a world where our children's mental health and emotional life is as important as their physical health and academic achievements. Reading these stories and recognizing our common humanity is an important first step.

Patrick J. Kennedy
Brigantine, New Jersey

The Honorable Patrick J. Kennedy *is a former member of the U.S. House of Representatives and the nation's leading political voice on mental illness, addiction, and other brain diseases. During his 16-year career representing Rhode Island in Congress, he fought a national battle to end medical and societal discrimination against these illnesses, highlighted by his lead sponsorship of the Mental Health Parity and Addiction Equity Act of 2008—and his brave openness about his own health challenges.*

The son of Senator Edward "Ted" Kennedy, he decided to leave Congress not long after his father's death to devote his career to advocacy for brain diseases and to create a new, healthier life and start a family. He has since founded the Kennedy Forum, which unites the community of mental health, and co-founded One Mind for Research, a global leader in open science collaboration in brain research. Kennedy is also the co-author of A Common Struggle, *which outlines a bold plan for the future of mental health and addiction in America.*

Patrick lives in New Jersey with his wife, Amy, and their three (soon to be four) children.

Editor's Note

Lee Gutkind

A couple of years ago, an episode of *60 Minutes* featured mothers from a support group for families confronting mental illness. One of them told journalist Scott Pelley about a letter she had received from an attorney representing her neighbors; they were requesting that she keep her mentally ill son in the house. Another mother observed that when her teenaged daughter came home from cancer treatment the family received casseroles and friendly visits and offers of support from neighbors and members of her church—but when that same daughter returned six months later from residential treatment for a mental illness, no one knocked on their door.

Unfortunately, in our society, there is a strong stigma attached to mental illness—in many ways, the worst part of a disease that affects every facet of our society.

In any given year, more than 50 million people in this country have a diagnosable mental illness, and 15 percent of those can be considered seriously mentally ill. By some estimates, nearly half of American adults will struggle with some form of mental illness in their lifetime.

And yet. Not only patients themselves but family members are often viewed with trepidation and distrust; a diagnosis of mental illness can threaten a person's relationships and even livelihood. As a result, few talk publicly about their experiences, and although successful evidence-based treatment models have been developed and researchers uncover new information about the brain every day, many people still blame themselves for their conditions. This stigma remains a major barrier for individuals and families who might otherwise seek help and treatment. Instead, embarrassed and ashamed, they struggle to recover without external intervention or support, as if their medical conditions were personal weaknesses or flaws.

I believe that one of the most important tools we have for combating stigma—by making it clear that mental health difficulties are not so unusual, and by fostering empathy and understanding and helping people appreciate others' experiences more fully and compassionately—is telling true stories. Specifically, personal narratives and memoirs can make a tremendous emotional impact on audiences. Even more compelling, recent research also suggests that people learn and retain more information when facts and ideas are presented to them in narrative form. And there are benefits for the storytellers, too; as a recent *New York Times* "Well" column pointed out:

> Studies have shown that writing about oneself and personal experiences can improve mood disorders, help reduce symptoms among cancer patients, improve a person's health after a heart attack, reduce doctor visits and even boost memory.
>
> Now researchers are studying whether the power of writing—and then rewriting—your personal story can lead to behavioral changes and improve happiness.

Personal narratives can be tremendously powerful and influential; this explains why creative nonfiction is the fastest growing genre in the publishing world, in the academy, and in fields as wide-ranging as history, law, and medicine. And while no one would suggest that storytelling can cure mental illness, it may have particular applications and uses in the field of mental health.

Lately, I am happy to say, a quiet but significant shift is occurring. People have begun "outing" themselves, resisting the shame and fear of isolation. Just like those courageous mothers on *60 Minutes,* people from all walks of life are telling their stories, in hopes that all Americans will begin to understand the struggle and triumph of those millions of people who have battled mental illness. As Patrick Kennedy puts it: "The only way for this to change is for people to share their truth. Total honesty is essential, not only for recovery, but also for changing societal attitudes and enacting public policies."

And this is exactly what I hope this book does. Here, we have collected twenty stories from writers experiencing various forms of mental illness—from schizophrenia to post traumatic stress disorder, from bipolar disease to suicide ideation and self-harm. They have all made themselves vulnerable by confronting the stigma and telling their stories in hopes that readers—you—might better understand the challenges they have confronted to live productive and impactful lives.

These storytellers are not alone. We received hundreds of submissions—thoughtful, powerful, honest stories from writers across the country, hoping to be included in this book.

The title of this collection comes from one of the stories we chose for this collection, and in many ways it signifies what all of these writers are doing. Whether visible or not, their scars can be seen as badges of achievement and sacrifice and courage—and maybe even hope. The author of the title story observes, "We understand that private suffering can be transformed, that it can have an impact on the world. We've learned the alchemy of pain, and some of us find that anguish does not always turn into violence. It can become something beautiful, too."

The writers in his collection have made their choice to tell their stories, despite the possible consequences. We must appreciate and embrace their journeys and their struggles to survive.

Lee Gutkind *has explored the worlds of medicine, technology, and science through writing for more than 25 years. He is the author of 16 books, including* Stuck in Time: The Tragedy of Childhood Mental Illness, *and the editor of nine anthologies about health and medicine, including* I Wasn't Strong Like This When I Started Out: True Stories of Becoming a Nurse. *His stories and op-ed pieces about mental illness and related issues have appeared in the* New York Times *and on National Public Radio.*

Take Care

Ella Wilson

She had to get to the Erie Canal. That much was certain. She had studied the maps closely. She knew the mountain ranges, the rivers and their tributaries, the font of the letters spelling out the words *New York*. She knew the palette of the states. She studied the map until knowing flipped to not knowing. After a while, she could no longer decipher a route to her destination. North, blue, Mohawk River, left, Catskill Mountains, Times New Roman, westward, onward, upward. No matter. She just had to get there; it was the thereness that mattered.

She didn't care when the Erie Canal was built or who had done the building. She knew only that the canal held what she needed: hard labor, honest days, moral values, common sense, perfect truth, forgotten youth. It would be her antidote to time, to all things lost. She wasn't worried about what she would do once she arrived; connection would be easy. Why, the very purpose of the Erie Canal had been connection! Freight moving from railroads to water. Making a connection, following the route, hollowing a root, striking a clue, drifting the blue, guiding the way, finding the day, shining above, sent with love, to New York.

From there, she could hop a boxcar, find a rail yard, talk to a jail bird, sleep on a mail sack, hide in a luggage rack, walk on the rail track. She would watch the stars in the sky barely moving as she rumbled *clickety-clack*. Nighttime on the city of

1

New Orleans, penny a point, ain't no one keeping score. Pass the paper bag that holds the bottle, feel the wheels rumbling 'neath the floor. She would talk to Willie Nelson, or someone who looked like Willie Nelson, and with just a few words and a threadbare smile, so much would be cleared up. Cleaned up. Understood. Overalls.

Emboldened by truth and clarity, she would continue westward ho across a country she had not been born to but had come to. But first, she had to get the kids from school.

The practicality of everyday life threatened to invade her calling as she drove to collect her daughters, but it was too late. The journey had begun. The world was keen to convey that message. Driving down the Brooklyn-Queens Expressway, she felt a profound sense of connection with the road. Every rise and fall she felt in her body, as if she were riding a bison or sitting atop a whale, a slap of the tail. Over waves in the sea, the water and me. Everything was a part of everything: her car, her body, the pavement, the air all moving together like one gigantic ripple through space and time. By the roadside stood a billboard for *Interior Vehicle Protection*. On the billboard was a woman with blonde hair wearing a pink sweater. The blonde glowed, beaming into the car. She was so much more than two-dimensional, and she smiled as she stepped out of the billboard to deliver a message. The car slowed to 40 mph. The woman reached out; now 30 mph. She was smiling; now 15 mph. She gazed up at the giant printed face, and everyone was honking. Cars swerved around her, the gusts shaking her vehicle. Sharply, she turned her eyes to the road, and the message dispersed like confetti. She rolled the words *Interior Vehicle Protection* safely into her brain, storing them for later.

Then there was a coat. Of course, a coat! Riding in boxcars was no mean feat. It was the day before Thanksgiving, and the stores were closing early. First, she called her babysitter, and then she called Barney's seventeen times. Seventeen times she called the store, but no one could verify the existence of this particular coat. Well, of course they couldn't. It was not that sort of coat. So she took the L train to the 4/5/6 uptown. Through Union Square station she tore, knowing what would be around each corner. She dodged and wove and knocked a man over. Backward he went and forward she flew; this was no time for manners. On the train, she used her cerebral cortex to push the wheels northward to Fifty-Ninth Street, Fifty-Ninth Street, Fifty-Ninth Street. Willing it past Twenty-Eighth Street, past Grand Central. The seconds clocked; ten minutes until the store closed. Eyes wide, she tried to judge which side of the train the doors would open. There was a pattern: left, left, right, or was it right, left, right, or left. She burst from the train and ran up the escalator out into the rain. Suddenly disoriented, she leapt from foot to foot, uptown, downtown, uptown. Panic was setting in: left, right, left; she wasn't going to make it. Over Madison, over Park, central reservation, no reservation.

She reached the door of Barney's at 5:58 p.m., two minutes, two minutes. Scared the security guard would turn her away, she tried to hide herself amongst the people exiting. Head down, her chest ripped with cold air and panic. She stumbled red-faced and shaking into the store. The guard touched her elbow and she knew it was over. They had found out. She had been caught. But no! He was offering her a chair. Was she okay? he asked. *Was she okay?* Ha! It was a trick. She would not fall for it. So she smiled at him: Yes, yes, I'm okay, nodding her way into the sea of people. In the elevator, she pressed the number six. The coat was just steps from the elevator door. She freed it from its hanger and paid for it, and then the coat was hers. She knew that, of course; it had always been.

Back on the train, downtown, homebound, goose down. A lady with hair—or was it hands, or maybe a smile—like her grandmother's got on the train and held on to the same metal pole as she did. The same pole! Their eyes met, and in that instant, something secret passed between them and she began to feel safer. At Union Square, it became apparent they were both transferring to the L train. Of course they were! She stood near the older woman, placing herself in peripheral vision so the stranger would know she was there, but without being too obvious. The older woman didn't look at her, but it was clear from the way she moved that she wanted her to be there. So when the hands, the hair, the smile, got off the train, she knew she had to follow up the stairs and out of the station into the cold rain until suddenly, she wasn't quite as sure that she knew what she was doing. The raindrops fell wetly upon her face and she faltered. Suddenly her bag felt too heavy. It was dark. The cold rain was soaking through her leggings. She looked around at the cars and delis, at the grid pattern of Manhattan, and she realized she had gotten off at the wrong stop. She lived in Brooklyn. Her momentum ground to a halt. She was cold. She wanted to go home. She was me.

To have reached thirty-seven without experiencing a manic episode made it all the more surprising when one barreled through my being.

I had been depressed. Many times.

Three years earlier, I had swallowed medication on medication. I was beyond tears. I was beyond most things. I was drifting. I had given up. It was in this place of certain uncertainty that I had slit my wrist; carelessly, I made a slash at death, but my ambivalence won and I lived. I would later see this suicide attempt, this escape route, as a turning point, not because I realized what I had almost lost, not because I had a near death experience or found God, but because my therapist fired me.

Trying to find a new therapist while nursing a slit wrist is like trying to sell a condemned building. It made sense that the only therapist comfortable making such an unwise investment was not typical. She didn't nod while I spoke. She didn't say, *And how does that make you feel?* She never once suggested I try holding an ice cube when I felt like dying. She brushed aside the stories I was used to telling. She dug around in the mess of my past, the terror of my present, and found things, new things. Some good, some worse than awful, but all the better for the love she used in ways I'd never seen. She used love violently, with spit and vigor. She used it gently, with embrace and calm. She used it with warmth and laughter. She used it with disregard and abandon. She had me between her teeth, and she was going to wrestle me to the ground.

With this woman I exorcised demons I did not even know I had. I found my spirit animal, a deer. I strode out into a field of pain and howled at the moon. I scraped the depression from my insides and holed it down into the earth. I let go. I grew wings.

Which is largely why, in April of 2014, I decided that I no

longer needed psychiatric medication. At that time I was taking Seroquel, an atypical antipsychotic used to treat schizophrenia, bipolar disorder, and major depressive disorder. It had been prescribed to me during one of my many hospitalizations. I took it at night and it made me sleep. Heavy, I logged through the nights like a felled trunk. My children would wake me for water or climb in bed with a foot to my chest, a shoulder to my face. I would wake none the wiser. I thought Seroquel was a sleep medication but, rather like calling a cigarette a finger-warmer, I may have been missing the bigger picture.

I had been taking 200 milligrams of Seroquel every night for three years. Three years during which I'd managed to stay out of the hospital. Three years when I'd had periods of depression that had passed. Three years when I hadn't cut my arms and legs, punched myself in the mouth, pulled my hair out, or burned my arms. But I didn't focus on the positive. Instead I pictured my spirit deer, drugged in the woods, unable to stand on her sticklike legs, and I knew this medication was no longer for me, for who I had become—a child of Mother Nature! A being of light! With my deer in mind, I decided not to taper the medication over the course of a year, as my doctor had recommended, but to stop taking it over the course of one day, as no one had recommended.

I wanted to celebrate the fact that there was nothing wrong with me. I wanted my elemental spirit to be stronger than anything cooked up in a laboratory. I wanted to be a warrior princess emerging victorious from a haze of misery and chemicals. So I prayed and meditated and visualized the angels' wings that would carry me. I ate kale! I made smoothies with chia seeds! I welcomed the flax!

At first I felt good, buoyed by rebellion and a belief in my ability to conquer mental illness. Sure, I was waking up early, but oh, the dawn! I sat in my kitchen in Brooklyn and drank tea and watched the dark turn to colors that I did not know came before the blue of day. Flocks of pigeons caught the early light like minnows. I loved my new life! When my children crawled into bed at five o'clock in the morning, I nuzzled them as they fell back asleep, marveling at their softness. I got up and made crepe batter. I read books. I was alive!

By day four, though, the shine had started to wear off. By

day five, I was desperate. I couldn't sleep, and this new life was starting to seem less magical and more frightening.

In the dark of night, the world was quiet. My husband snored; my daughters slept the untidy sleep of children: all arms, legs, and no fear. The night ticked deeper and took me with it. 1:00 A.M., then 2:00 A.M. The aloneness left me unmoored and scared. And so at 3:00 A.M., I raided the bathroom cabinet, washing Benadryl down with Nyquil.

Eventually, I found that by mixing melatonin and Klonopin I could get to sleep, but the longest I could stay there was five hours. So went the next several months.

October was month seven without sleep. The leaves changed colors and my husband, my children, and I drove to our house upstate with a friend for the weekend. With another adult to watch the children, I attempted to take an afternoon nap. It was here, in this nap, that I began to edge over the line from incredibly tired to mildly crazy. I lay curled on the bed, keenly aware of the mountains that rose up behind the house. I felt them bear down on me. They shadowed me with malice. The trees rustled in whispers, clouds loomed, and within half an hour, the very continent I lay on had become untrustworthy. I pulled the covers over me and drafted an open letter to North America and Those Who Call it Home to inform it that I, Ella Wilson, formerly of the United Kingdom, no longer trusted this great nation.

What followed was a manic episode. Suddenly I felt unsafe, hurtling forward into a dangerous unknown. In an attempt to counterbalance my present mania, unrelated parts of my brain sent out carrier pigeons with messages from the past. They tried to guide me to safety, leaving notes and clues. In England, perhaps, where I had been a child, where I had once been held so tight by my father inside his huge, dark green raincoat that I had wanted to live there permanently. Or was it on a canal boat where I had spent a summer watching my father, who for once was not sick, navigate artificial waterways from the back of a barge as we cut lazily through the countryside. My father had listened obsessively to Willie Nelson as cancer took him month by month, skin by hair, veins pulling him like strings away from life. As if, somehow, the world of which Willie Nelson sang might just rescue him. Time ago. Trains in the night.

Wishes and dreams. And now I too, at the edge of life for more cerebral reasons, searched my personal library for anything that could bring me back.

Going crazy was not at all like it appears in the movies. It happened slowly and with much more of my awareness than I would have thought possible. To know you're going crazy is a strange experience indeed. Like hiding behind a wall, jumping out, shouting *boo!,* and then screaming in fright.

Most mental health problems don't look like we expect. People with crushing depression still laugh and clap their hands. People with bipolar depression still go to work, order coffee at Starbucks, tread in dog shit, get married. The day I slit my wrist, I had gone down a slide at a children's play space with my younger daughter in my lap.

I had a psychiatrist, the regular kind, who I had known for seven years—since my first daughter was six months old and I was not feeling the way new mothers are supposed to feel. In fact, I was not really feeling the way anyone is supposed to ever feel. She was a smart woman with a penchant for bluntness that is helpful when you're floating at the end of a balloon string and mumbling about bridges or boxcars or some other topic incompatible with a balanced life. But I was hesitant to bring the Erie Canal to her door because, although she was a psychiatrist, a studier of the mind, she also seemed like she might own a new car and have a cupboard at home for bedding that actually had bedding in it. I thought, in other words, that she was too normal for my craziness. I was more than wrong.

I had tried to tell other people about my designs on the Erie Canal, but at best they had chuckled, and at worst, they had pretended not to hear me. But she did neither. *The Erie Canal? Yes, and what do you think you will find there? Are you receiving messages through billboards or commercials?*

I admitted that I was. I told her how I felt like my brain was a few seconds in the future, that I could actually feel the front part of my head further forward than anyone else's. I could see she understood. At work, I knew what people were going to say before they said it, so I could reply ahead of time, and sometimes the words that came out of my mouth were interspersed with words I was seeing around me, and can you believe that coffee? I know it! But what we can do is take it

7

smartly and just zip-drive it so great until everyone is in the same one and people will iPhone to all of us and shipping!

She nodded. I found relief in her certainty. Yes, she said, you are experiencing a manic episode. Yes, you are having psychotic thoughts, and that is why you are thinking about canals and billboards and following old ladies around the East Village. She even made that seem normal.

She suggested I start back on a low dose of Seroquel. But I wouldn't. I'd fought too hard to come off of medication to go back on it so readily. She called me each day to see how I was doing. Gently, she told me that what was happening in my brain was biological and the only way to stop it from getting worse was to take medication. I cried and didn't take it. She told me that it was okay for me to take the medication. She told me that she was on medication too, and that it helped her. I was surprised, but I still didn't take it.

There was a part of me that desperately wanted to go back on medication. I knew I needed help. Otherwise I would not have answered her calls. But I was in a place where I needed someone to take my hand. Going back on medication had come to mean failure. So I resisted. Then gratefully, if sadly, I surrendered.

The first night I took 50 milligrams of Seroquel and nothing happened. The next night I took 100 milligrams, then 200 milligrams. But I was not coming down. The further the trajectory skyward, the greater the force needed to stop the object in motion and reverse its path. We hit 500 milligrams and my husband had to carry me up the stairs. So we settled on 400 milligrams.

Finally, I could sleep. But as the brakes were applied to my speeding train of unhealthy thoughts, all my hopes and desires also came to a halt. I cried. I hid under the covers. I didn't want canals or expensive coats or old ladies or life itself. When you are on a train rolling away from everything you thought you were heading for—away from your great ideas, away from your plans, away from your family and friends, away from yourself—there is no telling the passenger that this train will turn around. Because trains don't turn around. The driver just switches ends. And the driver of this train was holed up in the bathroom with a list of things she had hoped for in her life, and the passenger had fallen asleep. So it was that I rolled slowly but surely into a dark tunnel.

Then my doctor prescribed lithium, which was supposed to balance my mood. Then Klonopin, after I had more racing thoughts. Then Wellbutrin. Then inositol, which I bought on Amazon and which tasted like icing sugar. But still I cried for the children in Russian orphanages, the forgotten plum, John Denver, the rising of the sun, my children's shoes, New Jersey. Nothing was beyond the scope of my misery.

My doctor, my therapist, my husband all told me this would change, that things would shift, that I wouldn't feel this way forever. It is the temporary nature of depression that the depressive cannot grasp. Like having your head held underwater for thirty seconds, it may be finite and most likely you'll survive, but that doesn't mean you're not going to panic as your bubbles of existence escape to the surface.

My psychiatrist called me daily, after my children were asleep. Sometimes I cried, and sometimes I didn't say anything. But still she called. Like a chime on a clock, like a hand on an arm, like a moon in the sky. She called and said, *Ella, it's time to brush your teeth and take your meds and go to bed.* And she'd stay on the phone while I swallowed the pills. She'd check that I'd had dinner, and if I felt sad, she would say to watch something funny on TV. If I couldn't fall asleep, she'd say to read a book till I was sleepy. If I felt like hurting myself, she'd say to make a cup of tea. It seemed too simple; it seemed too normal.

The idea of taking care of myself was foreign to me. I had grown up in a house of terminal illness: first my father, then my mother. I knew how to take care of other people. This was not because I was especially kind or altruistic. I was especially insecure and desperate. I did not feel at home in my family. I wasn't the first or the best. I wasn't especially smart or pretty; I couldn't do gym; I was scared of horses, dogs, school, other children, the dark, early evening, being alone, crowds, cheese, meat, milk, yogurt, sandwiches, anything that came in a can. But, it turned out, I was not afraid of sickness. When my father was diagnosed with cancer, I began to blossom. I took care of my father in obvious ways, in the plump of a pillow, the anticipation of a cup of tea, the willingness to play Scrabble at all times, the buying of magazines about vintage cars and Swedish furniture design, the listening to of stories about the time his brother had fooled him into thinking he could read Morse code on a sailing trip around Scotland. This was easy for me. I did not mind the low-ceilinged hospital wards, the barren car parks, the damp smell of cigarettes as those who had given up smoked in the designated room at the end of the ward. I did not mind missing parties and sleepovers. I did not mind missing my teenage years. I did not mind missing myself. In truth, it was a relief.

But something got lost along the way, as things are wont to do. Everyone loses something. Bag half-empty, items strewn by the roadside, we arrive disoriented, half-prepared for our lives or, worse, fully prepared for lives that have already passed. I arrived into adulthood, both parents gone, not knowing how to take care of myself. Moreover, I found the notion indulgent, embarrassing, and slightly grotesque.

If I tried to do something kind for myself, like make a cup of tea, I'd feel ashamed waiting for the kettle to boil and I'd click the gas off and walk away. Instead of watching something funny on TV I'd watch a documentary on Margaret Thatcher, because the idea of enjoying myself felt wasteful. If my husband was out I ate toast for dinner, because cooking seemed excessive and the idea of making someone cycle through the Brooklyn night that I might be full made me feel entitled.

One day, my doctor told me she loved me. It was not a dramatic pronouncement; rather, she was explaining that she cared about me, that she'd known me a long time, that she wanted me to be happy, that this was a caring relationship, and that she loved me. Things like this need explaining to those of us who do not trust love or understand caring. I had never expected that my psychiatrist telling me she loved me would be one of my happier moments, but it mattered, because I did not love myself. I was drifting. I was readying to untie the weights from my feet and float up into the sky to return to the dark matter from which I was formed. And this woman was reeling me back with everything she had: lithium and phone calls, Wellbutrin and kindness, Klonopin and text messages, Seroquel and love.

The shift that occurred was not what I had hoped for. But as my therapist had told me years before, it was best to abandon hope. In my hopes, I'd seen happiness and laughter, feelings of joy and love, maybe a floral dress, a sunny day, a skip in my step, and a healthy glow. In reality, what I got was not crying every time I was alone, wearing a different pair of black leggings from the other pair of black leggings I had worn for three months, occasional showering, and not sleeping during the day. That, it turns out, is what a shift looks like. It is slow, but it is real. Medication cannot cure you of depression. Like a seatbelt, it can save your life—but a seatbelt never brought joy to anyone's heart. A seatbelt never put a skip in a step.

And so it was in this new place of not-crushing-depression that I took my children to my friend's house for dinner. She has three children of her own and a colorful history of heroin addiction and bulimia. I felt safe with her. She knew the worst of it.

After the kids had eaten dinner and gone downstairs to watch TV, we sat around the dining table and talked. I may have even laughed. Her husband came home; we said hello. Her au pair had a friend over, and then my five-year-old daughter walked into the room and said, "My mum's going to kill herself."

She did not say it with fear or drama or sadness. She just said it. "My mum's going to kill herself."

Time stopped. My internal organs seemed briefly to fail and I feared I might just turn inside out on the spot. The fact that she was not wrong hung heavy in the silence that followed.

Things were breaking in places I had never been. A window shattered in Delhi; a vase fell in Tokyo; a star exploded in the ninth quadrant of the outer nowhere. I hunched over my daughter in sickness and shame while the world fell apart.

Not until that moment had I believed my inner well could spill over. My existential wanderings, my careless attitude toward life, my disbelief in myself as a viable human being, my starving, my cutting, my hitting, burning and bruising, my hatred, my mania, my depression—never had I considered that any of it could burst its banks.

My belief that as a mother, as the center of my children's universe, I could operate in a vacuum showed I understood little of physics and space. My daughter had inhaled my loneliness, my confusion and ambivalence. She had ingested my depression despite my singing and cooking and trips to the natural history museum, despite my book-reading and funny voices and last-minute sewing of monkey costumes. Despite it all, my death wish had found its way into the curly bouncing head of this child.

With startling clarity, I saw the link between myself and my children. What I did to myself mattered to them. In that moment an uncomfortable equation laid itself out before me: I mattered deeply and profoundly to my children, and they mattered deeply and profoundly to me. Therefore, I had to matter to myself.

A voice began to say, *When you are hungry, they are hungry,* and because I would never starve either of my children, I ate. *If you punch yourself in the face, you are punching them in the face,* and because I would never hit my children, I did not hit myself. I did not burn my legs on the bathroom radiator, and I did not press my arm into the 400-degree oven rack, and I did not slash my legs with scissors or tweezers or anything else. I did not. I did no harm. I took care. Beyond the fact that they were already picking up on my carelessness, I felt a cellular connection to them and I needed that connection, that canal, to learn to take care of myself.

I understood the message that I had been given time and time again. It landed in my soul with a thud to wake all cells. Take care. For yourself, for those you have carried, for the universe, for your deer, for your heart, for your angels, for those you love. There has never been a more selfless selfish act. Take care.

Ella Wilson *grew up on the Yorkshire moors in England and moved to New York in 2002. She has been writing nonfiction for the past twelve years and received her MFA from the New School, where she won the chapbook award. Ella has published work in several anthologies and is currently working on a collection of personal essays entitled* Existentially Challenged: A Merry Romp through Illness, Depression, and Death. *She lives with her husband and two daughters in Brooklyn.*

Chairs

Yvette Frock Gottshall

My mother and I waited outside the courtroom at Fort Meade, Maryland.

She was with me, speaking to me not so much in words but in more of a soothing *shhhh* as we sat on the bench. Or maybe it wasn't a bench but two hard plastic base-issue chairs; I don't remember. After some time, I went into that courtroom to tell the truth. My mother was not allowed inside. There was no one to sit with me then. I was alone. Once my name was called, the fading warmth of my mother's hand stroking my thin, straight blonde hair was the only remnant of her presence and protection, and it was not enough.

I was a good little soldier. The large courtroom was filled with uniformed soldiers and *the* uniformed soldier—the airman about whom I told my truth—was seated at the table behind me. He had someone sitting with him. The chair I sat in was too tall; my feet didn't quite touch the floor. If there had been someone with me at my table, I might have swung my legs out of nervousness, but alone, I was afraid to move. These were men like my father: starched, pressed, stern, with medals across their chests, their ranks displayed on their upper arms and shoulders. Men whose answers always included a "Yes, sir" or a "No, sir."

I answered the questions.

The ones about the airman.

The ones about what he did to me.

The ones about the "timeline." This term, timeline, had to be explained to me.

The events as they happened, in order, first to last.

The telling. It was necessary because this time I had told someone, and my father had called the MPs, the military police.

I was twelve, "eleven when he did what he did, I think."

I don't always remember everything exactly; I will come to understand this later. Even as a child, I knew the true answers were locked inside me somewhere and that I would eventually need help to open all the secret doors and hidden compartments in my head.

I began this work with a pastoral counselor nine years later, when I was twenty-one. Pastoral counselors are different from clinical therapists in their therapeutic approach: the shared religious values of counselor and client *as well as* behavioral-science approaches are both openly employed in the search for stasis or healing. This particular counselor had an office that was located quite a distance from where I lived, but she had been recommended to me by the director of my college's Baptist Student Center. So I drove alone from San Angelo, Texas, to Abilene—two hours each way—to sit in a wicker chair with bright, colorful cushions and unlock my grief. My mother had died in a private-airplane crash ten days before that Christmas, in 1982. *The San Angelo Standard-Times* printed a photo, both above and below the fold, showing the plane's burn trail. It was good to have four hours to think about things each time I went. The reason for the crash, which happened at approximately 11:01 P.M., was never satisfactorily determined. I will never know the truth about my mother's death, just as my mother will never know the truth about Bruce.

Bruce: our teenaged neighbor when we lived on base in Karamürsel, Turkey.

The truth: he had slipped three of his rough fingers into my vagina beneath the towel in which I was wrapped. I was sitting on his lap. He said, "Let's get you warmed up. You must be so cold."

I watched my little three-year-old sister, Glenna, and our friends as they continued to run back and forth through the sprinkler. Our parents, Bruce's and mine, were right there, laughing and telling jokes while they grilled steaks and hot dogs, drank cocktails, and occasionally yelled any time one of the kids veered too close to the barbecue. The barbecue sat on the edge of that square slab of concrete they called a patio, and I think Bruce might have been sitting in a lawn chair, the kind with the webbing woven across an aluminum frame, but it also could have been a base-issue dining chair someone had hauled out into the sun for this holiday get-together. I was five and a half and my mother was pregnant with my youngest sister.

My high-school students are usually high risk. They journal daily. I read their entries each night and I do not grade them for punctuation, nor do I grade them for grammar, although I do make corrections and will often write comments in the margins or draw a smiley face or a series of three check marks followed by an exclamation point. Sometimes I underline a section or phrase combination that I find particularly pleasing. I am teaching them the discipline of daily writing, of daily reading, and I'm gathering intelligence, if you will, about each student, about the class, and where they are particularly in need of more focused instruction. The usual suspects? Confusion about tenses and the proper use of *you're, your, and yore*, which will need some instructional attention and reinforcement.

One student, whose younger sister was also a student of mine, wrote faithfully and sometimes creatively to the daily prompt, but there was almost always a disturbing image or detail worked into her entry—details that would not necessarily be age-appropriate or common teenage knowledge, in those days before the Internet and easier access to every type of pornography.

WHAT I WANT TO SAY TO TRICIA
    who sits in the back row hiding
    in a hard green plastic chair
    behind a silken curtain of Texas
    sun-bleached hair is this—
    I recognize that look.
    The emotional flat line, numbing
    of the pulse of revelation, that visceral

delirium where nerve rats gnaw
at the edges of a darkened spine. It
says, Go away. You'll take a piece
from me I don't even know I
am already missing. Tricia, I want to
slap you. Hard. I want to slap you back
into life again, and have you say: This is
what hurts me. Dear girl,
it's supposed to hurt, those mirrors
appearing suddenly underneath
the bathroom door while you're
undressing. Those you have finally told
me about. There are other soul murders
you cannot bring yourself to write
about in your daily journal, except in slivers.
I want to say these things to you
while you can still
wake up and hear me. Honey!
You're sixteen and that isn't normal,
and it is okay to tell about it.
Keep back the rats of sublimation. Do not
let them eat you in the dark. You sit there, now,
a still, blank, lifeless mask where once there lived
a face, an easily given smile. I recognize that
sleepy look.
Oh, yes.

I read this poem to my current therapist.

She's been my therapist for coming on ten years now.

She listens, occasionally questions me, and sometimes helps reframe the way I am looking at a teaching or parenting situation or perceiving a person's intentions. Mostly, she asks how I am feeling.

"How did that feel?"

"When she said that, how were you feeling?"

"Tell me how you felt when all that was going on."

She is the fourth talk therapist I have had in thirty years, starting with that pastoral counselor back in Texas.

Ten years after my mother's death, while I was teaching Tricia and her sister, I had my first dissociative episode. It happened one Saturday afternoon while I was at home with my husband and our two children—a daughter, six, and a son, three. I think my husband and I were arguing about money as we often did in those lean days, like my parents had, and the kids started crying because they didn't understand why Mommy and Daddy were yelling, slamming things around, and not playing with them anymore.

Suddenly, I was no longer in Texas.

I was no longer a grown woman.

I was eight years old and standing in the next-door neighbor's base apartment on Okinawa. I was breathing too fast, clutching the kitchen counter for support, and listening to my parents scream at one another next door. My sisters had been rescued from the apartment with me. The neighbor had come to get us when the fighting escalated beyond the usual bickering, which was a constant thrum in our family's life. My sisters had calmed, and now they listened to the neighbor's husband read them a story, their hiccupping breaths and snotty noses the leftovers of heart-wrenching sobs.

I did not cry. I held onto the kitchen counter. The neighbor patted my hair and told me, "Everything is going to be fine; come sit down; I know it sounds bad, but everything is going to be fine; you'll see."

"Do you think he is going to kill her?" I asked.

"He's madder than I've ever seen him," I explained, refusing to leave the kitchen or let go of the counter. It was my anchor. Without the counter, I would have been lost. My stomach felt as though I had been kicked repeatedly and I was breathing like I'd been running dashes during school recess. Everything was coming apart. My parents. My body. My good feeling about the neighbors, because now I could hear what they always heard. I realized they could hear everything that happened in our house when my parents fought or slammed doors or threw things. I couldn't cry. I wasn't able to. Something must be wrong with me, I thought.

Someone began to shake me and I was back again, crying with deep racking sobs. David, my husband, held me. He was whispering over and over into my hair, "I've got you, I've got you, I've got you. You are safe, you are safe, you are safe." Our own kids had stopped crying and were hugging me, too. They were repeating the words their father had said, and I knew I needed help—if not for myself, then certainly for them. The buck would stop here. Whatever *this* curse or affliction was, I couldn't pray it or read it or work it or think it away. Not this. Not this time.

Despite my resolve, that night, I had the same nightmare I have had whenever under extreme duress since I was six years old—the dream of the dock.

In the dream, I am out on the boulder-reinforced, berm-like pier, which still extends out into the Sea of Marmara from Yalova in northwestern Turkey. In this dream, I am six and with my father, John; my very pregnant mother, Billye; and my three-year-old sister, Glenna. We are enjoying our walk out onto the far end of the pier. The salty sea air is lifting the dangling strands around my mother's upswept honey-colored beehive, and her skirt is making a wonderful swishy sound as she walks, holding one of my sister's hands and one of mine. My father is walking backward facing us and making my mother laugh. Suddenly, his face distorts and he rushes toward us and pushes us off the side of the pier. My mother lets go of me and grabs a handhold on one of the rocks lining the side of the pier. She is still holding onto Glenna's hand, so Glenna is safe for the time being, but I am trying to find purchase. My hands are too small to get a firm grip and my black patent-leather shoes have slippery soles, which are making it difficult for me to get a solid footing on the sea-slick, very wet boulders, so I am flailing. I am crying, Glenna is screaming, and my mother is pleading: *Why? Why? Why?* My father looks down on us dispassionately and then sticks his heel out over my mother's hand, which is just managing to hold fast to the rock, and he begins to grind her fingers under his shoe. She screams as she falls. As Glenna falls. As I fall. I always wake up screaming.

George, my second therapist, had a lovely, soothing space in a commercial building in Fort Worth, and I would tuck myself into the end of his lush green sofa and grab one of the pillows to hold over myself. He sat in a leather chair, opposite. He was the first to diagnose me as having post-traumatic stress disorder, PTSD.

"That's for soldiers that have seen or been in active-duty combat," I said in response. I would know, having grown up all over the world on military bases.

"Well," he said, "other people can have it too, although most people are only familiar with the term because of our soldiers' experiences."

"PTSD, really?"

"Yes," he said. "And I think you have some very distrustful feelings about your father, too."

I did not know then, as I do now, that all sorts of folks can have PTSD and for all sorts of reasons. I would discover that my myriad traumas, some ongoing since childhood, were the root of my diagnosis. Many other sufferers are likewise unsure of exactly what PTSD *is*. And those who do not suffer from PTSD do not always comprehend its debilitating effects. However, some, who, like my father, see anyone else's suffering as that of a hypochondriac or a malingerer, will scoff at the notion that anyone who hasn't survived active combat or a terrorist attack could possible suffer from: depression, anxiety and/or panic attacks; an exaggerated startle response; hypervigilance; bouts of rage springing inexplicably from the most benign of stimuli; bouts of inexplicable tears; night terrors; flashbacks; body memories; chronic headaches; and a myriad of other symptoms as unique to each person diagnosed with PTSD as the trauma(s) that precipitated the diagnosis.

Having PTSD, I learned, means that when a stressor in your present or something that reminds you of some trauma in the past, like a smell or a sound, acts as a trigger, you might begin to re-experience the traumatic event. You will be in the present physically, but emotionally and even in your physical body, you may feel like you are back in the time while the original event was happening.

"Okay," I said. "So what can I do to stop the stressors?"

"You can't stop them," George told me, "or at least not always, not at first. You must remember that although it feels as if you are, let us say, five years old and powerless, you are actually not five and not powerless. You are in the present. You have survived it, you are safe, and you can't be physically hurt by the memory. Even though it *feels* as if it is happening now, it isn't, so you have to remember and try to calm yourself."

"Okay," I said again. I felt like I was standing on the edge of a precipice and was about to go over. I asked George for a hug. When I am feeling very unsafe, as I was then in George's office, grounding myself, usually through reassuring physical contact with another trusted person, lets me feel that I am indeed safe and that the past is past and cannot harm me now. Back in the neighbor's kitchen, I think she understood this, but I didn't trust her to know how to make me safe, let alone *make me safe*. Instead of hugging the neighbor, I had held the counter.

George was a very calm, soft-spoken teddy bear of a man with a full beard that was turning gray. He was all loose-fitted shirts and khakis and cracked well-worn Sperry topsiders without socks; George was a person simply giving me information about myself. He explained that he understood that I probably felt very vulnerable just now and that he completely understood my need for a hug, but he could not cross that professional boundary. He did recommend that I see a psychiatrist for help with my depressive episodes and my anxiety in certain social situations. He would continue to see me for talk therapy, he explained, but I might need some medication to help my brain get some of its equilibrium back. This was when I learned the difference between a psychotherapist and a psychiatrist.

"You mean like I have brain damage or something?"

"Not exactly," he said. "More like parts of your brain have experienced some traumas and so some healthy connections that were severed as a result need to be reestablished."

I went to see the psychiatrist he recommended and was prescribed Prozac.

I was on antidepressants of one kind or another for the next twenty years.

Our children grew. David and I worked on ourselves and continued to process the implications of my mental health issues—and his. We processed together and tried to parse, with fear and trembling: what is mine; what is yours; what is ours, and what are we passing along to our kids in terms of nurture given our individual natures and our families of origin? Our marriage was built on a firm foundation of friendship, communication (even the most excruciatingly honest kind), and a shared love of books and ideas. We were best friends for five years before the thought of romance had entered our minds.

In 1997, we moved across the country in the midst of our own little family's recession. Within three weeks, we had both lost our jobs: his at a water-quality testing lab in Dallas and mine, a grant-funded instructor position at Texas Christian University. After months of unsuccessful searching in Texas, we cast the net wider and decided upon Vermont as the place we wanted to raise our children, now twelve and nine. We sold everything we did not absolutely need and moved—without jobs, but with a crazy, wild faith and hope—to Vermont. We packed up our two kids, two dogs, and two hamsters and arrived in the Green Mountain State with two hundred dollars. The kindness and generosity of strangers and a few dear friends housed us, helped us enroll our kids in good schools, located our first minimum-wage jobs, and eventually put us in a rental house where we began to rebuild our lives from the bottom up.

Before my mother's awful death, I managed quite well—through a combination of physical activity, youthful joie de vivre, and faith coupled with a voracious reading habit—to heal myself. However, as I grew older, I came to understand that, just like a regular trip to the dentist is a needful thing, just as a yearly physical is a needful thing, so too is a trip to a therapist. At least it is for me when things have gone awry. When what has been working stops working and I'm out of ideas or even clues as to what might be wrong with me, I will set off again in search of a therapist.

So much of my work in therapy has been focused on my childhood. In one particular session, my therapist and I began discussing games like musical chairs and Duck, Duck, Goose! Such group activities are fun and exciting and often provide what we think is a reprieve from more serious learning, but these games are, in actuality, a type of practice for very real experiences of exclusion. Through such friendly competition, ideally, we learn to manage feelings of alienation, anxiety, and sadness.

I considered my child self. In the courtroom, I'd sat in a chair that was too tall for me. With Bruce, I'd sat in a lawn chair or perhaps something base-issued. In the end, the details didn't much matter because, really, there had been no chair

left for me at all. Really, I'd always been the one left standing. At the core of my PTSD and so much of my mental and
emotional turmoil was the fact that I'd never properly learned
to manage feelings associated with being violated or traumatized, let alone the feelings of exclusion that so many military
"brats" share. I hadn't been allowed to work through my emotions and my experiences in part because our stern military
father prohibited such expression. Anytime I or my sisters
tried to talk about how we felt, we were reminded that we
were our father's three little "shitbirds," derogatory military
slang for screw-ups or persons always getting into trouble.
In this, we were not alone. There are, in fact, many military
brats who suffer in adulthood from the effects of PTSD, either
diagnosed with it themselves or as a consequence of living for
their developmental years with a military parent struggling
under its considerable influence.

I remembered my dream, the way my father made my mother
laugh just before he pushed her off the pier.

I still have stressors, many of which come from my family of origin. I have made peace, inasmuch as it has lain with me, with
those willing and committed to making peace. With those with
whom I cannot, I have also made a peace with myself. I have
erected safe boundaries and, though not always effective in
keeping them, I am learning how to let my yes be yes and my no
mean no without the need to justify why I choose to say either.

It seems miraculous, given my history of trauma, but I
have, with my beautiful partner of the last thirty-two years,
raised two amazing children who are now adults. I've continued a daily writing practice started when I was just fourteen
and our family was living in West Germany; I've become a
teacher, a responsive and intuitive one; I've earned my MFA
in poetry, after a twenty-year pause to raise our kids, and have
learned alongside some of the most amazing poets of our age,
including a few poets laureate. I write down the bones of my
torments in my poems.

I have a yoga practice.

I play with my grandbabies.

I sing karaoke off-key, and that's all right with me.

I belly dance like my mother taught me before she died too

soon, too young, at thirty-nine.

I walk miles in the summer thanks to the example of my sister Glenna, who raised four kids as a single mom and with her own torments from our shared history.

In the summer, I collect driftwood and make fences or sculptures for our yard, trellises upon which the clematis climb and bloom.

I carry huge stones from the river, load them into the back of my pickup, unload them into our yard, and build raised beds.

I practice thankfulness. It is a discipline when winter draws nigh; the days grow cloudy and the light of each day shortens to an almost unbearably pitched angle as far north as we now live.

When my equilibrium is thrown out of whack again by I know not what, as it has been yet again this past winter, I listen to my wise counselors, my sisters, and my familiars. I remain teachable.

After weaning myself from antidepressants two years ago, I'm exploring a new therapy called eye-movement desensitization and reprocessing (EMDR). It is said to be especially effective for folks with PTSD. My sisters have both experienced success with it and have, for a long time, encouraged me to try it. My husband was ultimately the one to convince me after hearing Dr. Bessel van der Kolk interviewed by *On Being* radio host Krista Tippett. David sent me the audio file of the interview and ordered van der Kolk's book, *The Body Keeps the Score: Brain, Mind, and Body in the Healing of Trauma*. EMDR, van der Kolk explains, reconnects the body with the mind and especially with the emotions. What George couldn't know back in the early nineties was that the body *does* remember what even the mind cannot, that what our emotions have locked away, our bodies will try to bring out of hiding. My therapist says that PTSD isn't mental illness *as such*, but mental health trying to work its way out of a troublesome past.

I am changing in body and in mind and growing more hopeful with each passing week. I am six months into weekly EMDR sessions and have begun doing Bikram yoga, which my EMDR therapist prescribed to help me heal my fascia, reconnect my body to my mind, and feel my feelings without becoming overwhelmed by their seeming enormity.

As an adult, I am finally learning how to be without a chair when the music stops. I am learning to stand strong.

Yvette Frock Gottshall *grew up in Turkey; Okinawa, Japan; Germany; and around the United States, including Texas. She earned an MFA in writing from Vermont College of Fine Arts and is a freelance interdisciplinary writer and artist who lives in the mountains of Vermont.*

A Little Crazy

Susie Meserve

I met Will in the summer of 1999 in Northampton, Massachusetts, when we both worked at Thornes Marketplace, a three-story building full of trendy shops and eateries in the center of town. I was in graduate school for creative writing and had applied for a job at the health-food store as a summer gig. I worked with Smith College students and locals who needed the 40 percent discount on their macrobiotic food. I was in a war with an unnamed eating disorder I thought of only as *control*. Earlier in the year I had been bulimic, but by summertime, I had moved on to severely limiting fats and running five miles a day. I hadn't had a period—or much of a sex drive—in over a year. The doctor said I had the estrogen level of a preadolescent girl. But Will, shelving novels at the bookstore when I descended the stairs of Thornes, inspired in me the faintest sexual stirring. He had long hair and a face that seemed world-weary and more than a little mysterious.

Will came into the health-food store while I was working the register one afternoon. He put some vitamins down on the conveyor belt and I nearly lost my nerve. Then I blurted, "You look like Elliott Smith."

"I do? Cool," he said, pleased and clearly a little flustered.

I spent the next week trying to catch his eye. There was a back way into Thornes, but I'd take the front entrance so I had an excuse to smile at Will as I made my way down the stairs. He bought a lot of vitamins that week; I decided there was a book I just had to have. Finally, we made a date. I can't remember who asked whom. I suggested a cocktail, but Will said he didn't drink. This was my first sign that he was not entirely like me. No one I knew "didn't drink"; my friends and I took ample advantage of the free wine at poetry readings and showed up regularly to Thursday nights at the smoky VFW bar. Will suggested dinner, but I didn't want to eat on a first date. Finally, we agreed on tea.

He told me, that first night, that he really shouldn't be dating.

"I'm a diagnosed schizophrenic," he said, and without pausing to gauge my reaction, asked, "Does that worry you? Does it worry you?"

Of course it worried me. It shocked me. I had no context for that kind of revelation. Schizophrenia was completely beyond the realm of my experience. I had only recently become acquainted with my own mental illness, something my therapist and I tentatively called *anxiety*, though she admitted that, on the form she would submit to my insurance, she had to write "anxiety" followed by "disorder." I was still processing the idea that the machinations I'd put myself through since I was seven—the hand-washing, the number games I played with the clock—were not exactly normal.

"A little," I said. "Yeah."

I didn't know what else to say. I considered ending the date. Mostly, I felt disappointed. But I walked with him to his place on the outskirts of town. He lived in an efficiency apartment, one room with no kitchen and old carpet. You could hear other tenants through the walls. Will told me he'd flunked out of a master's program the year before because he'd had a major psychotic break. He'd been hearing voices, suffering from paranoia, and having horrible visions; his fear, he said, was "out of control." Eventually, he ended up in a private mental health facility where they diagnosed him with schizophrenia. After six months, because he was in conflict with the program director and sure they would never make him well, he checked himself out. He'd briefly been homeless. He staunchly refused to be medicated. He had moved to Northampton to try to put his life back together. He was on disability and welfare.

I sensed that my reaction to Will's revelation was a kind of test I did not know how to pass. It was clear the date was over. He walked me back to the well-lit part of town, we said good-bye, and I strode the sad and confused walk up Main Street, to my bright, spacious apartment, alone.

I come from an East Coast family that's politically liberal and reasonably open-minded, but my parents might have freaked out if they'd known I was consorting with a schizophrenic. Part of Will's appeal, in fact—because I realized later that night that I *was* still intrigued by him, despite everything he'd told me, and that I would probably see him again—was that my parents would be terrified. In therapy I was working on separating from my parents, establishing boundaries, learning that it would not betray my love for them if I trusted my own decisions. So the possibility of dating Will immediately represented something risky, something almost out of bounds. That alone, of course, did not prompt me to say yes to a second date; when I waved to him on my way down the stairs the next day, a grin effortlessly presented itself across my face, and there was that faint stirring between my legs.

Will called me the next afternoon.

"Do you want to go for a trail run?" he asked.

I always wanted to go for a run, though I wondered briefly if being alone in the woods with a schizophrenic I did not know very well was such a good idea. Besides, it looked stormy, and I was not good with spontaneous plans.

"Okay," I said, surprising myself.

After a run in the hills behind Northampton in a thunderstorm—the two of us jostling one another playfully, panting, laughing, mud-splattered, soaked through—we showered separately and then met back at my apartment, where, on the floor of my living room, Will peeled off my jeans and put his mouth on me. The ceiling above seemed to twinkle with celestial bodies, smiling down, and afterward I felt tired, relaxed, hungry, and surprised. I could be inhibited about sex, but perhaps because I knew the biggest thing about Will already—and everything of mine paled in comparison, or so I thought—I felt absolutely no reason to withhold that deepest part of myself. I found myself shockingly willing to just let go. Very few areas in my life permitted me this kind of ease: certainly not my work, which a teacher had recently told me was *too perfect* (and thus, he said, not very interesting). Not my eating, nor my exercising: in those arenas I could not relax the reins even a little bit. That I might find freedom in this unlikely, mentally ill man, simply because he had no expectations of me and I had none of him, well—that was something.

But Will had no desire to be my boyfriend, nor the skills to be in a serious relationship with anyone. And his vast differences from me soon felt like a liability. I didn't want to tell my mom about him, didn't know how he would behave in social settings, at poetry readings, at a bar. One night, he told me he didn't think we should date anymore but that he still wanted to hang out with me, and I felt relief more than anger or sadness. I had always treated relationships the way I treated exercise or writing or food: with compulsion. I'd check my email every five minutes to see if a guy had written. I'd overthink every glance in the teaching lounge. With Will, it felt like being with him—or not—was my choice, and it was an easy decision to just be friends.

My friend did not seem like the stereotype of schizophrenia that I knew from movies and television. He did not hear voices anymore, at least as far as I could tell, and he was never violent. He was obviously depressed, though—depressed in a way that suggested sadness from some place far beyond the present. Sometimes he became slightly manic, and he frequently became confused. Often, when we talked, I wondered if we were having two separate conversations. He might, for instance, lapse into sullenness, into silence, as though he'd forgotten I was there; then, all of a sudden, he'd brightly ask a question only tenuously related to what we'd been talking about. Some days his veneer seemed so thin he was almost translucent, like the smallest insult or hurt would break him.

When he was up, Will was quick-witted; he could be hysterically funny. He was obviously smart. His decision to live an unmedicated life meant he took a barrage of supplements and carved away several hours a day for yoga, meditation, and acupuncture. His diet was so restricted it made mine seem hedonistic. He didn't eat gluten, soy, eggs, corn, sugar, meat, or caffeine (going out to dinner with Will was like a complicated three-act play). And he could be pedantic, overly direct, critical.

"You haven't read *Lathe of Heaven*? Seriously?"

"I can't believe you listen to NPR. Corporate media."

I accepted his bluntness with hesitation. Many times I wondered if our friendship was worth it: the bad moods, the sudden decisions that our evening was over, the weird outbursts of criticism.

But at other times, Will behaved like an endearing child, entirely genuine. Unlike most of the guys I knew, he did not resort to ironic retorts or mannered responses. He had the laugh of a ten-year-old, this sweet, bubbling peal. One day he invited me over to play a rented video game. It was a Saturday, and I had planned to spend the day relaxing after a week run like boot camp: exercise, teach, fast, write. So I said yes. Will couldn't handle any hint of violence, and the game was a lush but G-rated fantasy, something about a princess who needed to travel through a maze to reach her castle. We played it on his aging thrift-store television for hours. I remember the day as though we spent it happily, goofily stoned, but we couldn't have been: Will didn't put any substances into his body besides chromium picolinate and copious amounts of vitamin C. But being with him sometimes felt like an altered state.

After we played the video game, we pushed aside the controls and had sex on his bed. We had this implicit understanding: that we would still have sex. Not always; months went by when we were simply platonic friends. But then we'd fall into bed together again. I welcomed this. I had no compunctions about it, no hang-ups. I didn't care or know if he slept with other people. I didn't possess jealousy or longing where he was concerned. For the first and the last time in my life, I didn't equate a sexual relationship with love or the pursuit of partnership.

Not that I didn't love Will, in my way. We shared a rare kind of intimacy. We made gluten-free toast in his kitchen at 2:00 A.M., eating it, giggling, in our underpants. I saw him through a fractured, dissociated breakdown in my apartment after a thunderously loud Lucinda Williams show, the only time I saw him approach behavior I might call aggressive, though all he did was yell. We wrote an article together once. (He insisted I take the whole byline, though he had paced around my apartment feeding me lines like I were his secretary: "No wait,

29

write this, write this...") I watched him engage with the world as if he were doing everything for the first time: trying out a job, losing a job, finding a new apartment, beginning a new project. Because Will's life had once shattered to pieces, he didn't care what it would take to make it presentable, defendable, *normal*. For me, every venture felt like an obligation, a step on a ladder that led somewhere I was supposed to want to go. With my anxiety and my stupid eating disorder, I spent all my time climbing, and climbing, and climbing. What was at the top? I don't think I knew.

During my final summer in Northampton, Will and I made the ultimate intimate gesture: we shared a community garden plot.

Recovery is not linear, and Will had gone from a relatively good period to a bad one. Months earlier, I'd thought he might be "cured"; he had moved into a bigger apartment and taken a job at a better bookstore. He'd gotten off welfare and started various community organizing projects. He had introduced me to some new friends. But when summer hit, back into the depths he went. He stopped calling, and when I stopped by he'd answer the door with a faraway look on his face, like he wasn't sure who I was. In those periods we still saw one another, but he was not, it seemed, really there.

My problems were less serious but no less consuming. I had defended my master's thesis to very little fanfare or praise and left my MFA program with the sense that I might have blown it. I had plumbed the depths of my anxiety in therapy, which made me jittery around my family and jittery by myself. Most of my friends had graduated and left the area. I was hanging around the Pioneer Valley only because I had been offered a teaching fellowship for the fall.

So when Will asked me to share a garden plot, I said yes before I really thought it through. We drove up to the allotment on a May evening to check it out. It was not lost on either of us that we stood in the shadow of Northampton State Hospital, a psychiatric facility that had operated until 1986. With broken windows, rusty fire escapes, and rumors of hauntings, its presence across the field of plots felt comical, sinister, and a little too apt.

"What do you think?" Will asked of the dirt rectangle in

A Little Crazy

front of us. A lone mullein plant held court in the center. In my imagination, the plot flourished with more colorful fruits. I could see neat rows of tomatoes and basil, maybe a cucumber.

"It's great. I'm excited."

"Me too."

We must have hugged, though my memory is that we were awkward with each other that night.

The summer is short in New England; most gardeners take advantage of the brief season by planting in May. But we waited until the beginning of July to return to the garden. The mullein, ragged and graying, towered smack in the middle—the only living thing in that six-by-nine-foot desert. Coaxing a garden into shape in a month or two seemed like a real ambition. Around us, people happily tended their early peas, the first of the herbs, the tiny green orbs that would one day be edible tomatoes.

But in our plot, we bickered. Will sat on the sidelines with his head in his hands while I turned over dirt with some sense that I had to rush and resent the work. Will couldn't do any shoveling or heavy lifting because he said he wasn't up to it, but he did not spare telling me what to do. I did not feel kind toward him and soon turned martyrish and annoyed, wielding the spade, grumbling inwardly about the ridiculous proposition: What the hell had we been thinking?

And then I took the spade to the mullein. It had to be moved. The starts waited in their plastic pots to be planted in its place.

"Don't!" Will cried. *"Please.* Don't kill it."

"It's right in the middle of everything," I said. "I'm just going to move it so it's in a better place."

"Don't," Will said again. *"Please."*

"Come on!" I hollered. "Don't be ridiculous. I want things to be orderly. It's in the way!"

"If you kill it, I'm going to be really upset," he said. I thought he might cry.

More carefully than I had planned, I uprooted the mullein and moved it to the corner of the plot. I replanted it, went for the communal hose, and gave it a long drink.

When I came back from returning the hose, Will still sat in silence. I wanted him to leave, but I had driven him there and would drive him home. We were sharing a community garden

31

3 1328 00872 8741

plot at the top of a hill a mile outside of town, and only one of us owned a car.

Finally, he lifted his head from his hands.

"The schizophrenic and the obsessive-compulsive attempt to garden," he said wryly.

I did not laugh, but I was not too far gone to see the humor. I had missed Will's wit and lightness. I had missed being able to laugh at myself. I wasn't sure what, exactly, I was mad about. The mullein had not needed moving. We could have worked around it. We could have worked around many things.

We drove home in silence.

"Bye," I said when I dropped him off.

Several months later, I left Northampton and met the man who would become my husband.

I have often thought about the comment Will made. He equated us that day, diagnosed us, put us on the same plane, in the same handbook. At the time, I was angry and thought, *No way*. You're *the crazy one*. But if I was honest with myself, I'd spent much of our friendship noticing the ways that he and I were, to my great surprise, not so different. I'd never known a schizophrenic before I met Will. I never knew that someone with a diagnosis like that could play a video game, have sex, discuss politics, hold down a job, care about someone, hope. I know now that Will, despite the immense difficulty of his life, was one of the lucky ones: he overcame the worst parts of his illness. He was able to live, with challenges, in the same world I did.

Before I met Will, I thought being crazy was a binary: you were or you weren't. But Will and I were both at once, functional and dysfunctional, happy and sad, free and not free. We all live with this dichotomy. We are all at least a little bit crazy. The guy gardening in the plot across the way, staunchly pulling every last weed—maybe he heard voices too. The woman with the beautiful organic garden—the herb spiral in the middle, the sweet peas stanchioned up by bamboo stakes, the lettuces scattered just so—maybe she was a recovering alcoholic, bipolar, or just a little bit depressed. Maybe, like me, she suffered from anxiety and spent her life trying desperately to hide it. It was enormously freeing to realize I didn't have to hide anymore, that the things that went on in my head probably went on in someone else's. We were not bad people. We were not so beyond the pale. We were all just working in the shadow of the insane asylum, tending our desires and fears, our neuroses, our sadness, the strange things our brains did to make us suffer.

Will and I kept in touch. He left Northampton eventually, a year or two after I did. I visited him in Portland, Oregon, once with my husband and son. He started a nonprofit, got a master's degree, and now has a private therapy practice. He no longer believes in diagnoses like schizophrenia or anxiety. He's well known in certain circles for the work he has done around the possibility of treating mental illness without medication and without those kinds of labels.

He's still a pain to eat with. I know because he came to town recently and we met for breakfast. He brought his new partner and her two kids, and I brought my husband and son. He and I sat across from one another, and again, I felt like our friendship transcended expectation and normalcy. Will laughed his ten-year-old laugh. I teased him for reminding the waiter three times that he didn't eat cow dairy. Our spouses chatted; our boys shared pancakes. It was awfully good to see him. I thought that Will's decades-earlier self wouldn't recognize the put-together man sitting across from me.

I'm much happier than when I lived in Northampton. I'm still anxious, but I no longer have an eating disorder. My husband, thank God, is barely crazy—and patient. I anxiously watch our son for signs of anxiety. The irony is not lost on me. Maybe, like me, he'll grow up to have anxiety, but of course I hope he won't.

And maybe someday, I'll tell my son about the efficiency apartment and that strange first date with Will. I'll tell the story of the garden plot and that awful summer that ended with me harvesting ten bags of basil by myself at sundown on a September evening, in the shadow of a mullein that had survived its uprooting. Resenting Will, resenting being the one who thought she always had to manage things, I drove home to make pesto and, I'm sure, left tomatoes dying on the vine. Because I never went back there, and I doubt Will did either.

Susie Meserve *grew up outside of Boston and was educated at Tufts University and the University of Massachusetts at Amherst. Her poetry and essays have appeared in the* New York Times, Salon, Elle, Indiana Review, Cimarron Review, *and elsewhere, and she recently finished writing a memoir. She currently lives in Berkeley, California, with her husband and son.*

Goodbye, Suicide

Optimism One

One week after my eighteenth birthday, I woke in the county nut ward. Scuffed white tiles echoed the screams of a patient down the hall: "No, get away from me!" Spooked all night, I thought, *What the fuck are they doing to that guy?* My roommate, a stranger with a fishing hat secure on his head, snored like a motor trying to catch, failing, trying to catch, failing. A nightshift nurse tilted her head into our room, then disappeared. I later learned that her task was to tick a box on a sheet indicating that yes, the patient was still there, still alive. On my first day, they checked on me every fifteen minutes.

In the morning, the psych nurse asked, "Do you know why you're here?"

> *Marion Roberts—my grandfather, my mom's dad— called the sheriff to report finding a dead body in his field. He then walked out into that field and shot himself in the chest with his shotgun. I was seven years old, in my first year of Little League baseball.*

My brother Brian found me in the garage—unconscious, slumped across the console and passenger seat of my truck. White foam oozed from my mouth and pooled around my face. The engine was running. My head rolled and bobbed while he hooked his hands under my armpits and dragged me to the

35

front yard. As he ran into the house to call 911, I lay lifeless on the grass.

Voices faded in and out. "*Can* you *tell* us...?"

Betty Michael—my grandmother, my dad's mom—killed herself by overdosing on barbiturates. My dad was twenty-five. Five years later, I was born.

A paramedic scissored down the middle of my yellow Cheerios shirt. His partner placed an oxygen mask over my mouth and nose.

I kept hearing, "Can *you* tell *us* your name?"

Robert Nelson—my grandfather, my dad's dad—was an alcoholic. He fell off a trolley into the Feather River while drunk. He was found many days later. My dad was fifteen.

On a school day in the last month of my senior year of high school, I waited until my mom and brother went to work before parking in the garage. I duct-taped a garden hose to the exhaust pipe of my white Datsun pickup. Fed the opposite end of the hose through the just-open cab window. Inhaled the fumes as if I were hitting a pipe. Both sides of a homemade cassette repeated Metallica's "Fade to Black."

The resident psychiatrist asked, "Why do you want to die?"

Brian Nelson—my brother, nineteen months older than me—took two bottles of Nytol, 144 pills, hoping he'd never wake up. He was distraught over losing his high-school sweetheart, Debra. The doctor said the pills Bri took were not strong enough for his big, athletic body. That they would have killed somebody my size. That my heart would have exploded. I was fourteen.

The police dubbed me "5150." The California Welfare and Institutions Code allowed "a qualified officer or clinician to voluntarily confine for seventy-two hours a person deemed to

have a mental disorder that makes him a danger to himself."
The shrink declared that I was bipolar, prescribing lithium
and another antidepressant.

Confined to a wheelchair, my blood still saturated with car-
bon monoxide, I attended group sessions in the rec room. The
TV sat silent and the card tables hugged the walls to make
room for a circle of chairs. The female counselor—eyeglasses
at the end of her nose, clipboard on her lap—asked each of us
to "check in," to tell her and the other patients, especially the
new guy, me, why we were there.

Eve was my first "I love you," the first girl I became attached
to who became attached to me back. After ten years of abusing drugs and alcohol, another form of suicide, I'd been clean
and sober for a month and couldn't handle losing her. Couldn't
stand knowing she got together with J.R., one of my best
friends from childhood. Couldn't hear again that she lost her
virginity.

I didn't have my familiar coping mechanisms of dope and
booze. And since I felt abandoned and alone—a repeat of my
dad leaving the family, a repeat of so many relatives leaving
the family by suicide or overdose, which I thought was certain
to happen to me no matter what for the rest of my life—that
left no other option than to die.

That's when I made the Metallica tape. When I parked
in my mom's garage. When I snaked a garden hose from my
muffler into the cab of my truck. And that's when my brother
Brian saved my life.

Despite my passive approach to therapy, a peculiar hope
emerged after my failed suicide attempt. This odd, perhaps
not-quite-authentic giddiness might have been a subconscious
mechanism, an emotional reflex meant to hide some of the
embarrassment, which was a much darker shade of that feeling you get just after you trip and fall or almost fall and look
around with a stupid grin on your face wondering if anyone was
watching.

I might also have been avoiding the humility and hard work
of accurate self-appraisal, even if I didn't know I needed it.

There was a touch of fake-it-till-you-make-it. You say you

are fine, so you will be fine even when your ankle is twisted, your knee is wrenched and already throbbing. Even when you've just tried and failed to end your life. This strangely positive attitude worked to convince not only my family and my counselors but also myself—as if to say, "I'm okay. I just had a bad day. I wasn't seeing clearly. But now I am. And I'm ready to kiss life on the mouth. May I go now?"

If, after so much despair, hope seemed to come from some unfamiliar place wreathed with deception, there were times too when that certain brightness felt completely legitimate, so maybe it was authentic after all. A case of perception being reality.

Because along with the whirl of confusion and doubt, a new sense of possibility fireworked through me in ways more real and more freeing than I swear many humans might ever experience. It was like that Buddhist notion of dying in order to live. Surrendering to win. Letting go of everything. Now, with nothing more to lose, having hit the absolute bottom, there was, I came to believe, only one way to go.

Eleven days later, they let me out.

Eight months after that, on New Year's Eve, I dissolved two bottles of Nytol, 144 pills, in a tumbler of water. Sitting on the padded edge of my waterbed, I chugged and choked on what looked like a blizzard in a snow globe. In case the sleeping pills didn't work, I placed a wood-handled carving knife on the headboard to stab myself in the heart.

This time it was Kim.

A month out of the mental hospital, we hooked up drunk—a one-night relapse—and I latched on to instant love. I made her my antidepressant, but the prescription wasn't right. I made her my therapy, but she was unequipped to counsel me. I made her my booze, but she couldn't keep me intoxicated. I had to think and feel everything and, not having any tools to combat my self-destructive thoughts, I fell back into the same thinking I grew up with. All the hope I'd mustered in the hospital faded like the mirage I didn't know it was. Or if that hope was real, I had simply failed to sustain it with anything of substance, anything that addressed the root of my issues and tried to heal them.

Seven months later, on New Year's Eve, we broke up for the

twelfth or twentieth time, probably over her going out drinking with her friends, probably because I feared she would hook up with another guy, which would render me meaningless. Sober again but seeking no help, my mind was married to erasing myself.

On New Year's Day, confused, dazed, and disappointed that I still had a pulse, I picked up the carving knife. Thumbed the blade. Tapped the tip. But I didn't have the courage to push the blade into my chest. Instead I stumbled into the hallway. My mom rushed me to the emergency room.

"Can you tell me your name?" asked the ER nurse.

She made me drink liquid charcoal to absorb the toxins from the pills. The consistency of brownie batter, it tasted like a barbecue briquette and felt like a thick black cloud.

"This is disgusting." A ring of black circled my lips.

My mom's glassy eyes pleaded with me to drink it.

The nurse, looking down at her clipboard, said, "It's either that or we pump your stomach. And trust me," she said, looking up to meet my eyes, "you don't want that."

Modesto Psychiatric Center (MPC) had a little more shine than the county hospital. I did my time like a jail sentence: not wanting to change but attending groups and playing a lot of gin rummy with Julie, whose manic depression made mine look like emotional hiccups. I smoked a lot of cigarettes and had a short affair with a young woman named Dena. She was anorexic and bulimic, a victim of sex abuse, a cutter, and also suicidal. What I didn't do, what I never seemed to do, was listen.

I stayed for twenty-eight days.

Three months later, still eighteen, I reunited with Kim and with her return came a renewed desire to die—or, like a life sentence, it never left. But this time I told my mom, and she drove me back to MPC.

Julie, a fixture of the rec room, was playing solitaire in her usual spot.

"Hey, kiddo."

Her eyelids and cheeks, framed by her short bangs and long, black hair, drooped like a slow-motion avalanche. Once a week she walked out of the facility with an escort and then returned on a gurney, unconscious. The shock treatments stole more of her light with each volt of electricity that ricocheted through her brain.

This time, I listened. I observed. I was honest with myself, maybe for the first time ever. I could see and acknowledge that my way wasn't working. Recovering addicts like to say they're sick and tired of being sick and tired. I was sick and tired of wanting to die.

Frank, a cop and former marine, announced his hardness with shoulders thrown back and a flattop crew cut. In group, with a circle of padded chairs and no tables between us, he said, "I was trying to stop this girl, this young high-school student, from killing herself. She was sitting in her car and had a long knife pointed at her heart, the butt end of it pushed against the middle of her steering wheel. She had been crying, screaming, 'Leave me alone! Just let me die!' But I had talked her down, standing a few feet from the open door of her car, got her calm, when someone in the crowd who had assembled in the parking lot said, 'Fuck it, man, she's just a stupid kid.' That was the final prompt she needed. The paramedics couldn't save her."

Frank always wore black T-shirts—pro-gun, pro-military—that made it clear his mind and body remained armed and dangerous. When he told the story about the girl he tried to save from killing herself, he cried the way men do when they haven't done so in decades, or ever. It was an earthquake of convulsions, impossible to stop, his body wracked and his face distorted. The rest of us sat with our mouths open, our eyes transfixed. The next day in group, while Frank shared, he stood up and peeled off his black "Combat Veteran" T-shirt to reveal a white T-shirt with a single hand-drawn daisy.

"I know I need to change," Frank said, "so this is the new me."

If that guy can change, I thought, *so can I.*

I stayed, again for twenty-eight days, this time doing all the homework, opening up in groups and privately to my counselors, and actually earning my graduation from the cognitive-behavioral therapy (CBT) program. Like before, instead of receiving a certificate, they gave me a T-shirt. On the back, it read, "I Became Rational at Modesto Psychiatric Center."

Something had shifted in me. Something deeper than before. More profound. Not only was there hope, there were tools, ammunition to combat my maladaptive thoughts. I finally felt like I had a shot at a life free of self-destruction.

Four months later, my brother Kev and I hunched over our workstations in the backyard of Vital Services, a company that built and installed mailbox stands. He stood at the long table saw measuring and cutting four-by-fours and two-by-sixes while I painted the end products a dull white. My shorts, shoes, and T-shirt were splattered and smeared. Jane's Addiction played from a beat-up boom box.

"Dude, I think I'm gonna change my name," I told him.

"Oh, yeah?" he asked. "To what?"

"Optimism One." I stopped painting. My brush dropped to my side.

Kev turned to me, tucking a carpenter's pencil behind his ear. "Optimism what?"

"One," I repeated. "Optimism One."

"Optimism One? What's that all about?"

"It's the title of a book we're reading in class. It's by a guy who changed his name to F.M. 2030."

I listed my reasons: I wanted to signify the new me. No more past. No more Nelson. No more suicidal maniac. No more depressed drug addict and alcoholic. And a bonus: my new name fit with being in a straight-edge punk band.

"Dude," Kev said. "Mom and Dad are gonna freak."

"I don't care. Nineteen years of being Craig Nelson is enough, and it's not working."

Kev's eyes grew blank, distant. Perhaps he was thinking of his own life before he blinked back to the moment. "That's cool. Hey, whatever makes you happy."

"You did what?" my mom asked.

"I legally changed my name. No more Craig, no more Randal, no more Nelson."

Her lips pressed together, losing color. She let the magazine she was reading, *Good Housekeeping*, fall to her chest. "What was wrong with the name I gave you?"

41

I told her what I had told Kev. I wanted to change who I was, what I had learned, how I responded to life as it happened, not as I *wanted* it to happen. I wanted to distance myself from the legacy of suicidal self-destruction that echoed through my bones and blood, as if changing my name would change my DNA, change every lesson in escape inscribed and pulsing within me.

Seeing a shrink helped. Taking my meds did, too. But most of all, practicing the CBT taught by David Burns in *Feeling Good*, the book we studied at MPC, seemed to make the biggest difference. I could see where my thoughts were distorted. "Life is not worth living" was not a rational response to rejection. "Fuck the world" was not a reasonable approach to life's challenges. "I was doomed from birth" was not an accurate assessment of my circumstances. I could correct and redirect these thoughts in healthy ways. I could heal all that was broken in my default reactions to life on life's terms. With my new name and my new views, at nineteen, I thought once again that I had it all figured out.

A year later, I felt so confident that I stopped seeing my therapist. Stopped taking my meds.

Two years later, I had all but forgotten about CBT.

Three years later, I relapsed again, the Nelson in me waking up and numbing out with drugs, alcohol, food, sex, television— anything I could find and abuse. My family history reminded me that suicide was always an option.

> *Greg Michael—my uncle, my dad's half-brother—was a drug addict and an alcoholic. He went to prison for killing his fiancée in a head-on collision while driving drunk. I was nine years old. Fifteen years later, now out of prison, with the police surrounding his house, he rested a shotgun under his chin and pulled the trigger. I had just graduated from college.*

"I think about killing myself every day," Bri said to me when we were in our early thirties. Debra, his high-school sweetheart, was long gone, as were his star-quarterback physique and his abandoned doctoral dissertation.

My brother Kev and I were alone on a friend's porch when I told him what Bri had said.

Skinny with grief, Kev had just been kicked out of the house, had just found out his wife was seeing another man, his former workmate and poker buddy. Kev leaned forward with his elbows propped on his knees. He looked at nothing on the ground, nodded, and said, "Me, too."

At thirty-five, my name now just a name, I wanted to die. This time it was Diane. After two years and all my hopes that we would get married and live the rest of our lives together, she broke up with me. Again, I thought I was worthless, hopeless, helpless, doomed to be alone, an utter failure at life, so why keep living it?

"I need help," I told Joe after a recovery meeting. He had been clean and sober for over twenty years and appeared to live a happy, stable life with his wife and daughter. Three years sober, I said, "I can't stop thinking about killing myself."

"Okay, I'm glad you said something," he said, his faded red baseball cap pushed back on his forehead. "Look, you're going to be okay. Will you visualize something with me?"

"Sure."

"Close your eyes and just picture this: You're hanging from a bar in a huge storm, and it feels like if you let go, you will fall for hundreds of feet before you smash into the ground and die. But you're really only a few feet from the ground, and I'm right here to catch you. We all are. So you can let go anytime you want. You're going to be okay."

I breathed deeply, the weight of imminent death dissipating. Maybe I wasn't the first person Joe had talked down from the ledge.

"You feel better?"

"Yeah."

"Okay, buddy," Joe said and grabbed my shoulders. "You call me whenever you need to, day or night. You're going to be all right."

At thirty-nine, sober for eight years, I tied a noose.

A couple months before, I had driven toward the Golden Gate Bridge, planning to stop my car in traffic, walk to the barrier, climb to the edge, and jump. En route, my friend Mike had called to see how I was doing and I changed directions, driving to Shelley's, my almost-ex-girlfriend's, who had not been answering my calls or texts.

But now we had officially broken up, and she messaged me from a party to tell me her previous boyfriend kissed her. Part of her playbook was trying to make me jealous, but I didn't see it this time. Instead, I knew again that my life was over.

I retrieved a long, sturdy rope from my shed, followed every step of the instructions I found on the Internet, then searched my house for a strong beam. The narrow closet in my extra room looked like it might work, but I was afraid the short dowel would break under my weight. The back patio seemed the best, with its high roof and exposed supports, but I feared the neighbors would hear or see me before I expired. I didn't want anyone to save me. I already knew well the feeling of being a failed suicide attempt, a failure at failure.

I plugged in my drill, tightened in the thickest bit, stepped onto an old stool, and drilled holes in my hundred-year-old dining room ceiling to find a two-by-four beam. Every two inches a new hole, dry plaster snowing into my bloodshot eyes. Two feet across, nothing but what looked like thin slats, more like half-by-twos. I started in the opposite direction when Shelley texted and said she was coming over, saving my life for the moment.

Nine months later, Shelley gone for good, I finally interrogated my fear of being unlovable and alone. More therapists, more self-help books, and the patient counsel of Michael, my sponsor, buoyed me. I examined Shelley and all the others as an addiction, something I had to have, something that controlled me, that was ultimately destructive in the way drugs and alcohol had consumed me because of the way I consumed them. But now, single, alone, and not looking for another woman to fill the need for companionship and affirmation and escape that I had felt for so much of my life, I didn't want to die. I didn't feel that familiar family pull, even if my brothers didn't share the same sentiment.

Brian Nelson—my brother—drove to a park on Debra's twenty-fifth wedding anniversary. He finished off an unmarked bottle of prescription pills, drank straight from a plastic bottle of vodka, walked to a picnic bench, and shot himself in the temple with a .45 caliber pistol. I was forty-three.

I had tried to save my brother's life like he once saved mine. I had sat with him in the hospital for seven straight days the year before, when I found him overdosed, suicide notes placed all around his house. Tried to show him the way of sobriety. Of happiness. Of acceptance. Especially of loves lost. Tried to show him that even without medication for more than twenty years, teenage diagnosis be damned, I had fought, I had finally surrendered, and I had, I thought, found peace. All with continual sobriety for the previous eleven years. All with continual help. All with continual work—reading, writing, talking.

Now, every day, my name and the scars on my patched-up ceiling remind me: look back, but don't go back. Every day Brian's face stares from his memorial poster. He and the other overdoses and suicides in my family warn:
Don't do this.
Do the opposite.
There's another way.
Go.

Optimism One *earned his MFA in creative nonfiction from Sierra Nevada College. He is a Buddhist, a triathlete, a world traveler, and a tenured writing professor who lives in Modesto, California, between August and April. "Goodbye, Suicide" is part of a memoir-in-progress called* How to Swallow a Black Cloud and Exhale Light.

Show Me All Your Scars: Why People Hurt Themselves and What They Can Teach Us

Jane Campbell

When she was twelve years old, Chloe got a paper cut on her finger. That was how it began for her. She was raised in Toronto, the high-achieving daughter of high-achieving Chinese Canadians, and on the outside, she looked the part. She sat in class, primly dressed in her private school kilt, and picked away the scab. A few delicate ponds of blood pooled on her fingertip.

In the spring of Grade 8, Indu dug her fingernail into the flesh of her forearm, leaving noticeable raised marks on her skin. She grew up in the neat, evergreen suburbs of Vancouver, British Columbia. Her parents had grown up in India. They were products of a different world and they didn't, couldn't, understand her. When she started scratching herself, it was just an experiment of sorts. Just to see if she had the nerve. Just to see what it felt like.

Jeremy was six years old the first time he curled his finger around a strand of hair and pulled, hard. He was born into a violent marriage in a gray working-class city a couple of hours outside Toronto. By the time he was six, his abusive father was long gone and his mother had remarried. When she asked him about the bald patches on his scalp, he told her he'd gotten into a fight at school.

Chloe felt a sense of release when the blood broke through her skin, the way you feel when you come up from underwater and draw oxygen back into your lungs. She picked at herself until that didn't do the trick anymore. She moved on to sharpened pencils, school scissors, a razor blade, a knife. Soon she had to be alert all the time. She rolled up her knee socks, pulled incessantly at the hem of her skirt. She didn't want anyone to see the open gashes that crisscrossed her thighs.

Indu went from fingernails to pen caps—they actually have enough of an edge to break the skin if you've got the time and the willpower. Eventually, she bought an X-Acto knife and a box full of razor blades.

In his early teens, Jeremy started making cuts on his legs. He didn't bother trying to cover his tracks by using pen caps or pencil tips; a lot of teenage boys mess around with knives. In Grade 9, he thrust a blade into his chest with such force it bounced off his breastbone.

I cut myself for the first time when I was fourteen years old. A few months later, my desperate, unnerved parents put me in the care of a nationally renowned psychologist who specialized in treating adolescent girls. She'd testified before Congress and held senior positions at some of the top mental hospitals in the country, but the first time we met, she sheepishly confessed she knew so little about self-injury, she'd had to go to the library and take out all the available books on the subject. There were two. I told her I'd already read them and found them inaccurate and sensationalized. She could only offer a sympathetic shrug.

More than fifteen years later, self-harm remains understudied and poorly understood. "Even within the academic world, self-injury is often stigmatized and perceived incorrectly," says Sarah Victor, a PhD student in the psychology department at the University of British Columbia who is writing her dissertation on self-injury. She chose the topic specifically because there was so little pre-existing research on it.

Until 2013, the only place where self-injury appeared in the *Diagnostic and Statistical Manual of Mental Disorders (DSM)*, the so-called bible of psychiatry, was as a symptom of borderline personality disorder, a condition characterized by intense anger, impulsiveness, and fear of abandonment. In the most recent edition of the *DSM*, "non-suicidal self-injury" was listed as a "condition for further study," but it's still not considered a disorder in and of itself.

Despite its relative absence from psychiatric texts, self-injury is not rare. "Studies of big populations of high-school students show self-injury rates between 15 and 20 percent, which is huge," says Sarah Victor. The rates are lower in adults, but they're still significant. A large-scale phone survey conducted in 2011 by Dr. David Klonsky, a psychology professor at the University of British Columbia, found a prevalence rate of about 4 percent in American adults.

When Dr. Mandy Hawkins, now a practicing psychologist based in West Vancouver, was in graduate school, she led a support group for university students dealing with stress and depression. One day, a young woman told the group she was hurting herself and wanted support. Another student admitted she also self-injured. Then another student came forward—and another. It turned out every single person in the group was either currently self-injuring or had done so at some point in their university career. An entire room full of people: all of them had hurt themselves on purpose and all of them had believed they were completely alone.

Self-injury occupies a curious place in North American popular culture. On one hand, many people view the behavior as singularly troubling and shocking, a sign someone is in extreme emotional distress and quite possibly on the verge of suicide. It's the stuff of "scared straight" after-school programs and very special episodes of television shows. In November 2014, the Canadian Institute for Health Information (CIHI) released a report showing that hospitalizations for self-injury have risen more than 85 percent in the last five years, and media outlets across the country picked up the story. A November 18, 2014, headline in *Global News* warned of an "epidemic" of self-injury, and in the same week *Postmedia* announced a "surge" in self-injury among teenage girls and called the news "disturbing." In fact, according to Sarah Victor, there's ongoing debate in the psychiatric community about whether self-injury rates are actually rising or seemingly alarming statistics like those recently released by CIHI just reflect increased awareness among health professionals and the general public. Nonetheless, the language in these reports is typical. When mainstream media outlets do cover self-injury, they typically characterize the behavior as a virulent and spreading contagion, one that poses a particular threat to vulnerable young women.

In other corners of the cultural landscape, especially the teen-centric free-for-all world of Internet memes, subreddits, and Tumblr posts, self-injury couldn't be taken less seriously. The entry for "self-injury" in *Encyclopedia Dramatica*, an irreverent catalogue of offensive memes and flame wars gone by, "Sixteen-year-old girls cut, cut, cut the pain away because they are usually rich, privileged, lucky, well-financed kiddies who just don't have anything serious left to bitch about . . . Some argue that we should let them play Russian roulette and see if any actually kill themselves, ridding the world of their butthurt whimpering once and for all."

On *Encyclopedia Dramatica, Urban Dictionary,* and elsewhere on the Internet, self-injurers, more often referred to as "cutters," are often associated with "emo," the post-punk teenage subculture best known for whiny music, asymmetrical haircuts, and a general embrace of sadness and self-pity. Some emo bands do reference self-injury in their lyrics, but this doesn't explain the strength of the association; other bands like the Foo Fighters, Nine Inch Nails, and Eminem have all released well-known songs that explicitly describe self-harm, yet people don't assume their fans cut themselves. The connection between self-injury and emo music can likely be traced to the mid-2000s, when emo became successful in the mainstream for a brief historical moment and then, like so many MTV-era music fads, quickly wore out its pop-cultural welcome. "You're so emo" became an insult, meaning that, just like the music, you're so melodramatic, cloying, self-indulgently sad. The term "emo" now seems to be only loosely affiliated with a music style. It's become a word used to express disgust with an entire class of people: stereotypical emo kids are white and upper middle class, from stable, loving homes. They're so sheltered and naïve that they don't realize how lucky they are, so they mope around listening to sad music and talking about their feelings. They also cut themselves not because they're seriously mentally ill, but as an ultimate act of melodrama. This behavior doesn't make them insane or dangerous; it makes them the punch line of a joke. "I wish my lawn was emo so it would cut itself," says one popular Internet meme.

As gossip spread in Chloe's private school, she found that her behavior inspired both disgust and ridicule. People were afraid of her. When her friends found out she was cutting, they told their parents, and their parents told them to stop hanging out with her. At the same time, her older sister rolled her eyes at the cuts and the scars, thinking Chloe just wanted attention from their parents. Her classmates called her "emo" and said she was imitating the sad-eyed girls she'd seen in music videos.

It's true that in many ways, Chloe was the very picture of the hysterical teenage girl cutter. She was privileged, well-educated, born into a stable family, but her self-injury was not some sort of melodramatic performance. She kept cutting deeper, and she couldn't stop. She didn't want to. Her parents and doctors were worried she would commit suicide. She was hospitalized repeatedly and missed so many of her high-school classes, she wasn't sure if she would be able to graduate.

Like Chloe, I found my self-injury shocked some of my peers and bemused others. I was never sure which was worse. I stopped hurting myself about ten years ago. I still have scars. I don't know if people notice them. If they do, they never ask. I'm not sure what I would say if they did. I have no qualms about telling people I've struggled with major depression and severe anxiety, but if the subject of self-injury comes up, my throat tightens and my fingers go numb. After all this time, I'm still not entirely sure how to explain myself. I keep circling back to this question: Why do people hurt themselves on purpose? This mystery seems to lie at the heart of the stigma against self-injury, of both the horror and the derision. Our most basic instinct as human beings is to avoid pain and injury. Hurting yourself intentionally seems so illogical and unnatural. What could it possibly accomplish?

Klonsky has published groundbreaking work showing that

while self-injury has a number of possible functions, almost all people who hurt themselves on purpose do so at least in part to regulate their emotions. Self-injury seems to help people cope with overwhelming feelings of sadness, frustration, and anger, perhaps by creating a distraction from internal pain. Self-injury can also be used to create feeling. People sometimes self-harm to shatter the sense of detachment and suffocating numbness caused by severe depression.

Researchers are only beginning to investigate whether genetics or environmental conditions make certain people more prone to self-injury; however, psychologists have long observed marked similarities in the upbringings of self-harming patients. "A high percentage of people who self-harm grew up in families where they were discouraged from expressing or talking about their emotions," says Dr. Mandy Hawkins. "As they grow up, they often have difficulty correctly identifying their feelings—for example, they may not be able to tell the difference between anger and sadness—and this makes emotions harder to deal with."

Some, like Chloe, who describes her family as "traditional Chinese Canadian," are raised in environments shaped by cultural strictures against showing emotion. Indu had a similar experience. "My parents believe we are purely intellectual, spiritual beings," she says. "When I was growing up, I always felt that in Indian culture, feelings don't exist."

In some cases, self-harmers have parents whose own coping abilities have been stripped away by abuse or tragedy. When Jeremy was a child, he watched his mother nervously pick at her arms until they were covered with open sores. People used to ask him if she was a crack addict. In fact, she'd never touched drugs, but she'd spent years trapped in a marriage to a violent man who beat her and her young children on a regular basis. She escaped when Jeremy, her youngest child, was three years old, but to this day her arms are a patchwork of wounds and fading scars.

Jeremy is thirty-seven years old now and studying counseling in Vancouver. He is very skinny and vibrant with frenetic energy. His hands and forearms are covered with tattoos. Is his body art an elaborate form of self-injury? He's quick to deny it—he doesn't find the tattooing process particularly painful.

He explains that he knows when people see his tattoos, they assume he's been in prison. They are correct, but he actually got them after he was released. "These are my armor," he says. "People think I'm a convict or a biker, and they won't stand up to me. I'm not a big man, but I don't get any flack." When he speaks about his mother and the phantom of his long-gone biological father, he digs his fingernail into the flesh of his earlobe. He doesn't quite register what he's doing until he pulls his hand away and sees his fingertip is stained with blood.

The idea that people use self-harm to regulate intense emotions can still be hard to swallow. It makes sense that people would try to escape pain through pleasure—by drinking or getting high or having sex—but why fight pain with more pain? People who self-harm can speak eloquently about how it makes them feel—the sense of release and even comfort, the stark beauty of pain made visible in the flesh, the addictive rush of blood surging through the skin—but they often can't explain how they got the idea in the first place and why it ever made sense. Perhaps the problem is that there is no logic or reasoning: they're trying to explain a behavior that goes deeper than conscious thought.

People fear self-injury because it seems unnatural, but is it really? Self-injurious behavior has been observed in animals. Distressed cats and dogs have been known to groom themselves obsessively until their skin is bald and raw. Captive parrots pluck out all their feathers and bang their heads into cage bars. Tilikum, the orca who famously killed his trainer during a live Sea World performance, ground his teeth against metal pool gates until they were worn and broken, as Tim Zimmermann has written in *Outside* magazine. People with autism and other severe developmental disabilities often harm themselves compulsively; so do prisoners and patients in psychiatric institutions. Some psychologists argue that people who are institutionalized usually self-harm for attention from guards, not in response to emotion—but Jeremy, who spent three years in Vancouver Island Regional Correctional Centre on a robbery conviction, tells a different story. He reports that his fellow prisoners hurt themselves constantly and that, while some were trying to get moved into the segregation unit— just for a change of scenery—many took pains to hide their behavior from the guards.

According to the popular stereotypes, self-injury is an elaborate indulgence of the overprivileged and the overeducated. In fact, there seems to be something deeply instinctual about the desire to inflict pain on oneself. People who self-injure typically suffer from mental illnesses that cause them to feel overwhelming emotions. Because they did not learn how to talk openly about their feelings as children, they are particularly ill equipped to cope with intense anger, sadness, and guilt. When words fail, when words are not enough, self-injury may seem like the last and only option. As Indu says, "Nothing screams louder."

People who hurt themselves usually can't explain their actions because they never made a conscious choice. Slightly hysterical media reports often warn parents that their children might fall victim to a self-injury epidemic caused by YouTube videos and Tumblr posts that show emo kids cutting. In fact, self-harmers usually can't pinpoint where they got the idea to hurt themselves. It just came to them one day, an innate longing as inescapable as hunger or lust. "I have no idea where it came from," Indu says of her desire to cut herself. "It really seemed like it came out of nowhere. I had no idea it was a thing." Jeremy had seen his mother pick at her skin, but when he started actually cutting himself as a teenager, he thought he'd invented the behavior. He'd always felt so isolated and different from other people, it seemed possible he was the only one.

One of the most commonly held stereotypes about self-injury is that people do it for attention, in much the same way a toddler throws a tantrum or a cat pees in its owner's shoes. Much of the online vitriol leveled at "cutters" stems from the perception that they're trying to manipulate people or selfishly garner pity. According to Sarah Victor, this is a misconception. "The research shows that people who self-injure for attention are relatively rare, statistically," she explains. "It does happen, but it's a small percentage of self-injury."

Self-injurers themselves have a more ambivalent response to allegations of attention seeking. They bristle at the suggestion that their pain is all for show or that they're trying to manipulate people around them. They point out that they don't broadcast their behavior; in fact, many go to obsessive lengths to conceal it. At the same time, they can't honestly say the attention doesn't matter. It's true there are times when they hide their behavior, but there are also times when they "forget" to wear long sleeves to cover the cuts on their arms, and some even hurt themselves in the presence of other people. "On one hand, it was a very private thing," Indu says. "I didn't want other people to see it, but at the same time I've always had this strange sense of wanting to share it, of wanting to just let it be out in the world."

The phrase "just doing it for attention" (emphasis on "just") seems to imply that people who hurt themselves are seeking special attention, an undeserved level of attention—but don't people in extreme psychic distress legitimately need extra consideration from those around them? Sarah Victor contends that people who do self-injure for attention should not be seen as manipulative or dishonest. "If this is the best strategy someone has to get care and compassion from other people, then I think they deserve my care and compassion," she says.

Self-injury forces us to look pain in the face, to see physical evidence of conditions that are usually personal and private. Mental illness is a difficult, confounding subject, one many of us would rather ignore. Self-injury draws our attention to something we don't want to see, and perhaps this is why it makes so many people so uncomfortable.

When considering the stigma against self-injury, it's important to note the persistent association between self-injury and women in both popular culture and the psychiatric community. The earliest case studies of self-injuring patients in medical texts from the 1960s and 1970s describe women almost exclusively. When doctors do mention men who harm themselves, they make a point of labeling such patients effeminate and "sexually confused." This understanding of self-injury as a largely female problem has spread to modern popular culture. The stereotypical emo cutter is either a female or a feminine male—emo boys are known for wearing eyeliner and tight jeans, having long hair, and being girlishly emotive. Barbara Jane Brickman, a media-studies scholar, analyzed hundreds of portrayals of self-injury in popular and medical texts dating back to the 1960s for a 2004 article in the journal *Body &*

Society. She concluded that "the white, suburban, attractive teenage girl persists as the face of self-mutilation," despite an increasing number of studies showing that men and women have similar rates of self-injury. In Klonsky's survey, for instance, nearly 40 percent of respondents who admitted hurting themselves on purpose were men.

The evidence shows that self-injury is certainly not an exclusively female problem, so why does the association persist? It may be partially due to the different means by which men and women tend to hurt themselves. Researchers have found women are more likely to cut, while men are more likely to self-injure by burning or hitting themselves. Cutting creates more obvious, less explicable wounds. Men are also more likely to self-injure by proxy: that is to say, by going out and picking fights. Jeremy reports that in prison he often witnessed other prisoners act out intentionally in order to provoke beatings from guards. People are also more apt to excuse aggressive and violent behavior in men. If a teenage boy punches a hole in his bedroom wall, his parents may shrug their shoulders and say, "Boys will be boys." If they discover their teenage daughter has sliced up her arm with a razor blade, they'll probably be less sanguine.

Men are also less likely to seek counseling in general and more self-conscious about admitting they suffer from mental illness. Joseph Chastain, a California-based filmmaker, harmed himself regularly for more than ten years. He's currently finishing a documentary about self-injury entitled *Not Without Reason*. He had no shortage of female interview subjects, but he struggled to find men who were willing to speak with him. "Women are more likely to talk about their feelings," he explains. "In this society, we're taught that emotions are feminine."

Would self-injury be so reviled if it weren't so strongly associated with women? The same charges leveled against teenage girl cutters are often directed at women in general: dramatic, out of control, unreasonably needy, and "attention whoring." Feminist scholar Susan Bordo has argued that contemporary women live in fear of being "too much." Too hungry. Too sexual. Too emotional. In her book *Unbearable Weight: Feminism, Western Culture, and the Body,* Bordo contends that anorexia isn't stigmatized to the same degree as other mental illnesses because it is associated with the traditionally masculine traits of self-discipline and self-control. By starving themselves, women can subvert deep-seated cultural stereotypes that they are slaves to their desires and emotions. While anorexia is often glamorized in contemporary culture, self-injury is denigrated. It's taken as proof that women are hysterical and irrational, given to indulgent, over-the-top displays of emotion.

Most people who self-injure don't do it forever, although the urges may never completely go away. The behavior is more common in teenagers than in adults, and many people who struggle with self-harm in their teens stop sometime in their early twenties.

Some people stop self-harming because they grow weary of leading a double life. "I can't afford to do it anymore," says Indu, now an expressive twenty-three-year-old with a wide and easy smile. "I just hate hiding it. I hate the paranoia and the vigilance." She no longer cuts herself; she's switched to hair pulling because, she says, it's less messy and unlikely to result in serious injury. Although she's given up cutting, she's not ashamed of her scars. In fact, she wishes she had more. She appreciates the way they challenge people's expectations about mental illness. At first glance, she is put together, polished. Her clothes are neat; her earrings match her top. Only after a few minutes do you see them: dozens of ghostly lines running up and down her arms.

Other people move away from self-injury when they adopt more destructive coping mechanisms. By the age of fifteen, Jeremy was addicted to alcohol and drugs. When he was twenty-seven and living in Courtenay, British Columbia, he contemplated suicide and became desperate to get sober. He went to a crisis center, but the nurse he spoke to treated him dismissively and suggested that if he were serious about committing suicide, he would have done so already. He walked out of the hospital and into a restaurant where he'd had a job interview the day before. For several hours, he sat at the bar and ordered drink after drink. Then he handed the bartender a note demanding money. The bartender complied, but Jeremy didn't make it very far. There was no way he'd get away with it and he knew that. Now he sees his crime as his ulti-mate act of self-injury.

Jeremy got clean and sober after he was released from pris-on. He spent three years trying to get a scholarship to attend counseling school in Vancouver and finally succeeded. He still struggles with his mental health and urges to harm himself. He's currently in his third year at a degree program that's only supposed to last a year, but his school has been under-standing and lets him retake classes he hasn't been able to finish. He's not sure if he'll get certified as a counselor and knows his career opportunities may be limited by his criminal record, but his studies have finally given him a sense of struc-ture and purpose in life.

In some cases, people who self-harm gradually develop the coping skills they never learned as children, either through life experience, therapy, or some combination of the two. Chloe did graduate from high school, but she spent much of her uni-versity career in and out of mental hospitals. When she was twenty-one, a doctor recommended that she enter a Dialecti-cal Behavioral Therapy (DBT) program, an intensive form of therapy that combines individual and group counseling. Chloe had been diagnosed with borderline personality disorder in high school, and DBT has shown promising results for pa-tients with this condition, which is otherwise difficult to treat. Chloe eventually completed the six-month program twice. In therapy, Chloe began to realize she'd spent her whole life fo-cused on other people's expectations and desires for her, and for the first time she started to think about what she wanted: a career, a stable relationship, a puppy.

Four years later, she has all three. She lives in Vancou-ver with her fiancé and their two dogs and cat. She works from home in the health and safety industry. On weekends, she dons Hunter rain boots and yoga pants and heads to the dog park, where she's indistinguishable from all the other fit, twentysomething doggy moms. Almost indistinguishable. She still has scars on her arms and legs. She spent thousands of dollars on creams and laser treatments, and the scars got fainter, but they didn't go away completely. Now she wouldn't wish them away if she could. "It was a part of me," she says. "People can assume all they want. They probably think, 'Oh, she went through an emo cutting period' or whatever, but they have no idea what happened."

Even people like Chloe who no longer hurt themselves don't necessarily look back on the time they self-injured with bitterness or regret. Chloe admits that she doesn't feel like she should tell people who are currently hurting themselves to stop, because she knows they may not want to and she understands that. Even now, she thinks people overreacted to her behavior. "There are much worse things in this world," she says. Her self-injury never put her in any real danger; most of her wounds were superficial and healed on their own. Far riskier behaviors like binge drinking and promiscuous sex are seen as much more socially acceptable. She understands now that self-injury was a distraction that prevented her from dealing with her underlying emotions, but at the same time, she admits, "When I think about it, I don't really think there's anything wrong with self-injury," at least as a temporary coping mechanism in times of severe distress. Her advice to people who are currently hurting themselves is only this: "Stop judging yourself."

It's probably going too far to try to see self-injury in a positive light; it's disfiguring, potentially dangerous, and distracts from emotional pain rather than resolving it. However, perhaps it's worth considering that people who have struggled with urges to self-harm may not necessarily be damaged by the experience, that they may acquire unique perspectives on the place pain has in our lives.

After speaking with Chloe, Indu, and Jeremy, after listening to their stories and telling them mine, I've gained a new perspective on my own embarrassment about self-injury. I'm not ashamed that I hurt myself. I'm ashamed that I don't regret it, that the tidy narrative of illness and recovery never quite made sense to me. Even with the benefit of age and hindsight, I cannot see self-injury as a mistake or misfortune.

Those of us who self-harm learn to survive by making psychic pain tangible. We understand that private suffering can be transformed, that it can have an impact on the world. We've learned the alchemy of pain, and some of us find that anguish does not always turn into violence. It can become something beautiful, too.

Chloe, who grew up feeling isolated and misunderstood, has now created her own family with her fiancé and their pets. Her family dog comforted her in the darkest periods of her illness, and now she adopts and cares for abandoned animals. Indu is studying creative writing and often discusses self-injury and mental illness in her work. She loves writing about her personal struggles "because then it's more than just my own weird shit; I can turn it into something meaningful for other people." Jeremy doesn't know exactly what his future holds, but he's determined to make a difference for other people like him who live on the margins of society and have difficulty accessing treatment resources. "I believe I went through everything I went through to help other people," he says. "We suffer for a reason. What we do with it is our choice."

Jane Campbell *has an MFA from the University of British Columbia. Her work has appeared in* Grain, Revolver, The Impressment Gang *and the BIG TRUTHS food anthology* Nomfiction.

Flying High

Andrea Rizzo

Mom is lying on the bed with her head slumped down and eyes closed. Her thin, silvery hair is greasy and slightly tangled, and her light-blue hospital gown sinks below her clavicle. There is a faint trail of tan-colored food caked in each crease of her mouth, leading to a patch of white chin whiskers that make her look like a catfish. Her enormous belly protrudes to meet the particleboard tray hovering above her, on which sit an empty plastic glass and straw. A white plush dog is haphazardly cast on her left side, near a festive red envelope with "To Someone Special" written in thick black strokes. I feel a pang of guilt. As 400 miles now divide us, I haven't seen my mom since the spring, and now it's nearing Christmas. In those months, her life has been reduced to warm things, pillows, and water. I rest my hand on her shoulder and gently touch her.

"Mom?"

I lean closer.

"Mom?"

She wakes with a start and looks up at me. "There's nothing wrong with me except I have bad dreams," she says. Her blue eyes grow big and optimistic, focusing into wakefulness.

"What did you dream about?" my brother Douglas asks.

"Different things... Grady... and Andrea." She looks up in recognition with her eyes twinkling, acknowledging that I am there to see her.

"Was I really in your dream?" I ask. I wonder if she dreams of me often, even though I don't visit but a few times a year.

"How you ran away, I think. And who else? I don't know, all kinds of people. And I passed all these tests that... the doctors here... the one I went to that one time, I've gone to so many," she starts mumbling, becoming fully awake and aware of her surroundings. Her dream, I realize, was of being sane.

When I was twelve years old, I watched my mother's dense, milky white arm flap in the breeze from the Kmart parking lot. Lifted high above her head, her hand flowed from side to side in a graceful Miss America wave. Her square face beamed at the private plane flying thousands of miles above us. The sun was bright, the day was clear, and my mother believed a millionaire pilot was following her around, secretly in love with her. He was too shy to say hello, but if the pilot saw her wave, he might dip his wings in admiration.

"Mom, nobody's following you! Why would they?" I was mortified but used to it. This wasn't the first or last time I impatiently watched her wave, praying that nobody I knew from school could see her doing it too. Mom's confusion between what was real and what was imagined had been going on for years. I pointed out reality whenever I had the chance.

Mom's mental illness burned more brightly than anything else in our lives. From the time I was a little girl, I knew my mother was not like anyone else's. She didn't worry about mundane events like grocery shopping, keeping house, or playing with me, her youngest daughter. My mother's life was full of imagined glamour, potential parts in Broadway plays, and the boyfriend she could have married before my dad, the one who believed she would be a star. She could have had her moment in the sun. But marrying my father and living with his constant realism had put an end to it, she thought.

Everyone in the neighborhood knew my mom was different. Her vocabulary lacked sophistication, and she would tell people they were "good" and "smart" and that she wasn't, while compulsively rocking back and forth on her heels when she was standing in line at the bus stop, the department store, or the bank. She wore an auburn bouffant wig and painted tight circles on the apples of her cheeks with bright red lipstick, roughly smearing the color into the bones before stopping to gaze at her image in the mirror with a lusty, open-mouthed stare. I watched the reflection and thought, *I don't want to be like you. I never want to be like you.*

It was my biggest fear to go crazy like my mom. I worried about waking up one day and no longer understanding reality in quite the same way, being lost in the black hole of madness. The thought of never being taken seriously again and becoming a cartoonish figure like her was terrifying. Mom squeezed herself into too-tight, garishly colored polyester pantsuits. At home, she only wore a white full-figured cotton bra and gargantuan nylon underwear, keeping Hershey's kisses between her breasts for convenient snack storage.

Her clothing taste, or lack of it, inspired a horrific but wonderfully fun fashion show. My best friend, Jennie, was in my kindergarten class and lived right down the street within Beech Lake Estates. She often came over to play. We donned Halloween masks backward in an effort to mimic my mother's wigs. I wore the Alfred E. Neuman mask with stacked red hair, and Jennie chose the witch face with curly brown ringlets. We also tried on Mom's floor-length chiffon nightgowns and pretended to be lounge singers. The one fashionable find I truly coveted from her closet was a pair of Candie's high heels that reminded me of the ones that Sandy, Olivia Newton-John's character, wore in *Grease.* They marked Sandy's shift from wallflower to sexpot, when she stamped out her cigarette and said longingly to Danny Zuko, "Tell me about it, stud." I put those shoes on and did reenactments of the scene-stealing carnival song, "You're the One That I Want," on top of the kitchen table, with my accommodating brother Kevin down below.

My mother started having nervous breakdowns in the 1960s, well before I was born. The doctors gave her a schizophrenia diagnosis due to hallucinogenic features—what later became the millionaire pilot—before settling on manic-depression, now known as bipolar disorder. It flung her toward the two polar opposites of depression and mania. Every few years, she would stop taking her medication, and after a fairly significant display of mania, she would spend about a month away from home getting her chemistry regulated.

After having me in 1973 as an attempt to save the marriage, neither parent could handle the union for much longer. My dad would not and could not deal with the course of her illness. And my mother stopped putting up with his short temper and constant concern that every joke or off-color remark she made was because she had stopped taking her medication. After several years of grumbling, my mother decided to let my father know she really was unhappy, mental illness or not.

Just about a week after Easter Sunday in 1980, while my dad was out of the house, my mother packed up our two-tone brown Pontiac Safari and took me to live with a friend of hers whom I had never met. She bundled up an assortment of loose clothing, drapes, curtain rods, and paintings she had created or just liked. She was focused and muttered that she'd had it with my father, that twenty-five years of marriage was all she could take. I didn't understand what was happening and wanted to stay at home with my daddy and brothers. I called Jennie to let her know that I was being taken away. She wanted to know where, but I wasn't sure. My brother Douglas was at home with a broken leg and just watched us leave, helplessly propped up on his crutches.

We ended up living about ten miles away, at the house of an ancient lady named Ione. I did not remember ever seeing this woman and wondered if she was someone my mom had met through her local shopping trips. Mom talked with everyone everywhere, which also embarrassed me. This tiny dwelling was filled with plastic-covered furniture and a small, unfriendly toy poodle that growled from under Ione's chair.

My mother was lucid enough to take me out of my first-grade class at Saunders Elementary in Newport News, Virginia, and enroll me into Captain John Smith Elementary in the nearby city of Hampton. Before long, I was running with the bad neighborhood kids, who were very different from the upper-middle-class crowd I was used to. The leader of our group of misfits was a ruggedly gorgeous girl named Bonnie, who was tall and lithe and somehow elegant in her flannel shirts and torn jeans. She commanded us weaker ones to do things like steal from our parents and local stores. I took Ione's checkbook and tried, with a crayon, to write a check at 7-Eleven. The cashier just laughed and put my purchases back on the shelf. I tasted my first cigarette butts during this time, digging them out of car ashtrays or off the sidewalk, smoking that last little bit. Although it was fun walking freely around the streets and skipping school, I missed my dad desperately, and my mother wouldn't let me see him.

I regularly told Mom how much I hated her and loved my father. I thought she was punishing me by taking us far from him, my siblings, and my home. I now know that she wanted out of the marriage and had every intention of taking care of me, but the timing was bad. Her act of leaving came unfortunately in tandem with a nervous breakdown. When I was able to visit my father one time during those few weeks, he was very interested in recording my narrative about my new life. We sat in the gold-and-white kitchen, the cassette recorder placed between us on the same table I used as a platform for performing the carnival scene in *Grease*. Dad was more like a reporter than my father. I told him about skipping school, drinking chocolate milk and eating candy bars for dinner, and how Mom wanted to go live in outer space, a place she talked about often.

"Andrea, where does your mother want to live?" he asked, while the tape recorder softly clicked and whirred.

"She wants to live on the mooooooonnnnn," I delighted, playing with *moon* in order to get the maximum absurdness.

After we were gone for three weeks, Ione called my father and said that Mom was not functioning. I was not eating properly or going to school. My father contacted Smith Elementary and confirmed that I had only attended about one-third of the time since I was enrolled. He went to social services with this information and the taped recording of my story, and a day or two later a policeman knocked on our door while I was watching daytime television and my mom was lying in bed. They took Mom away in handcuffs to the mental hospital. I was taken to social services and picked up by my moist-eyed father.

After my parents divorced the following year, my dad was given full custody of me due to my mother's mental state. I still spent every weekend with my mother until I was able to drive. When it was just the two of us, I was able to more clearly see the full spectrum of her mental illness. The continuity of her lingering depression was the most obvious trait. It was as though she were allergic to the sun. Her apartment was always dark, with the heavy mustard-colored curtains drawn tight. I could see a tiny bit of the backyard through an imperfect slit in the drapes: a steel drying rack, the apartment behind us. My mother slept intermittently on the couch in the living room or in her bed, with her huge bottom rising up like some nylon-covered monument. Her snores were great and loud, and at times she woke herself up due to their sheer volume. I peered into the small sliver of sun and ached to be bathed in its light. Mom didn't want me to spend too much time outside and away from her, not because she was afraid for my safety but because she couldn't expend too much energy watching me.

"I wish I were dead," Mom said, with her head stuffed into the couch or a pillow. "I miss your father."

"Mom, can't we do something? I'm bored. I want to play with my friends... or something, anything..."

"It always has to be a three-ring circus with you! I drive you up and down the Peninsula with Jennie. Why can't you just be quiet?"

About once a year, she would stop taking her medication and be thrust, lightning-fast, into mania. Sometimes, she was influenced by a well-meaning friend or churchgoer who told her that pills were the work of the devil. Other times, my mom just felt better and wanted to put an end to side effects that included extreme lethargy and weight gain. The intensity of bipolar disorder made her daily life pretty grim—she lived at a rundown, tired apartment complex and was hardly able to maintain a job as simple as pouring iced tea at the mall cafeteria—and to compensate, she filled her life full of fantasies. Not all of her illusions were as hopeful as the romance with the millionaire pilot. In fact, many of her fantasies were macabre; she thought a cat had infected her through a simple bite and obsessed over potentially losing her hand or even her life. Another time, Mom was convinced she had poisoned my brother with a homemade dinner and wanted to contact the president of the United States and tell him what she had done. Just as frequently, though, her dips into surrealism could be magical and bright.

"When I'm manic, I can play the piano beautifully," she would say. She was the only painter in the family and depicted richly colored flowers in vases, along with tranquil gazebos and natural landscapes with oils, watercolors, or pastels. This artistic tendency seemed to calm her mind, and within it she found a place of confidence and beauty. Like many people with bipolar disorder, she craved the manic high that allowed her to be creative and exempt from the boring tasks of daily home life. Her tales from spending weeks at a time in the state hospital included fighting off murderers from death row and the countless men who were interested in her sexually, including doctors. Ironically, Mom was becoming stronger than she had ever been when she was with my dad. She almost found a sort of independence in this institutionalized life. It was hard to understand as a child, but my mother proved that living a standard and safe existence was not the only way to navigate through life, even if only her mind was free to wander.

In the summer of 1993, I was nineteen years old. This was the same age Mom had been when she had her first bout with mental illness. For months, she'd become convinced that a chicken bone was lodged in her throat. Not long after this episode, she married my father. I still feared I would fall into the dark funnel of madness and become just like her. My anxiety only increased when, in July, my mother experienced yet another nervous breakdown, this time with the drastic consequence of never being able to live alone again.

The final apartment complex she inhabited was a humble lower-middle-class place where transient military families came and went and less fortunate single parents stayed. She was standing outside naked and looking up to the sky when her neighbors called the police. Maybe she was still hoping the millionaire pilot would swoop down and save her. Maybe she thought a Hollywood director would drive by and see a young starlet instead of a sagging, middle-aged woman. Maybe this was her ticket out of the mundane life as a divorced mother of four and into a spectacular new existence. At the station, she attacked the pre-screener and police officer. When Mom was admitted to Eastern State Hospital in Williamsburg, they noted that her "thought content was bizarre and paranoid. She stated that she was pregnant and that her seventy-eight-year-old mother was poisoning people. She denied hallucinations. Memory was fair. Insight and judgment were poor."

"I'm sitting in the middle of the desert, trying my best to get it down on the typewriter," my mother had said on the phone a few days before.

As it turned out, she'd developed a conspiracy theory of some sort, something only the government officials and she knew about. I should have known by the way she held her hands in my car earlier that week: she pressed her index finger to the top of her thumb in the same way a praying mantis might hold her forelegs in anticipation of a kill. She sat quietly but was very alert, as if all of her senses were sharpened for an impending attack. Mom did this every time her mania reached a breaking point. Then back to the hospital she would go.

Dad and I had the daunting and unenviable task of clearing out her apartment. In her mania, Mom had erected a giant mound of stuff in the middle of the dining room. In the pile were clothes that she had worn throughout her life—the powder-blue chiffon nightgowns with which Jennie and I played, along with polyester day slacks from thrift stores and the Haggar Clothing Company catalogues. Wire hangers and walking shoes. Even some gold necklaces and costume jewelry. To the massive heap, she'd added the contents of the refrigerator—rancid bacon strips and monochromatic leftovers. She had a lifelong habit of tearing herself and others out of pictures—particularly my father, her mother and stepfather—and several headless bodies and heads made up the pile. Some of the best wares from the china cabinet were in there too, including pieces from my parents' extended stays in Germany and Japan, tiny statuettes of Asian fishermen, and Hummel children with cheeks like cherubs, all smashed to bits. It looked like a bonfire of bad memories ready to be stoked.

I was relieved to find that the full twelve-piece set of Rosenthal china, which had always been promised to me, was still intact. The mocha-colored flowers on a bone-white background with a delicate gold line had somehow made it through the storm. We packed up seven boxes of china that day, then secured the spared Hummels, miscellaneous porcelain and glass figurines, and crystal bowls. The glass pipe I had spent many

Saturday afternoons filling with tap water and dishwashing liquid, making a never-ending string of bubbles, slipped out of my fingers and broke. I couldn't believe it had survived Mom's mania but not my own hand. We took most of her furniture, clothes, and valuables to a storage unit and brought my china back to my father's attic. The apartment my mother had inhabited in both her manic and depressive states was ready for the next tenant.

It has taken me most of my adult life to forgive my mother for her mental illness and to see her as a woman I can respect, one with intelligent thoughts, wild hopes, and an artistic nature, just like me. My mother talks about a cat she owns that does cartwheels. She says the Queen of England wants her to come live at the royal carriage house. She tells history as if she could rewrite it. ("I remember Anne Frank wrote letters... Was it to Hitler?" she wonders.) But mostly she talks about Grady, her fictional husband, who is also the father of her imagined infant triplets. Every time I ask to meet him, she says he is working on building a home for their new family. She frets about nursing the babies and packing up her belongings so they can move. I used to correct her and let her know she was mistaken, but I know it doesn't matter now. Seeing her like this, unable to walk, go to the bathroom by herself, or even trim her own nails, I am thankful her daily life is wrapped up in a surreal and fantastical world.

Here she is at her final resting place before death, a nursing home, no more or less sane than the other people with dementia or an altered sense of reality. It reminds me of visiting her in mental institutions as a kid and young adult, when I just tried to ignore the insanity all around and get through the hour. A woman in a red "Happy Holidays" sweater keeps walking past my mother's door and scowling at us. A flat, repetitive "help, help, help" chant drones from somewhere, while the aides are talking loudly about a new Lil Wayne video and big butts. A young, beautiful nurse with bright pink lipstick comes to check on us and tells me that my mother surprises her every day, in a good way.

I rub lotion on my mother's paper-thin skin, marveling at her well-preserved coloring. Will I be as lucky in almost forty years? Her nails are brittle and yellow, so I clip, file, and clean out the beds, almost gagging at the various food particles that have worked their way underneath her nails over the last several days, weeks, or even months. Much of the residue is chocolate. It is one of her favorite vices, one that my brother Douglas is happy to indulge during these visits. He suspends a mini Hershey's bar in the air as if presenting a treat for a dog, and she greedily snatches and consumes it. Somehow the tiny bar ends up everywhere, and chocolate creases the soft flesh of her jowls.

I clean her face with a damp cloth and get to the task of plucking her whiskers, starting with the ones that protrude from her chin. She makes funny faces and sounds in concert with each rip, as though she is sucking on a lemon while giving an animated, "Oh! Ah!" I try her eyebrows next and get the longest strands out before she pleads, "No more." I move down to her feet, which are infant-like, with soft soles and heels because she hasn't walked in quite some time. I clip her toenails and massage lotion onto her swollen ankles. I don't remember a time in my life when I've shown this level of kindness to anyone, especially to her. As grotesque as she has always been to me, it's surprising to both of us that I am grooming her. I rub her back and shoulders and brush her scraggly but beautifully silvered hair. She doesn't ask me to do any of this, but I want to. Instead of being embarrassed or bewildered by her madness, I see her as innocent and renewed. It's as if Mom has come full circle back to the stage of infancy and needs my compassion. She stares at me with wide eyes.

Before I head back home, I lean in to give Mom as much of a hug as a hospital bed allows.

"I love you biiiiigggg much," she says and holds out her arms with trembling girth. It is a family phrase of endearment, although I don't remember her ever saying it. I look at those dense, milky white arms that are now withered with wrinkles and time.

"Aw, I love you too, Mom," I say.

"Do you want me to walk you out?" she asks. I look at her carefully, dressed in a thin hospital gown and almost completely horizontal on the bed. She can't walk me out any more than she could take that trip to the moon, as she wanted to do a few decades before. Her bizarre nature has finally given way to old age and physical disability, neither of which I imagined her ever reaching.

"I'll pretend you're walking me out," I say. We both laugh. And then I walk into the bright sunlight.

Andrea Rizzo *has an MFA in creative nonfiction from Goucher College. She is the senior editor of a mental health and wellness website for members of Beacon Health Options. Andrea has been a music writer for twenty years and was co-director and associate producer of* Hardcore Norfolk: A Story of Rock'n'Roll Survival, *a full-length documentary about the underground music scene in Norfolk, Virginia.*

How I Became an Angel

Jennifer Metsker

My last psychotic episode started a few days before Christmas several years ago, and whenever I look back on it, the memory begins *in medias res*. There I was, curled up in the passenger seat of a car late at night in a snowy parking lot. I couldn't see anything and no one could see me because I had my eyes squeezed shut. You see, I had recently become an angel, and I believed this transformation had given me the power to become invisible. All I had to do was close my eyes. Imagine my surprise when this didn't work. The car door opened. Medics and policemen began discussing how to get me out of the car and into the ambulance waiting nearby.

I had been running on adrenalin for days, and my senses were keen and animal-like. My body was paralyzed, but with my eyes closed, my ears had developed superhuman capabilities. The voices of the people outside the car became exaggerated, like those you might hear in a cartoon. Syllables revealed intense displeasure and distaste. A certain tension in the dialogue, flattened vowels, words clipped off at their endings—these were danger signs. I believed I could hear entire lives in inflections. The woman with the nasal voice who spoke about me in the third person—I pictured her small kitchen: a pile of dirty dishes in the sink, children bickering at the kitchen table, one child putting her fingers in her ears and closing her eyes, singing out "la la la la la." This woman's exasperated words were like flat hands ready to slap me, and I refused to move.

My psychiatrist says it's rare to be able to articulate what happens during psychosis, let alone what you were thinking. "You remember everything?" she asks me periodically, leaning over her desk.

"Yes," I say.

"You'll have to tell me sometime," she says. But then she turns back to my chart, asking about symptoms and side effects. Her small therapy dog wags her tail and jumps up from her pillow to weave around my ankles, as if she knows I need comforting. I pat the dog as I recount my concern over the slight elevation in my mood. I know the language. Even though my psychiatrist is curious and kind and I'm willing to tell her whatever she wants to know, it still seems like what happens in psychosis is expected to stay in psychosis. *Are you feeling an unexplained sense of euphoria? Are your thoughts confused?* These are yes-or-no questions. So these half-hour sessions never seem like the right time to explain it, the way my mind once reshaped reality into a story so complicated I didn't believe that I was the one inventing it.

There have been many attempts to define psychosis, but today that definition is narrowed mostly to, as Rudolf Cardinal and Edward Bullmore put it in a recent book, "the presence of delusions and/or hallucinations . . . without insight into their hallucinatory nature." This might aid diagnosis, but such dry, distant language doesn't really capture the vividness of the psychotic experience. In 1968, Gerald Vogel made a connection between psychosis and dreams in his paper on rapid eye movement (REM) deprivation:

> There are many similarities between dreams and the symptoms of psychosis... Both often display hallucinations, delusions, loss of capacity to test reality, implausible thoughts and implausible thought connections, loss of volitional control over onset or termination of an episode, etc. Because of these similarities, it has been suggested that the same mechanisms may underlie both states. Hughlings Jackson expressed this notion in his famous dictum, "Find out about dreams and you will find out about insanity."

It's true that the psychotic episodes I have experienced were a lot like dreams—stories woven together in an incoherent fashion from a gathering of fractured data. Here is a voice, here is a gesture, here is an inaccurate map on the wall. Just as the dreamer does, I did my best to make sense of the world I inhabited. But the nature of that world was, in the words of T. S. Eliot, "a heap of broken images, where the sun beats."

Psychosis differs from dreams in one essential way—the dreamer is not safely cocooned in bed, head resting on a pillow while the brain concocts its terrifying alternate reality. The psychotic is awake. This is why it's not entirely accurate to say psychosis is like a dream. It has the qualities of a dream, but you are living it, and that is very different.

I teach fiction writing classes, and one day while outlining a lesson plan on craft, it occurred to me that psychosis has many similarities to the craft of fiction. Psychosis has plot and characters. It has rising action and builds toward a climax at the end. Or should I say: The End. The psychotic story is often apocalyptic in nature. As the mind invents its fantasy world, the self becomes a character in a fractured narrative, fraught with intense distress as impossible plotlines collapse in a world that is not as malleable as a dreamer's mind.

Thus, when I return to the story of what happened to me, it's dangerous. I'm an unreliable character plotting an untenable story in the real world. There I am in the parking lot with my eyes squeezed shut, refusing to move, believing entirely in my powers of invisibility while those around me try to figure out how to cart me off to an institution with the least possible resistance. I can't help but think now how tragically creative it all was.

It's hard to see it coming—the thickening of a psychotic plot. The episode that landed me in the parking lot that night was not the first I had experienced, but it was no less confusing or convincing than the others. Like most breakdowns, it happened during a stressful time. I had dropped out of a graduate art program in Chicago and moved with my boyfriend to a small college town in Michigan, where he would begin his own graduate study. I was working as a secretary, a job at which I did not excel, and the dull days at my desk depleted me. In June, after another serious breakdown, I had

75

been diagnosed with bipolar I disorder with a susceptibility to psychosis. Reluctantly, I began taking medication, but became severely depressed once again.

At first the depression altered my perceptions only in ways that slowed my thinking and made my life hopelessly grim. I didn't believe I could fly or that I was a messiah. The television wasn't speaking to me. I couldn't read people's thoughts. I could barely get out of bed each day and a blanket of sadness covered every object I touched—the staplers, the bowls, the bus seat—but it was winter in the Midwest, and perhaps, I reasoned, winter encased the world in sadness the same way it encased the world in snow. I blamed myself for being sad. I secretly believed I had, in some way, failed at life, that I had made some terrible misstep in order for my mood to be so irreparable. Then I was beset by terrible visions. At work, on walks, at home in bed, I would close my eyes, and there they would be: skulls and dead people and demonic faces. Though I didn't know this at the time, research shows such themes to be common in individuals with my diagnosis. "The delusions usually involve ideas of sin, poverty or imminent disasters, for which the patient might assume responsibility. Auditory or olfactory hallucinations are usually of defamatory or accusatory voices or of rotting filth or decomposing flesh," according to Jenny France and Sarah Kramer. Without this knowledge, I suffered shamefully, assuming I had somehow caused the darkness. Ultimately, I couldn't sleep or eat for days at a time. I began pacing the apartment, unable to read or focus on the television—nothing made sense. Long story short, the medication I was given didn't work at all (and was later taken off the market). But psychosis never follows the short version of the story.

I called my therapist. She told me not to call my psychiatrist, not yet. She wanted me to see her first. This baffled me. When I asked my therapist why she wanted to see me so urgently, she told me we would talk about it when I got there. *Just come*, she said. We planned to meet the next evening.

In my fiction writing classes, we often talk about how the plot in any good story is driven by character desire. If psychosis is a narrative, the desire driving the psychotic character is a desperate need to make sense of what is happening. He or she wants nothing more than to understand the reason for his or her suffering in order to put an end to it. This is the essential flaw in the psychotic character that leads to his or her downfall: There is no reasoning with mental illness. It's unreasonable. But the psychotic mind does not accept this. The short story: The brain is suffering from an imbalance of chemicals that cause intense confusion and eventually delusions. Desperate to be well, the psychotic mind looks for clues, if not miracles, that will lead the brain out of its confused state. Because the clues are often based on delusions, the story arranges itself around false premises. This is how the longer story, the psychotic story, begins.

After I got off the phone with my therapist, I began the long wait for my appointment. Waiting in a state of mania is no simple task. I paced around the house as my mind raced. I began talking constantly, to myself and to my boyfriend, who followed me around our apartment trying to calm me down. Periodically, I would get down on my hands and knees and sob, overwhelmed because I could do nothing to stop the hallucinations. Meanwhile, my mind reached for answers—was it the weather, was it my boyfriend, was it a vitamin deficiency, was it my family, was it my therapist? In time, the delusions became too great and I began making strange connections.

Because my therapist hadn't told me much over the phone, I reasoned that whatever was going on with me must be a secret. Perhaps I was special in some way, and the information was privileged. In fact, perhaps my life was filled with senseless mental pain because I didn't belong in this world. Perhaps I came from another world—a heaven-like world filled with angels. Maybe angels had left me here as a test to see how much suffering I could endure. Over the course of a day, it became quite clear that I was an angel, a very special one, and now the others were coming to collect me. I was a practicing Buddhist at the time, but it was the Christmas season—allusions to angels were everywhere. Like Christ, I reasoned, perhaps my time on Earth was done. That explained why the therapist, who had told me several times she was a very devoted Christian, needed so urgently to see me. The angels were going to meet me at her office. The terrible visions of death were replaced by glowing beings with open arms illuminating the snowy clearing behind my therapist's office. I could even hear the angels speaking to me, calling me home. Revealing none of this to anyone, I asked my boyfriend to drive me to my therapist's office.

After my therapist called me into her office, I sat down and began talking excitedly about how much better I was feeling— so much better, I told her. I was in a state of euphoria. I didn't reveal the secret about the angels. I thought it was important that I show I could keep the secret and still play my earthly role until the right time was revealed. The therapist seemed pleased, likely believing that her therapeutic methods had cured my depression. She began to talk about the joys of the Christmas season and a certain carol she had heard on the way to the office. As she talked at me, rocking in her absurd rocking chair and barely letting me speak (she was clearly not a very good therapist), my plotline began to falter. Where were the angels coming to receive me? Why wasn't she mentioning them? I searched the window that looked out over the empty lot behind her office, but it was pitch black. As she babbled on, I began to notice how messy her office was, documents and folders and food wrappers heaped high on every surface. Anyone who consulted with angels wouldn't have such a messy office, would they? Doubts crept in, and my story began to warp.

The plot of any good story is made up of external conflicts that thwart the main character on the path to his or her desire. This creates suspense. But to the psychotic mind, external conflicts warp the very fabric of the story. It's like discovering you have walked through the fourth wall of a novel to end up in an unfamiliar sitting room in another novel you have never read. Everyone is staring up at you in fancy period clothes, and you've upset the teacart. Your basic desire remains the same—figure out what's wrong with you—but when you're faced with a deluge of angry characters, you must improvise, devise a new story.

For example, let's say there is a character named Mary. Mary loves John, with whom she has spent one beautiful night, but she faces one critical external conflict: John has a wife. Mary must make a decision: she can confront John, or his wife, or pretend like nothing happened. That's the way an ordinary story goes. But the psychotic story offers other options. Mary loves John, but John has a wife and also, as it turns out, John is the devil, which explains the intense suffering he has caused Mary, which also means that John's wife is in danger, which is why Mary must corner John's wife at a faculty party and warn her about her husband. The wife doesn't seem to believe Mary, so Mary grabs her arm and shakes her hard. The wife is terrified and calls for help. People descend on Mary, dragging her away. As Mary is being roughly escorted from the party, she realizes the reason John's wife and the party guests are frightened of her is because it's not John who is the devil, but Mary herself. How did she not see that before? The external conflicts Mary is faced with—the terrified wife and the angry party guests—have altered the very fabric of her story. Who can she trust now? No one. Not even herself.

When the angels didn't come, I lost faith in my narrative as well as my therapist. I was frantic. I stood up and began pacing the room. The therapist had a map of the world hanging on the wall above her desk. Large swaths of tan countries taunted me from earthly continents. While the therapist chatted away, I searched for some sign that heaven was located on the map— perhaps I could still find it. But rather than finding heaven, I discovered that the map didn't contain the country of Tibet. The place where Tibet should be was simply part of China. The short story: Likely this map was made in China, a country which lays claim to Tibet. The long story: Somehow I'd ended up in a parallel world where Tibet had never been—there was no Dalai Lama, no Buddhism. I became certain this was a sign that it was wrong of me to put my stock in angels—I was a Buddhist after all. I still believed that I was an otherworldly being of some kind, but it was clear I had somehow sunk into an alternate reality where angels couldn't reach me, and I was sent to this dark place to be punished for (a) believing in angels when I was a Buddhist or (b) being a Buddhist.

I began screaming about everything: the messy office, the missing Tibet, Buddhism, angels, Christianity. The therapist opened her door, trying to find a phone in the front office to call 911. I saw people in the waiting room. Why there was such a crowd waiting to see her, I don't know, but no one seemed worried that this world was not the real one; they only seemed alarmed by me. Their bodies sat heavily in chairs, their coats lumped around them, their eyes wide with fear.

My boyfriend was waiting outside the office; he was now trying to get a handle on the situation. I pulled him aside and told him we had to get away before the police came. He rushed me out of the office and helped me into the car, likely because he knew the kind of rough treatment patients received in mental hospitals and wanted to help me avoid it. But we didn't make it out of the parking lot before cop cars blocked our path. That was how I ended up trying to disappear—it was the only way left to escape. If it hadn't been for the man with a compassionate wheeze of a voice, a voice that emerged from the babbling fray and coaxed me out of the car, I might never have gotten into the ambulance voluntarily. He could have been a medic or a passerby, I'm not sure—I never even knew what he looked like. But he became a key figure in my story for that moment, the only round character in a flat world. Something about his calm, reassuring voice made me believe that this man was the only one who believed I was an angel. I held out my hand to him, and he took it. I kept my eyes shut as he led me to the ambulance.

Each psychotic break I have experienced borrowed its material from whatever I had come into contact with during those initial moments. The story about the angels was the last psychotic story I would ever concoct, but it wasn't the first. The first episode arranged itself around the voyages of Columbus—a concentration of my undergraduate studies. The next focused on my apartment building and its radiator troubles. The loud knocking in the pipes became evidence of ghosts. Another one blended Allen Ginsberg and the water shortage in California—I had been reading Ginsberg's poetry as well as a book on hikes in California that happened to mention the periodic droughts and how they affected the landscape. I was visiting my parents during that episode, and I remember standing up at the dinner table to announce that I had spoken to Allen Ginsberg and he had told me the world was going to end.

But the stories weren't just predicated on these details; they also arose from the pain of the illness itself. Mental illness is immensely isolating. At the time of the angel episode, I hadn't spoken much in months. I had no friends aside from my boyfriend, and I had been ostracized at work for my sullen behavior. I imagined I was a lonely angel left behind because that was precisely how I felt.

I used to wonder why insanity had such religious overtones, but after my experiences, such allusions are easy to explain. Quite literally, God is the *deus ex machina* in a psychotic story. When my students' fiction stories get too complicated, extreme things happen. Murderers come out of nowhere or a new character enters to save the day. Why is the crazy man you've seen roaming the streets screaming quotes from the Bible? Because his plotline has gotten out of control, but there are no fictional devices left.

Eventually, psychosis becomes less like a dream or a narrative—it becomes a prayer. Who can protect you from ghosts? God. What can you do when Allen Ginsberg has returned from the dead to tell you all the oceans have dried up? You must pray to God for rain. It's easy to get from ghosts to Holy Ghost and from worldwide drought to the Great Flood.

Once I was in the ambulance, the medics discovered my blood sugar was so low that I was near death. I entered the ER singing gospel songs, according to my boyfriend; I have only a vague memory of bright lights and sharp things. But even after a Haldol-induced blackout and days of medicated confusion, pieces of my story still held.

I woke up alone in my hospital room, confused about what had happened. I had an IV in my arm and my clothes had been replaced by a hospital gown. I tried to account for these new details in my fallen-angel narrative and, eventually, I was able to make them fit. Of course I would be in a hospital—I had been captured, and now they were running tests on me. Doctors and staff members came and went, pretending that they didn't know my special status or, if they knew, that they just didn't care. They had dour faces and distant attitudes. They stared at me blankly when I spoke or made notes without telling me what they were writing down. They not only made me feel ashamed of my story and even more alone with it, they became part of it.

In art therapy, we colored in coloring books with felt-tip pens. I chose a picture of horses and a brown pen, but the ink in the pen came out teal blue. With every stroke, I checked the casing of the pen. Brown. Then the ink that came out. Blue. Short story: There was likely a problem at the factory—blue ink ended up in a brown pen. The art therapist hung the colored horses on my hospital wall and told me that I had done a good job. But why, I asked myself, were the horses blue? In what world are horses blue? By praising my blue horses, she became just another figure in the plot to convince me that this hellish parallel reality was real.

And then there was, as there always seems to be, the mean nurse. When I got scared in the middle of the night, she yelled threats about more medication. Medication seems like such a scary substance in a psychotic nightmare. As your mind searches for who or what is to blame for what is happening to you, the pills get caught up in the narrative. You're terrified that they might be making you worse, and every time you express your fear, the staff bring you more pills or inject you with something without explaining what it is. The medications make you slow and confused, and now you can't protect yourself from the experiments they're doing on you. This is how hospital staff members become the villains of the story.

Luckily for me, in the end the villains won, though by the time that happened they were no longer the bad guys. Once the medication fought off my delusions, the hospital employees were just ordinary people doing their jobs, albeit with minimal transparency and kindness. I woke up one day and understood where I was. I looked out the window of my hospital room—it was still gray and snowy; there was a rose garden below in a courtyard—and I understood that I wasn't stuck in a hellish reality. I was only stuck in the hospital (though some might argue there is little difference). The doctor came in and explained that I'd had a psychotic break because my medication didn't work; I needed to be on a different regimen. He gave me instructions for the coming weeks and let me know what side effects to expect. For all my delusions about becoming something greater than I was, my story's happy ending was an unhappy reality. Now I had to return to my life and job with another psychotic story lodged inside of me that had no place in the real world.

I would spend years trying to find the right medication to balance my moods and prevent delusions for good. During that time, I feared the most minor of confusions—simple things like forgetting a date or missing an appointment still feel like signs that I'm losing my mind. And there is a terrible shame that comes with having stepped outside the reality everyone else seems to navigate with ease. Eventually I learned to distinguish reality from fiction. I have what is referred to in psychiatric terms as insight—the ability to know that delusions are part of my illness rather than believing in them wholesale and refusing my diagnosis. I take my medications willingly and have come to trust that they will keep away stories about angels. In this sense, I'm lucky. Not all those with mental illnesses can so easily separate fiction from reality.

But even today, when I think of all the creative energy that goes into the stories of those who are subject to madness, I'm both endlessly sympathetic and impressed. The stories represent the war going on in the mind as the self desperately tries to make sense of what's happening. Some say that psychosis is a personal crisis, that delusions are based on the suffering of the individual. Yet, personal relationships have a significant impact on those experiences of psychosis, as Richard Bentall explored in *Madness Explained:*

> Invariably . . . delusional beliefs are . . . redolent with social themes. Patients rarely profess bizarre ideas about animals or inanimate objects. Instead they believe that they are being persecuted by imaginary conspiracies, that they have been denied recognition for inventing the helicopter or the pop-up toaster, they are loved by pop stars or their doctors, or that their partners are conducting numerous affairs despite compelling evidence to the contrary. . . . Michael Musalek, a psychiatrist at the University of Vienna, has suggested that psychotic symptoms therefore reflect the core existential dilemmas experienced by ordinary people.

For those suffering with psychosis the world is distorted, but they still want to take part in the story, whether they seek recognition or an explanation for their collapsing world. They are not just trapped inside a story created by their illness; they are trying to save their own lives. If you were susceptible to slipping into a fictional world, wouldn't you try to be the hero of that world? Whether we become angels or messiahs or aliens, it's all in the interest of escaping something that seems even scarier—a life with an illness that makes it difficult to take part in the ordinary stories of the world.

Jennifer Metsker *received an MFA in poetry from the University of Michigan. Her poetry has appeared in the* Seattle Review, Whiskey Island Review, Michigan Quarterly Review, Southern Review, Cincinnati Review, Gulf Coast, Cimarron Review, Verse Daily, *and many other publications. Her work often explores issues related to psychology and psychiatry and, through her writing, she aims to foster greater compassion and understanding for the struggles faced by people with mental illnesses. She currently teaches writing at the Stamps School of Art and Design at the University of Michigan.*

True Americans

Andy Smart

About an hour after we found Dad's body, I made a decision that has shaped much of my life since then—I told the truth about his death. I called work and told my boss I was going to need some time off. When he asked what happened, I told him point blank: *My dad shot himself this morning.*

Dad was always a big guy who often said pizza was the perfect food. Had I told people he died of a heart attack, they'd have believed it. Such a story would have made some things easier, but then I would've been left with the lie and the Herculean task of convincing myself that the worst day of my life went differently than it did.

My father was born in the fifties. He was everything a "man of a certain age" was expected to be—stoic, brooding, unavailable. He was beaten as a child and bullied in school, and sought refuge in the Army, where he adopted a domineering drill-sergeant persona. Dad's thirty-year career took him from Fort Leonard Wood, Missouri, to Barksdale Air Force Base in Louisiana, then to the border of a Korean demilitarized zone and back to the United States. Back home, he joined the National Guard as a reservist and worked as a full-time mechanic for the US Postal Service. "Death before dishonor" remained his personal catch-phrase, and *Full Metal Jacket* was a film he knew by heart. In fact, he modeled himself after R. Lee Ermey's character in the film, Gunnery Sergeant Hartman.

I came home from playing outside once—I might have been twelve at the time. I arrived half an hour before curfew and Dad met me on the porch. Not good; this much I knew.

I tiptoed up the cracked concrete steps. If he didn't hear me, I thought, he might not see me. As I reached the top step, however, Dad had me in missile lock. He popped the knuckles of his right hand by clenching it into a fist. This was followed by a long, disgruntled sigh. Finally, he stood, straight-armed and squared up.

"What is your major malfunction?" he demanded. "Do you or do you not have a curfew?"

"Yes, sir, but..."

"Shut up. Are you or are you not wearing a timepiece?"

"Yes, sir..."

"Shut up!"

Behind the smudgy glass of the storm door, my mother sighed sympathetically.

It was a familiar episode, emblematic of my old man's character—his idea of manhood and leadership. Even of love. He'd delivered some variation of that same speech to platoons and individuals for years. He'd motivated people that way, successfully, throughout his career. If the in-your-face, shut-your-mouth, salute-your-commanding-officer approach was good enough for Dad's soldiers, it was certainly good enough for his son. His son who, even as I crept into my teenage years, was expected to cry about these incidents. Dad would call me a pussy, but he'd accuse me of challenging his supremacy if I didn't get upset.

I don't recall what happened that particular time on the porch. Part of me says it doesn't matter. What's true is that I came home on time and was punished anyway.

Later that night, I heard my parents talking, in muted clips, through their bedroom door. My father had apparently decided the conversation was over; I heard the creaking of a door being half-opened, the thud of his bare feet padding into the hall.

"I know how old he is, Janet," Dad said. "But you bust his ass for being early, and he'll never be late."

He retreated to the basement. When he wasn't at work—

serving Guard drill at the armory or bending a wrench at the post office—Dad was downstairs playing soldier. First it was board games, like Risk and Axis & Allies. He could singlehandedly plan sieges of every country on the planet. While these were games designed for at least two players, Dad didn't care. There was no one against whom he'd rather strategize than himself. In the concrete bunker of our unfinished basement, my father was a one-man army. Then along came Nintendo, with games like *Silent Service* and *1942*.

"Can I play?" I asked him once.

"Huh?" he grunted, then shook his head. "This is one player."

On the rare occasions Dad was upstairs, he was entrenched on the yellowing Naugahyde sofa, usually asleep. He lived in the house with his wife and his child, but he was an entity unto himself. The reclusive warrior, the great provider. Him from whom sensitivity and positive engagement couldn't rightly be expected.

"You know I love you," he'd tell us, "because I pay the bills." *You eat because I love you. You have a house because I love you. You wear the clothes on your backs because I love you.* The litany usually concluded with a section saved just for my mom—how lucky she was to find a man who loved her despite all her "issues." How he didn't drink, gamble, get high, or cheat. How he was, after all, a marked improvement from his own father. Someone, he told us, had to be strong. Men don't have the luxury of emotionality, especially not when people depend on them.

But, for all his blustering, Dad watched his body decay from indiscriminate diet and laziness. His was not the hard body of a soldier in his prime but the soggy physique of a reservist whose days were spent primarily behind a desk. After Korea, Dad left active duty to—in theory—spend more time with Mom. To do so he joined the National Guard, which, in short order, became an all-consuming endeavor. For a position that only officially required one weekend a month, it certainly seemed like a career. My father had a gift for convincing young soldiers who were on the fence to stay enlisted and for keeping old-timers in until they could draw a pension. Though his service to his country was well documented, it wasn't the type of Gunnery-Sergeant-Hartman impact he'd dreamt of.

But with a Pepsi in hand and a McDonald's Quarter Pounder in front of him, my old man soldiered on.

Several years before his suicide, Dad actually retired from the service, before he could be retired by an Army that didn't have much use left for him. By the time he died at fifty-two, he was nearly toothless, pre-diabetic, morbidly obese, and had two bad knees. His mobility and muscle strength were those of a much older man. My father died decrepit and alienated from everyone, much as he lived.

I didn't know until after he died that my father was mentally ill. I didn't know much about suicide at all, let alone that aging white men are the most likely demographic to take their own lives. I also didn't realize gun ownership increased one's risk of killing oneself—that the availability of lethal means plays a major role in suicide completion. And of course I didn't know that a man like my father, who refused to go to the doctor for routine physicals, was evidencing a potentially lethal fear of illness and mortality. His moodiness—the isolation he preferred—was mistaken for masculinity, his irascibility for strength.

Mental illness carries a stigma, true; suicide casts an even darker, more all-encompassing pall. Both my mother and I felt the judging eyes on us at my father's wake. Surely, some people thought, Dad's suicide was a reflection on us—we'd failed him in some way and he'd preferred death to life with us. Several times I thought about denying that he killed himself. As soon as we left the funeral home, I considered rewriting history in order to spare myself the awkwardness and insinuation. Instead, I got mad. I got mad at Dad for being depressed and not telling me, mad at myself for being mad at my father, and mad at everyone else for casting aspersions on my family. I would not lie, I decided. And I never have.

But what they don't tell you about the truth is that it's almost as lonely as a lie. If you insist on telling the truth, you will eventually be pained by the consequence that others are uncomfortable hearing it. Even if they don't actively participate in maintaining the all-too-prevalent stigma attached to suicide, people as a rule are reluctant to talk about it.

While I've never overtly denied how Dad left this world, I occasionally skirt the issue with metaphor. When someone asks if my father was sick, I tell them he was; the American

Foundation for Suicide Prevention (AFSP) states the vast majority of suicides are the result of mental illness. So, yes, my father was sick. AFSP also implicates chronic pain as a risk factor for suicide; given Dad's orthopedic condition, it stands to reason he was in at least some nagging discomfort. So, yes, my father was sick. Other times, when the inevitable direct inquiry comes along—*How did your father die?*—I'll simply say it was sudden. No lie there.

Only once has Dad's cause of death been seriously misrepresented. Greg, our funeral director at Gebken and Sons, called Jefferson Barracks National Cemetery to arrange Dad's burial.

"They asked if he died of natural causes," Greg said. "I said yes." Greg anticipated my protest and explained that Dad's military honors may have been delayed or denied had we declared his death a suicide. Greg's thinking ran thusly: Dad shot himself in the head. Naturally, it killed him.

Something else about the truth: Eventually you'll want a safe place to tell it. For me that safe place was, for a time, Provident Counseling's Tuesday-night support group for survivors of suicide. For the first few weeks, group was a searing pain in a still-open wound; Dad had only been dead four months when I started going. But everyone in the room was in a similar position. We'd all lost someone dear to us by suicide—a father, brother, son, daughter, a spouse. Only after a dozen sessions did I notice the disparity between the stigma-conscious and people like me. One woman, referred to here as Robin, insisted her husband had slit his wrists because of withdrawal from chewing tobacco.

"I looked on the Internet," she said. "It can make you do things."

I don't remember the color of her eyes, but I remember them scanning the room. I remember them pleading. I remember those eyes and the desperate desire for comfort.

Her husband, she told us, wasn't "the C word."

In group, the C word wasn't cancer, it was crazy. Some of us balked at the term because it insulted the mentally ill and perpetuated the stigmatization of psychological disorders. Others disliked the word because they rejected mental illness as a possible diagnosis of their loved ones; they felt that to acknowledge it would be to dishonor the memory of the dead.

While I never called Dad crazy, I called him irrational. It wasn't reasonable to punish children for transgressions they hadn't yet committed. Nor was it logical to expect a family to feel loved just because they had food, clothes, and a house. I knew, and told the group, that Dad couldn't possibly have been in his right mind that morning.

"There's no way," I said. "There's no way in hell he'd have pulled the trigger if he knew it would do this to me. Dad was smart, but he did something stupid. He was good, but did something bad. He might not have been nuts, but what he did..."

Trying to parse Dad's reasoning felt like a rabbit hole of contradictions.

A man I'll call Jacob denied his wife's suicide to his friends and family. She accidentally drowned, he told one distant cousin. Another piece of family lore was that she'd fallen down drunk and hit her head. Jacob's lies were spread thin and far, such was his need to avoid the truth.

"I don't understand," I finally said one night. "We come here every week. We say it every time. We're survivors. Of suicide. If we don't hide in here—why out there? I have nothing to be ashamed of."

I tried to meet the gaze of everyone all at once. There was creaking of seats. Somebody coughed. Finally, I was rebuked.

"We don't judge here, Andy," warned the moderator, who that week happened to be an older Jewish woman named Sandra. She often told us about her Shabbat prayers for her deceased daughter.

"I know," I said. "I'm not judging anyone. I'm just saying..."

"But that's because you're one of us," Jacob said. "You don't judge because you don't have room." He stirred his now-cold coffee with a plastic spoon. Little caffeinated ripples lapped at the cup's rim, never quite spilling. "Other people," he said. "Other people judge."

"Not all of them," I said. "Not the ones worth knowing."

"Whatever, man," Jacob said. "It's my call."

"Yeah. Yeah, it is," I said.

"Maybe Andy only admits it so freely because he's so guarded in here," someone posited. "Maybe you could live without telling everybody if you were a little more involved in group."

In that little room with its big oblong table, the Kübler-

Ross stages of grief were traversed in all directions and to varying degrees, always—at least to my mind—falling short of the last one: acceptance.

My mother, throughout the marriage, wanted to ask my father about his problems, but didn't. My father pretended to listen to his wife confess her emotional turmoil, while at the same time allowing her the illusion that he was okay. I grew up watching one parent be crazy out loud and the other be so in private.

My childhood was spent witnessing the struggle for propriety—when to speak or be silent, when to confess or deny. When I was young, I'd busy myself with toys. As an adolescent, I'd lay on the floor pretending to read *The Godfather* or something else beyond my scope. Mom and Dad would dance clumsily around one another, each afraid of stepping on the other's land mine. But no matter how hard I tried, I couldn't avoid either one. My father, far from garrulous, would occasionally talk to me.

"I love your mother," he'd say. "But goddamn it." He would take off his thick brown glasses and drop them in his lap.

"Every day it's, 'I'm depressed,'" he would say. "Bullshit."

I winced or blinked or sat perfectly still. More than once I'd come close to telling Dad that I thought I too was depressed.

"What's the real problem?" he always wanted to know. "But all I hear is this depressed routine."

I would nod my assent, feeling all the while like a traitor.

Most days, Mom had me to herself, especially when I was too young for school. Sometimes she'd offer her opinion on Dad. Sometimes I'd ask.

"He's just Jeffrey," she'd say. "He wasn't raised to talk about his feelings. Or to know how to listen." She brushed my wavy brown hair across my forehead. "I don't want you to be like that. You don't bottle it up if it hurts, okay?"

"Okay." For a moment, I recognized her as the girl in the hand-sewn wedding gown whose picture sat on the mantle.

"You promise?" she asked.

I can't remember if there was a pinky-swear. There might have been. I know now that my mother was sexually abused by her grandfather but never told my father. I know that it pained her to make love to her husband, because he didn't understand her.

Even before I knew there were limits to her transparency, I understood my mother was unafraid of herself. I understood that, while I loved my father, I did not want to be like him. I've tried to emulate Mom in her honest admission of her depression, generalized anxiety, and obsessive-compulsive disorder. I've gotten the lion's share of my fortitude from her. Maybe it comes from watching her unabashedly take Zoloft at a restaurant, so she wouldn't forget it later. Maybe it comes from her continued acceptance of a chemical imbalance, of diagnosis and treatment, of Social Security disability payments. But the tolerance and honesty with which my mother accepts the realities of mental illness comes with another dilemma: how to be brave without being too vulnerable, how to gauge when and where to unburden oneself. And to whom.

I don't remember when Dr. McKinney first started treating my mother, but I was no older than three. He continued to treat her until about the time I turned eight. Dr. McKinney was a psychiatrist, and my mother was the first member of my family to see such a doctor.

I remember precious little about the things I most want to understand. How did Mom convince Dad that treatment was necessary? She had a checkbook, but Dad was the sole breadwinner. Did he not object to this? Did she always drive herself to the appointments? Was I ever with her?

Then there's the lingering issue of "so what?" Would knowing that I sat in the back seat of our silver Ford Mustang while Mom drove to McKinney's help me in some way? Would I feel complicit in an act I was far too young to comprehend, let alone to have stopped? And would it do Mom any good to tell me if I was?

What they don't tell you about truth is that it's slippery and sharp. Truth cares less for you than you care for it.

I remember some things, but nothing haunts me the way William McKinney does.

I was just a kid. I didn't know his credentials or where exactly his office was. I didn't know how my mother found him. All I knew was what I saw: my mother, a naturally slender woman who loved to exercise, sleeping more than a cat and gaining more than a hundred pounds; my mother, passionate but predominately gentle, turning violent toward her son and husband; my mother swallowing fistfuls of Xanax, Librax, Tofranil, and God knows what; my mother on the phone, sobbing that the medicine wasn't working; my mother filling prescriptions, going back to the doctor. The doctor, for his part, continuing to write scripts. Three hundred milligrams of this, forty milligrams of that, ten more milligrams if the forty didn't work, whatever. He just doled out pills.

The use of antidepressants, according to the Centers for Disease Control and Prevention, increased nearly 400 percent between 1988 and 1994—precisely when Mom was going to McKinney. Perhaps, then, some of the doctor's overzealousness can be attributed to the culture of the time. Millions of Americans were beginning to take antidepressants. Why shouldn't Mom?

They were ugly, my mother's drug years. But the ugliest season of all was the nine-month winter of fluoxetine—otherwise known as Eli Lilly's wonder drug, Prozac. For some, Prozac was a legitimate miracle; for others, it wasn't. But for a few, like my mother, Prozac was a catastrophic pharmaceutical failure. Mom's volatility increased exponentially on Prozac. It happened only once, but once was enough—she flipped the sofa over, with me on it.

When the couch tipped, I yelped something that sounded like "Whoa!" I was still too young for profanity, though it abounded in my house. "What was that for?"

I still don't know what triggered it. Part of me remembers her saying I'd laughed at her. Another part thinks she just screamed unintelligibly. But I know we were alone. Dad was at one of Dad's places: the barracks, his two-week-long annual training, drill weekend—which one, I don't recall. It was just Mom and me.

She looked at her finger and said, "You made me break a fucking nail." Her shoulders squared to me, her pupils dilated and nostrils flared. "Why are you doing this to me? I didn't have any of this until I was pregnant with YOU."

You've heard the old riddle: Do crazy people know they're crazy? Of course it's not that simple, but still we try for parity, like scientists.

For me, the question: Should I tell the truth about suicide?

For my mother: Is the chemical I've introduced into my body producing a violent reaction that will threaten to destroy my family and my life?

And for Dad: Am I representing myself as stronger than I am? Do I feel an abundance of shame that will eventually cry out in the form of a gunshot?

The self, *en medias res,* can't always answer these questions. Truth, that great and noble-sounding abstract, can't exist for us at times. My mother, at that moment with the couch turned on its back, could not have known what she was doing.

But soon after, Phil Donahue saved Mom's life.

In 1991, *Donahue* aired an episode decrying Prozac as a catalyst for murderous rage and a precipitator of suicides. No psychiatric professionals were interviewed, Eli Lilly was not represented, and anyone wishing to defend the drug was silenced or passed over. Some say this made the episode an exercise in sensationalism and bias—that it proved nothing. In this case, I didn't care about truth—not in a scientific or universal sense. I wasn't concerned with the burden of proof and whether Donahue met it. I cared about what was true in my life. I was simply grateful my mother saw the show.

When did Mom give up fluoxetine? After *Donahue* and before *Jeopardy!* No phone calls were made to Dr. McKinney or the Walgreens pharmacist. She quit Prozac on my father's thirty-sixth birthday because a talk-show host and his guests told her she should and because some buried self-confidence told her she *could.*

Since that day, Mom has worked closely with two doctors, Stanley Wald and Scott Groesch. Neither of these men are psychiatrists. Wald was—sadly, he passed away—an internist. Groesch is a general practitioner; he's my family doctor. These men have increased Mom's mental health and decreased her reliance on drugs. Wald initiated a gradual weaning off of Tofranil, withdrawal from which greatly, though temporarily, exacerbated Mom's panic disorder. He stood by Mom as she slowly left the medication—and all the weight she'd gained—behind. Groesch introduced Mom to her personal wonder drug, Zoloft. Two hundred milligrams, or two pills, a day; that's one-tenth of Mom's daily pill count at the apex of the McKinney regime.

Some truths about the present day:

Like my parents before me, I am mentally ill. I take Zoloft, or at least I try; I'm forgetful, so I take it only sporadically, which negates the cumulative effect of the drug. I stopped going to the Provident group after seven months. It outlived its usefulness, for me at least. Every session was an exercise in negative time travel—each of us transported back to the day our loved one died just to begin the healing all over again, the scab having been torn from the wound. Any time I expressed a desire to push forward and focus on recovery, I was chastised. *This is a place for grief,* I was told. Too much grieving was doing me no good, so I took my leave of the group. I am not one for spending time in such places.

For this reason, also, I don't frequently visit Dad's grave. But a week or so after he died, Mom and I went together. The meandering roads of Jefferson Barracks are lined with modest white headstones, some dating back to the Civil War. In his suicide note, this is where my father asked to be buried.

There's the usual information on Dad's tombstone—his birthday and the day he died, but when we arrived at his gravesite that day, we were confronted by another glaring addition. *Vietnam,* the tombstone read. Mom and I exchanged glances in silence. She didn't seem to have any answers, but I knew my father was never in Vietnam.

I lost sleep over the headstone issue for a few days before I called Dad's buddy Dan, who was our point of contact with the Army following Dad's death.

"Hey," I said, "can I talk to you about Dad's marker?"

"Yeah, sure," Dan said. Before I could answer, he asked, "What's wrong? They didn't boot the spelling or something, right?"

"Not exactly," I said. "Dan, they've got it on there that he was in 'Nam."

I could hear Dan breathing into the receiver.

I went on. "You and I both know that's not true."

Dan was quiet. Then, finally, he spoke. "I wouldn't worry about that," he said. "He served during the Vietnam era."

Clocks ticked. My stomach gurgled.

"He was a good soldier," Dan said.

I didn't argue. Everything about that was true enough. It was as true as Greg's dubious definition of "natural causes," as true as when Mom tells me she doesn't know why she's depressed.

"I just am," she says with a defeated shrug. "Does there have to be a reason?"

I've spent almost three thousand days living in the wake of my father's suicide. I've spent more than three decades living with and around mental illness. And the constant, the thing I thought was concrete, was truth. Honesty, I believed, was noble, but it was honesty that almost cost my mother her life—honesty and a blind belief in the authority of a doctor. On the other hand, *dis*honesty killed my father. He could never quite own who or what he was. He had his vision of manliness and projected an image that complied with it. But that wasn't Dad. Not really. Dad was scared of things like old age and sickness and not being the right kind of man.

Rectitude. That was big with Dad. So he made a life giving orders and issuing critiques that he himself didn't follow.

In the end, it isn't always simple to tell the difference between what's true and what isn't. It's even harder to know when or how to tell even the portion of truth we know. Standing next to Mom at the cemetery that day, I don't remember what was said or if we spoke out loud at all. I stared at the headstone. *Staff Sergeant Jeffrey M. Smart, US Army.* On that wet-hot afternoon, I met my father for the first time by reading the words Mom and I had chosen:

Dearest Husband. Beloved Father. True American.

As Mom and I drove away, past the graves and the giant American flag, we too seemed new. Our ordeal had changed us, I thought. We were no longer either mentally ill or not. No longer simply a mother and son. We were something else. We, too, were good soldiers.

Andy Smart *lives and writes in Saint Louis, Missouri. He is passionate about relieving the stigma of mental illness, especially in an attempt to prevent suicides. His work has appeared in several journals, in print and online.*

'Scuse Me While I Fuck the Sky*

Ryan Bloom

    *(A substitute lyric tossed off by Jimi Hendrix as a downpour drenched the Seattle concert stage ~~where he was playing~~ on which he played, which seems an appropriate title for this essay because of the ~~confusion~~ contradiction born ~~from~~ of a love ~~and~~ [+ that ~~soaks~~ grows inevitably into a] despair beyond the individual's control, beyond, even, [keep reading without commas though I want them here; does that mean I should get rid of them?] the control of a rock g.d [fill in "o" for final draft, keep "g" lowercase], [+ as if simultaneously anointed with gifts from the ~~Heavens~~ sky {parallel title} and touched by the fires {ok to echo Jamison's title?} below,] the dualism condemning the individual [+ to love and accept, to *need*, that which should be ~~despised~~ ignored and exorcised, exorcism being a thing the individual will not countenance ~~because of~~ due to the {+ unbearable level of} uncertainty it would entail], control of the uncontrollable being, no matter what is said below, the absolute, rock-bottom cause of everything, of every recurrent bit of anxiety, of every unwanted, intrusive obsession and compulsion, good or bad, positive or negative, whether to create or destroy.)

[+ When you're born] ~~No~~ one tells you ~~that~~ you're different.
[+ Or, to be more accurate, that you *will be* different, will, suddenly, on what is likely to be an otherwise drab and ordinary October day, *become* different {<u>note to self: average onset of mental illness very approximately seems to occur between twelve and twenty, though probably shouldn't include stat here, because intend to focus on the one illness, and don't want to be so specific as to say what that one is, yet, so can't say the average onset of O.C.D. is (X) because, even if I did want to name it at this point, the explanation required about different studies finding average onset ranges from age nine to twenty-four would be too distracting</u>}, and that when it happens, when, at eleven, walking into your second-floor bedroom, the same bedroom you walked into the night before, and the night before that, the week before, the year before, when you crumple to the floor because, somehow, the things on your dresser—your CDs and books and the two superhero folders you use for school "completely" rearranged, that *all* of the angles are things are not where they—have been when you see off, that should be, you will, from your dampened spot on the ground, begin to count—one, two, three, tap the right bedpost, one, two, three, tap the left bedpost, circle the mattress, circle the mattress, get in bed, two sips of water from the jug on the night-stand, no more, not another sip no matter how thirsty, how incredibly parched and desert-dry your throat, because if you take another sip you'll cause yourself to have a heart attack or cause Mom to have one, or Dad, so put the glass down, just put it down, *now*: five, four, three, two—and when this no one will tell things could be [+ , that things] fact, different for happens, you] ~~That~~ different~~:~~ ~~Are,~~ in 99 percent make up 70 population, men and women, dexMundi, the C.I.A.'s IndexMundi counting for of adults (who percent of Earth's 2,648,092,799 2,661,529,094 according to In- which pulls from World Factbook, and Factbook ac- the *approximate* population numbers, not the 99 percent O.C.D.-free figure, which comes from the NIMH and The Kim Foundation, and which speaks more specifically to the United States, rather than the world) **[ax this <u>highlighted</u> section, I think, right?]**, because when you're born, as you grow up

in your modest-but-nice home in Metro Washington, with

normal,
parents—
one tells
this stuff
different,
possibly
incorrect
word like
you'll end
in some
[+ and]
way, such
example,

because how are you, at eleven years
old, to know that 45–65 percent of the
symptoms seen in childhood ~~O.C.D.~~
cases appear to be attributable to
genetic factors, and so maybe one or
both of your parents is maybe not so
"well adjusted," and maybe if you knew
that you could talk to them, or they
could talk to you, or you could talk to
each other, and maybe, before this thing
gets out of hand, it could be addressed,
because it also appears that the earlier
you learn to ignore the intruders, the
better, maybe, the results

well-adjusted
—because no
you any of
about being
because it's
too politically
to use a
"different,"
up finding out
painful ~~or~~
embarrassing
as when, for
in homeroom

a friend flashes a newly acquired driver's license and says,
"Let's skip," and on the way to the car, a threadbare

Volvo 240 DL—
your ~~chauffeur~~
"What do you
before getting
and after an
of confused
friend, who
encouraging
school, is a
a best friend,
not begin to
you purposeful
"Excuse me?"

somehow instinctively knowing that what you are about
to say is vaguely, amorphous-
ly embarrassing, yet also,
oddly, not thinking much of
it, because even the big-time
athletes you watch on TV do
these sorts of things, these
rituals and routines, adjusting the straps of their batting
gloves twice on each hand,
then the helmet, once, twice,
three times, then back to the
gloves, twice more on each
hand, then again the helmet

—you ask
friend,
count to
in the car?"
initial period
silence, your
despite
you to skip
good friend,
one who would
consider doing
harm, says,
and "What do

you mean?" and "Tell me more," which you do, giving just a

couple more examples—
could you have known
ing this, that also ex-
every time you walk down
hall in your apartment,
specific part of a specific
on the wall, and if you
because someone else is
you're afraid they might
what you're doing, you

how the pencils and
pens and postcards, the
"Out, Damned Spot"
eraser and X-ACTO
knife on your desk are
all aligned in specific
ways, at specific angles,
and if one of them is
moved, even just a
little, the compulsion to
use the X-ACTO knife
for a purpose other

—and how
that reveal-
plaining how
the main
you tap a
painting
don't do it
with you and
catch on to
then feel

as if you're going
out or throw up or
if both, it's possible
choke on your own
die, and this is why,
said person is dis-
must go back to tap
center of the paint-
you're being honest,
really telling your
of this, which you're
not, you'd say that
in said example
random person at
in fact, your sig-
other, and even she
know about these
yours, about any of
of it that she hasn't
figured out on her
nine years together,
you are too fucking
what might happen
her, though you
positively know, as
a person can ever
thing about another
you absolutely know
no way whatsoever
of you or laugh or
your face, yet, none-
are convinced you
her, despite the fact
know she will say
the most intelligent
things, because the
if you tell her, no,
she'll break up with

than that for which it is
intended becomes so over-
whelming that you have to
fix the overwhelming that
you have to fix the mis-
aligned object as quickly as
possible and get out of the
room before you maybe do
something you'll definitely
regret, and then, even once
you're out of the room, the
thought of the blade dragging
across your skin, the palm
of your hand, the webbing
of your fingers, a wrist, both
wrists, your Adam's apple,
of how the skin won't open
at first, because the slit is so
incredibly precise, so perfect
that it's not until the blood
begins to force its way out, to
burst in propulsive gushes,
that you know it's real, even
though it's not real, but
the thought is so insistent
that you have to check your
extremities to make sure,
despite, even while you're
checking, knowing how
ridiculous and absolutely not
real the thought is, knowing
it's just a thought, knowing
you did not and would not
drag a razor-sharp blade
across your skin, somehow,
still, you have to check to
make sure, and, okay, so you
don't really tell your friend
all of this, you stop right
after the bit about things
needing to be appropriately
aligned on the desk, because
already by that point you are
staring at disbelief and you
know it would be a mistake
to keep talking, so you don't

to pass
both, and
you could
vomit and
as soon as
tracted, you
the exact
ing, and if
if you were
friend all
obviously
said person
is not a
all, but is,
nificant
doesn't
routines of
it, or any
silently
own after
because
scared
if you tell
absolutely
much as
know any-
person,
she will in
make fun
throw it in
theless, you
cannot tell
that you
and do all
and caring
problem is,
it's not that
you, it's

that, maybe not right away, but soon enough, if you tell her,
she'll have a heart attack and die, because she's a runner,

and so even though she won't break things off, she will still *leave you forever,* all alone, abandoned— [You *will* lose control] —and anyway, all those years ago, long before your significant other, the whole reason you were even willing to try to explain some of this **[though clearly not all of this, and not this specifically, as that makes no chronological sense]** to your now wide-eyed friend is because you just couldn't quite process, "Wait a minute, are you really saying you don't do these things, too?" and how could you have known that the explanation would result in your well-meaning, not-hurtful, truly good-natured friend— who, remember, does not actually know as much as it now seems, and is truly not the jerk this recursive, asynchronous telling may indicate —spending the next twenty years switching things around on your desk, shifting pencils and pens, adjusting the carefully positioned angle of the postcards, sometimes a lot, sometimes a little, tilting hallway paintings, trying with faux absentmind- edness to rush you into the car before you can finish count- ing, rearranging books on your shelf, flipping a facedown copy of Italo Calvino's *Difficult Loves* **[while true, does it seem too much here, too much of an authorial wink; would changing it to a different book to avoid pre- ciousness be dishonest?]** so that it's face up, just to see if you'll notice, if you were telling the truth all those years ago, or if the whole thing is some elaborate ~~ruse~~ joke and you can be caught off-guard, flushed out like a snake from a hole **[would rat give a better sense of the self-disgust felt; does snake seem too strong, too much a predator, ver- sus rat being prey (weak)?]**, and when you do notice, your friend will laugh or chuckle or poke you in the ribs, as if hit- ting the punch line of a long-shared joke, an inside joke, and that's okay (not ideal or perfect or good but okay), because your friend truly does not intend harm, and even if "not intending harm" seems kind of like "not understanding," still you would much, much rather your friend think the situation humorous instead of pitiable, no question about it, but de- spite that, you know in the central core of your mind, in the same place you know there is absolutely nothing the voice

in your head—
nothing Not Voice
actually, legiti-
you or any of the
love or the people
know in some An-
far, far away, you
of the problem
**emphasis on
one problem,**
may in fact be just
your friend's
humoring and
is possibly a result
culture, of Woody

not a crazy-person voice,
not a voice that ~~I~~ [+ you]
believe is some other
person or being speaking
to **me** [+ you], rather more
as if ~~I~~ [+ you] were to poke
~~myself~~ [+ yourself] over
and over again with **my**
[+ your] own finger, able,
somehow, to make it seem
like, simultaneously, it
is and is not **my** [+ *your*]
finger doing the poking,
while, in a way that seems
impossible to explain, still
knowing it is definitely,
absolutely just **me** [+ you]
poking ~~myself~~ [+ yourself]

—there is
can do to
mately harm
people you
you don't even
dorran village
know that part
**[too much
"the," as if it's
one solution]**
this: maybe
reaction, the
jesting, which
of popular
Allen or *Monk*-

type portrayals ~~of O.C.D.~~ (the latter of which, I'm told, is
fairly accurate in its depiction of obsessions and compulsions,
yet, despite this, because it is a TV show meant to entertain,
it still plays those afflictions for laughs, and in one sense,
the main sense, who cares, it's just *entertainment*, but in
another sense, one I have a hard time accepting, because not
only is it immensely bothersome but it's also potentially a
real problem, in this other sense in which people take every
little thing so damn seriously, to the point that every word or
phrase that might potentially, maybe, possibly, perhaps, by
some off chance be less than 100 percent politically correct
and establishment codified is thus received as another hammer blow to the eggshell heart of some poor, helpless ~~chick-
adee~~ soul, who will now, as a result of societal carelessness
(or callousness or worse) grow up broken and unable to cope
with the world, in this sense, which is near-impossible to
accept) **[ax highlighted?]**, maybe ~~your friend's~~ [+ this]
harmless humoring, maybe the popular-culture conception
of ~~O.C.D.~~ [+ this thing] really does perpetuate "potentially,
maybe, possibly" harmful lenses and beliefs, and not only
among the general public to which your friend belongs, but
maybe also among some non-specialized caregivers, such that
a person dealing with a case of ~~O.C.D.~~ [+ this thing], a case
that to that person is horrifyingly not funny in its time-con-
suming, life-altering grip of again and again and again and

over and over and again and over and over and again, maybe
someone will refuse the opportunity to seek seriously needed help ~~for *a serious problem*~~ because ~~Not-Voice knows
that~~ it's possible even the docs may think of ~~O.C.D.~~ [+ this
thing] as more pop Woody Allen than depressed-in-the-oven
Plath, more itchy Monk than double-barrel Hemingway, and
why pay for a sort of humoring you've spent nearly every day
of your thirty-four years of life getting for free **[note to self:
if it didn't surface until eleven, it's really twenty-three
years]**, a humoring that, while better than the alternative,
the pity, does nothing to still the spinning circular loops of
compulsion and do it and don't do it and go and stop and sit
and stand and run, walk, leap, tap, wash, wash, wash, turn,
drink, again, check, check, again, again, again, again, again,
again, because while it's true and clear as day that Not Voice
is not real, is neither a schizotypal voice nor a unipolar voice
of oblivion, while it's obvious that everyone occasionally has
"weird" thoughts like yours, and so, it stands to reason, your
thoughts are actually pretty normal, and thus the problem is
really— because it's all very straightforward — that you're simply focusing
too much time and energy on thoughts every-
one else has and effortlessly
ignores, because of the kernel of validity in this psychological
wisdom, a wisdom now cherry-topped with the aforemen-
tioned "potentially, maybe, possibly" harmful humorous
lenses and beliefs, it's not so hard to understand how a
person, a doctor or friend, may not realize that every ~~single~~
time ~~I get near~~ a ledge [+ approaches], whether attached to
a high-rise balcony or a baseball-stadium bleacher, Not Voice
whispers— jump —not once, not a simple, staccato jump,
but a steady, droning, pounding, bleating
rhythm of jump, jump, jump, jump, jump, jump, jump, jump,
jump, jump, jump, jump, jump, jump, jump, jump, jump,
jump, jump, jump, jump, jump, jump, jump, jump, jump,
jump, jump, jump, jump, jump, jump, jump, jump, jump,
jump, jump, jump, jump, jump, jump, jump, jump, jump,
jump, jump, jump, jump, jump, jump, jump, jump, jump,

j

     u

          m

              p

                 p

                   p

                 p

                     p

                       p

                     p

                       p

                        p

                        p

                       p

                       p

the repetition so in-
cessant that the only option, despite Not Voice not being real,
is to, as quietly and surreptitiously as possible, white-knuck-
le the railing or the arms of the metal seat or whatever is
available, anything at all **[explain pretending to be dizzy,
and other lines of reasoning used in these situations,
or no?]**, because even though the problem may be one of
simply paying too much attention to a rather mundane and
quotidian thought, still, nonetheless, Not Voice knows that if
I'm willing to one, two, three, tap the right bedpost, one, two,
three, tap the left bedpost, circle the mattress, tap, circle the
mattress, get in bed, take two sips of water from the jug on
the dresser, then, finally,

get ready for sleep—
thought goes, if Not
make me do all of
night just to get into
to say, completely
my rational, think-
beyond my control,
say that one day,
in the future, who's
won't listen to other
pounding, bleating

Not me. No. Not

So I humor Not
I always have: I
to tap and twirl and
like a circus lion,
who knows when
might decide to pull
cat o' nine and get
Today? Tomorrow?
Month? Year?

[+ The truth,
that none of this is
on with the game of
tricks on command,
my own prodding
Way back at the
introductory note
"love" as being part
and that may, by

and, to be even more honest, to
add what I left out earlier, after
doing all of the above, to then
get back out of bed, ~~because,~~
~~yes, I have to get back out, I~~
~~cannot do it ahead of time,~~
~~before getting in bed in the~~
~~first place~~ to peek through the
window blinds in order to reassure myself that lights are on in
other apartments, that should I
need help, should I suffer a sudden, out-of-nowhere embolism,
someone will be there to save
me, or possibly save me, and
then, because I'm up, I should
try to take a leak, again, even
though I just did a minute ago,
I should try again so that once I
do settle in bed I won't have the
urge and then have to get back
up and start the whole process
over, and for the same reason,
before getting back in bed, if
the water jug on the nightstand
is less than half full, I'll need
to go fill it up, because what if
I wake up gasping in the middle
of the night and need an *entire*
jug of water just to keep breathing, and if I don't go fill it up,
if I let it get too empty, then I
could die of my own stupidity,
and what could be more stupid
than that

—the
Voice can
this every
bed, who's
beyond
ing mind,
who's to
some time
to say I
droning,
commands?
me.
Voice as
continue
perform
because
the voice
out the
serious?
Next week?

though, is
why I go
performing
a slave to
finger.]
top, the
mentioned
of this deal,
this point,

seem curious: what could one possibly love about ~~O.C.D.~~ [+
this ~~illness~~ thing]? Maybe—
just out of my depth here [or 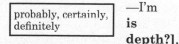 —I'm
the phrase "beyond" my   is
                                                              depth?],
because as much as, given the chance, given some breakthrough in science, I would say, "Yes, dear Lord, touch me
with your curing hand," [should I insert "delayed sleep
phase syndrome" and how when I was little I'd be
awake all night praying for things to change even
though I didn't believe in *that* voice either?] I would

be lying if I didn't admit what is likely another pernicious and wrongheaded belief, what is certainly a widespread and not wholly inaccurate belief **[is the difference between "wrongheaded" and "not wholly inaccurate" clear {i.e. it's harmful to believe vs. there is some scientific evidence to support}]**, which is that, despite the fact that the MacArthur Foundation **[is the foundation's association with creativity and genius well-known enough?] [insert somewhere (?): O.C.D. hits all socioeconomic levels (53.97 percent middle class) but seems to occur alongside high verbal IQ, though, paradoxically, maybe also with poor verbal memory (poor organizational memory abilities in general)] [not the place for it, but maybe insert how O.C.D. is neither new nor a first-world-only problem]** is not likely to come calling anytime soon ~~(or ever)~~, despite the fact that Mr. Nobel and Mr. Pulitzer, that Man Booker and Mrs. Whiting, that chances **[I really want to be able to calculate this, but ten minutes of my math-deficient searching has gotten me nowhere; ask Buddy or Dad]** are none of them will be knocking down the door in the near future, ~~or ever~~, **[insert how I can't write things like this {ever} because by writing them down I make them "true"]** despite all of this, I cannot help believing, because personal experience makes it seem so very obvious, that whatever iota of writing ability I have, it is *because of* ~~my O.C.D.~~ **[+ this thing]**, because I can't stop obsessing over every single word of every single sentence, because I can't stop reading each one over and over, speaking them into my palm, aloud **[I think it would be too distracting to sidetrack into the whole writing in public thing, hence speaking into the palm so others don't hear, and how this is part of the O.C.D. routine, how I can't write if I break the routine, even if I'm a few minutes off my schedule; consider if there is a way to add this somewhere else]**, mouthing them, silently, writing and rewriting, again and again and again and again, for hours upon hours upon days and weeks and years, until the sentences lose all meaning, and then I think, "Boy, you really wrote a nonsensical piece of shit

there, didn't you?" and as a result of this obsessive loss of
meaning—

in a drawer
three, and
back to it,
all of the
sentence
the like),
able to see
and so, as
non-MacAr-
I will be able
again, and
the sentenc-
better, such

not the traditional
English-language sense of
obsession but a more clinical
obsession, which is to say my
own finger acting like a large
needle taken to my water-bal-
loon brain, trying to poke as
many holes as possible, watching as I try, compulsively, to
stem the flow of liquid from a
hundred holes at once, which,
yes, does also get in the way
of writing, so that there is, at
once, plus and minus, though
I allow myself to believe the
minus is really a plus

—I'll stick the thing
for a year or two or
eventually I'll come
having forgotten
specifics (as far as
construction and
and I will then be
the words anew,
best as my limited,
thur abilities allow,
to obsess over it all
in so doing make
es just a tiny bit
that in the end,

whatever all of this work amounts to, it will have been possible only and solely *because of* O.C.D., not *despite*
it, and if it's O.C.D. that has given me this thing that I
love so— my modicum of writing ability —how could I possibly
not love it back?

This belief, I realize, is dangerous, because if the thing I
associate with the deepest, most worthwhile, most gratifying
and life-giving part of my self— my writing — is burnished
by, or, worse, created by, my illness, then, in
a way, I become my illness, and if I don't *have* O.C.D., if I *am*
O.C.D., then I excuse all of ~~the~~ [+ my] myriad obsessions and
compulsions as necessary, and if these things are necessary
in order to write, the thing I want to do more than anything
else, then I will cease to fight them, I will give into them,
and, worse, I will not want them to go away, I will reject that
deus ex machina breakthrough in science as incompatible
with my [+ very {seems unnecessary, but leave to em-
phasize the deep-rooted nature}] core being, and if I'm
not willing to accept even the no-effort breakthrough cure,
what on earth would make me fight and struggle and sweat
and grapple and beat and beat and beat [that is: beat and
struggle not to beat and struggle] against the reality of
an incredibly insidious disease that is spending every ounce
of its effort not to be defeated? A thing that is by its very

nature unhealthy and problematic becomes the image of healthy functioning, and that sort of Orwellian contradiction, given time to grow, if one accepts the one, two, three, circle, circle, tap, tap commands as necessary to their purpose in life, that's the sort of belief that seems at least vaguely capable of leading one to also accept other, more drastic things, compulsions, words and actions, as necessary, too. And I don't mean to come off— | it's the last thing I want | —as theatrical or alarmist or over the top, because it's probably true that a person who is forced to pay such hyper attention to his [+ their] mind, despite his [+ their] fears, probably has [+ have] *less* chance of losing it—

most likely every- will just keep on on (though maybe necessarily a good because the

unlike in The Far Side cartoon that haunted my childhood, where the curator walks into the snake house and suddenly, out of no-where, comes down with an "attack of the willies"

—and thing keeping that's not thing either), statistics

indicate that taking Not Voice up on its more extreme suggestions— alone rarely or it's true that with O.C.D. tendencies, tually make

to swerve the car to run down a person on the side of the road, to slice open your palm with an X-ACTO knife, to jump off your friend's eighth-floor balcony

—as a result of O.C.D. never happens, though 50 percent of those do experience suicidal and 15 percent even- an attempt, and even

if that attempt is to escape the mind rather than to follow through on a compulsion **[in other words, the attempted suicide is not actually because of O.C.D. but to escape O.C.D; another way of thinking about this would be to imagine that the attempt is not because the voice tells you to jump but because you want the voice to stop telling you, so that, in a way, the fulfillment is the rebellion; maybe it's easier to consider this with another base example: you're not following through on the compulsion to slice open your hand, which, if you did, would be *because* of O.C.D., rather you're taking action *against* O.C.D., saying, "not another lash; *I'm* in control here" {this can't be inserted into the main text until clarified, because it's a fine point that may not seem to make any difference}]**, still I feel compelled to disagree with Nietzsche, because even if O.C.D. potentially, maybe, possibly *won't* cause me to throw myself from a tall building, ~~and while I do worry about the writing/O.C.D. connection, it is for that very reason that~~ still it's hard to accept, I cannot accept, won't let myself accept his what-doesn't-kill-me-makes-me-stronger mantra, because that would mean O.C.D. is, in some way, good for me, good for my writing, which is what I want so desperately to believe, because if that's true, I can stop fighting not to fight, I can accept O.C.D. as who I *am*, and so I'll never be forced to confront it, to burn and itch and do the hard work of grasping it by the neck— as it sometimes —and I'll never know that maybe way back suggests I do to at the beginning when I said all that stuff small animals, about nobody telling me I was different, dogs, cats maybe all of those people already knew more about this thing than I do: maybe they didn't tell me because I don't *have* to be.

[+ Maybe.]

Ryan Bloom *is an English lecturer at the University of Maryland, Baltimore County. He has written for the* New Yorker, Guernica, PEN America, Salon, Black Clock, *the* Arabesques Review, *the* American Prospect, *and other publications. His translation of Albert Camus'* Notebooks 1951-1959 *(Rowman and Littlefield) was nominated for the 2009 French-American Foundation and Florence Gould Foundation's Translation Prize for superior English translation of French prose. In 2014 he was awarded the Eli Cantor Fellowship by The Corporation of Yaddo, an artist's colony in Saratoga Springs, New York.*

One of Those

Annita Sawyer

May 2001

The entry area was packed by the time I arrived. A crowd of psychiatrists, psychologists, social workers, politicians, religious and civic leaders, and community members was gathering for a benefit conference to celebrate the fortieth anniversary of the founding of Fellowship Place, a community center in New Haven for people with mental illness. Eminent faculty members from my years in graduate school nodded and smiled as I squeezed past. *You're okay,* I told myself. *You're a psychologist now.*

Tables filled with hors d'oeuvres and wine rimmed the rotunda of an elegant oak-paneled Yale reception area outside the auditorium. Two Fellowship Place violinists playing Mozart greeted enthusiastic guests, although chattering voices quickly overwhelmed the music. As we all flowed into the auditorium, I met a social worker I recognized from my Quaker meeting. She and I found a spot on the far side of the room where we could lean against a wall. All the seats had been taken.

Famed authors William Styron and Kay Redfield Jamison sat at a table onstage. They were there to discuss the ways that social stigma complicates the identification and treatment of mental illness. Each gave harrowing examples of personal experience with depression and bipolar disorder and the shame that made already heartbreaking emotional pain even worse.

Then they turned to the stunned audience and implored each of us to consider our own psychiatric history.

"How many of you have recovered from depression, schizophrenia, severe anxiety, or other disabling mental illnesses?" Kay Jamison asked. Self-conscious rustling rippled through the room. A few well-dressed individuals froze. Some sneaked sideways glances at the crowd. Except for a few Fellowship Place graduates, no one raised a hand.

"Fear of stigma keeps you silent," she continued. "But unless you speak up, the positive influence of your success is lost." If accomplished men and women shared their stories of recovery from mental illness, she told us, stigma and hopelessness could be modified, even overcome.

Inspired, I turned to the social worker standing beside me. "I'm one of those," I whispered, barely inclining my head so she could hear. Clara spoke without moving, her face straight ahead. "Me, too," she said.

I'd volunteered several of those whispered confessions over the years. I'd admitted to a few trusted friends, or people I'd met with similar pasts, that I'd been troubled as an adolescent, hospitalized even, although I kept the schizophrenia diagnosis to myself. Two or three decades after the fact, that didn't sound so bad—dismissible as a youthful indiscretion, not unlike my friend who crashed the family car the first time she got drunk, or the one who spent the summer after her freshman year of college at her boyfriend's apartment while her parents thought she was in the dorm.

Yet Clara and I never pursued our revelations further or referred to our brief exchange again. I didn't tell her that I'd sent for my psychiatric hospital records a few weeks earlier, and that I was expecting them soon in the mail.

Even from a distance, I could identify the small white truck making its way down the narrow country road. Spring's afternoon light had drawn me out for a walk, and I was on the return stretch. Yellow primroses and multicolored pansies brightened yards around the modest raised ranches, colonials, and split-levels scattered along the quiet street. I enjoyed my neighborhood. Children played hopscotch and catch in the road. Dog walkers stopped to chat. Most of the houses were around thirty years old, and several families had lived there almost that long. For my husband Bill and me, it was twenty-five.

I tried to focus on the day, breathing in the color of the Japanese maples, which shone like red glass in the sunlight. Spirea bushes taller than me bowed with blossoms—they looked like they were covered in snow. But as the truck moved closer, I walked faster. I needed to get home. Maybe the package was already there.

The young woman who delivered our mail slowed the truck and waved when she saw me. She picked up a large gray envelope, which she held out the open door. I felt a jolt—the scene jumped, as if time had burped. *What does she want?* I thought. As the letter-carrier handed me the envelope with "New York Presbyterian Hospital" printed in a corner, I recovered some presence of mind. I thanked her for the personal delivery. Ears ringing, I finished my walk, feigning calm. I smiled and waved as I passed two of my neighbors.

In the house, I ran straight to the sunroom, tearing open my envelope along the way. Breathless, I flopped onto the couch. Then I paused. Forcing myself to inhale, I slowly moved to sit upright. Heady perfume from fat pink and white peonies crowded into a vase on the glass coffee table suffused the air. The room glowed, lit by late-afternoon sun. With the reverence of a midwife delivering her first baby, I lifted the heavy folder from its package. I moved my fingers across my name and case number on the label. I held my breath as I raised the cardboard cover and confronted the first page. Awe became voraciousness as I began to read.

After the admission note came the hospital's psychological assessment:

New York Hospital—Westchester Division
Psychological Report: June 7, 1960:
Miss Perez is an intelligent, creative, and imaginative youngster who seems to be slipping into a quicksand-like illness . . . deeply depressed with suicidal preoccupations and fantasies. She has been able to maintain a facade of functioning, but is paying dearly for it in terms of the energy consumed by her obsessive patterns. On the Rorschach, there are indicators of catatonic turbulence, deep depression, and suicidal concerns.

The general picture is one of an insidious illness made some-
what more hopeful by some still remaining signs of vitality.
— J.D. PhD

Whoever wrote this sounds kind, I thought. *Although she's a*
bit overboard with the illness imagery.

Transfixed, I continued reading all day and into the night.
Other than occasionally interrupting myself to pee, I didn't
stop. Bill's concerns were dispatched with a wave of my hand:
"Don't say anything. I need privacy. Please just leave me alone."

Our little calico cat, Fuegito, kept me company. She tucked
herself under my arm. She climbed up my back to sit on my
shoulder. When I slumped into the pillows, she cuddled in the
crook of my neck. She never left me.

Several psychiatrists had written detailed notes.

New York Hospital—Westchester Division
June 4, 1960: patient notes:
Since her admission the patient, to the extent that she was
allowed, spent a great deal of time by herself in her room and
when she was asked to come out with the group has furtively
occupied herself on the outskirts of that group in such solitary
activities as reading. She has likewise, in the therapy program
of the hospital, given minimal participation, protesting her
gross lack of ability. In psychotherapy, she displays the same
kind of passive resistance. Though obviously a girl of consid-
erable intelligence, her productions, even in answer to specific
questions, are of an obviously sparse and intentionally uncom-
municative sort. Thus, although she obviously commands a
superior vocabulary, she can only describe herself as "crumby"
and it may be said that her participation in psychotherapy is
indeed no more than a crumb of what it might be.

Diagnosis Offered: Dementia Praecox,Other Types, Depressed
APA Diagnosis: Schizophrenic Reaction, Schizo-Affective Type
—Dr. Smith

I'd long dismissed my diagnosis as misguided, a mistake
of the times. But seeing Dr. Smith's note in print dismayed
me. His frustration with my difficulty speaking and his lack

of sympathy for the paralyzing fear he characterized as hostile resistance filled me with shame. I felt profoundly misunderstood. Despite all the professional perspective gained from twenty years as a therapist, I couldn't separate my essence from his contempt. Nevertheless, mesmerized by these reports that transported me directly into the early hospital years, I read and reread through to the last page.

New York Hospital—Westchester Division
August 10, 1960; Mental Status:
The patient was neatly groomed, fearful but cooperative. Voice was a barely audible whisper and there was much blocking. There was little facial expression other than a vague sadness. She kept her hands rigidly clasped. She looked much younger than her age and appeared to stare off into the distance as though unable to converge her gaze on nearby objects. (Arieti has described both of these physical characteristics as frequent findings in catatonic schizophrenia.) She stated that she was depressed and longed for death so that she could cease to be "a bother." Her feelings of worthlessness amounted to an obsession to which she made continual reference.... Judgment and insight were lacking.
—Dr. O'Connell

I dragged myself to bed in the dark early hours of morning.

With daylight, I returned to the sunroom. Wrapped in an old blanket, I huddled on the couch, shivering. Under a clear blue sky, purple and white pansies, yellow begonias, and vivid pink impatiens fluttered in window boxes just outside the glass. The beautiful world around me seemed far away—unreal and meaningless.

What's happened? I wondered. *How can I be like this?*

Get a grip, another voice responded, not unkindly. *You have responsibilities; you have work to do. You've got to get a grip.*

But I had no answers and no grip. I sat, barely moving. Hours passed.

"How about some tea?" Bill offered. His face looked pale and tired. "Can I help?" he asked again. "Anything I can do?" he asked a few hours later. "Tea?"

"Tea is good," I said. I could tell he needed some way to feel relevant. Sometimes I could only nod. "I need time to process," I said, when I could speak. "I still need to be alone, if that's okay."

"Sure," he said. It wasn't really okay. He didn't understand why I was so upset or why he couldn't help; I hadn't found words to explain. I worried he was angry, but I didn't, couldn't stop.

I pored through the thick chart several times. I recorded dates and the number of shock treatments received. I calculated the total. I double-checked. I checked again. The sum was eighty-nine. Eighty-nine electroshock treatments.

Eighty-nine shock treatments. For the rest of the week I walked around dazed and preoccupied—counting, counting, and counting some more. I made charts and diagrams and lists, which I arranged and rearranged. No matter how I tried, the number didn't change. *Eighty-nine shock treatments.*

June 17, 1960: Has started on shock.
August 28, 1960: Course of 25 EST completed this month.
April 18, 1962: Electroshock therapy stopped after twenty consecutive treatments.
November 18, 1962: EST series started and completed after 18 treatments.
April 17,1963: After a completion of a regular series of 20 EST treatments two months ago patient was placed on weekly maintenance EST treatments which were discontinued 2 weeks ago after a total of 6.

Once my stunned disbelief wore off, I sank into mourning. Imagining dead tissue where vital cells should be, I grieved for what I might have been. Nevertheless, I had to bring myself to function in the present world among my colleagues, and my patients, and the everyday strangers in the supermarket or on the street who had no idea of my situation. They couldn't see the hospital pajamas or the terrified girl. They didn't know what was missing, what possibilities had been burned away inside my brain.

Exactly one week later, a second package arrived. These were the records from the hospital I'd been transferred to after New York Hospital gave up. Thanks to my mother's best friend's political connections, the director of the New York State Psychiatric Institute had been required to accept me as a patient. This facility, generally known as PI, was a teaching hospital affiliated with Columbia-Presbyterian Medical Center. PI was the hospital I eventually came to think of as home. It was where I'd learned about the world. Its staff and patients had been my family. In a trance induced by the records I'd already read, I consumed this next set like an insatiable addict, the words an irresistible drug. Nothing mattered but learning about my past.

Again I found myself sucked into a time warp, transported backward, as if I'd become that twenty-year-old woman who looked and acted like an early adolescent girl. I lost my bearings. At times, I felt as if I were pulled underwater by the weight of it. I feared I'd drown.

Another part of me observed what was happening. I was impressed with the detail in the handwritten records—no one I knew kept notes like that. As an experienced clinician, I could see troubling implications in the descriptions of my symptoms and behaviors. I appeared more disturbed than I had believed. My old explanation—that there had been some misunderstanding and I had been hospitalized by accident—no longer sufficed.

For days after the records arrived, I rarely left the house. Grief weighed so heavy I struggled to move from one room to another. I pulled myself together for my patients and collapsed at home.

A few weeks later, Bill left for a week's sail with friends. Initially, I felt relief—one less responsibility. And I enjoyed the quiet—I had no need of conversation. I liked eating whatever and whenever I chose. I fixed myself popcorn; I ate ice cream straight from the carton while reading magazines and newspapers. I fried onions with peppers or tomatoes from the garden. Often I settled for cereal—I didn't have to cook.

Soon, however, harsh thoughts began to intrude, questioning my integrity and taunting me with images of dead animals and babies, calling me a whiner when I became upset.

The psychologist part of me knew that this hostile invasion was provoked by reading the records, triggering old memories and associations. Clinically, I was revisiting what likely had been my condition years earlier as a young patient in the hospital. I'd regressed to a state of constant self-attack.

Without Bill, without any actual interactions to provide distraction, it wasn't long before these thoughts and images had invaded every open space. As another Sunday arrived, I realized that I needed wholesome, live voices to counter the toxic ones in my mind. I missed the nourishing silence of Friends Meeting, and I craved the company of good people I could trust.

The grim cloud that had enveloped me at home persisted as I drove to the meeting house. I watched myself fake a smile as I shook hands with the greeter at the door. Like a child who knew she should seek help from a neighbor if a hurricane threatened and her mother wasn't home, I turned to those Quakers for the security and acceptance I could not give myself.

I found a seat in the farthest corner of the large meeting room. *I'll be safe here*, I thought.

It was a beautiful June morning. Sun shone through the trees, making golden patches on the hardwood floor. The day's heat hadn't yet struck, and the various people assembled there—families with little children, elderly couples, widowed women, single adults of all ages, most familiar to me, some troubled, some odd, most accepting and caring—appeared comfortable in T-shirts and trousers, maybe shorts, occasionally sundresses. Although some of the children wiggled in their seats or pawed their parents, the peaceful quiet central to Meeting was settling over the room.

As the silence deepened, I felt myself sink into another reality—a scene barely formed, a memory just beyond reach. A foggy mist developed, surrounding me. Vague figures slowly, incompletely emerged. Whispery voices and auditory shadows brought me to an old puzzle: it was almost twenty years earlier. My daughter was young, in elementary school. Her best friend's mother was dying. *Did I promise Catherine I'd take care of her daughter after her death, or I had only thought to promise? Did I give my word?* Later... voices in unintelligible language, sounding like trouble, frantic exchanges between my daughter and her friend. Did these things really happen? I couldn't say. The figures had no faces, the words had no syllables, the gray cloud muffled everything, and it all seemed far away.

An elderly man rose to speak. I adjusted my attention and

half listened. "My back has been so painful I can barely walk. This morning I had planned to stay in bed rather than come to Meeting, but I thought I'd at least step outside for some sun. That's when I saw the bird. She sat on a nest she'd made in the eaves of my porch." He went into some detail about the intricacies of the nest.

"So today I bring hope," he said. "Her work inspired me to come."

Hope, I repeated to myself. *Hope?*

I slipped back to the memory of another summer: My family and I were visiting Cape Cod with friends during a vacation. We were taking a walk. My daughter, still young, listed all of her transgressions in life, as if expressing some profound anxiety about herself. *Why? Was she worried about going to a new school? Was there anything else?* My heart trembled. Was there something I hadn't seen? As my own mother did when I needed her, had I looked away? Fog rolled over me again, while on both sides and in front of me, the community of Quakers continued in silent worship.

Earlier memories appeared. The night was late. I was a child—maybe ten, maybe twelve—in my bedroom in White Plains. The house was quiet and dark. I heard the bedsprings creak in my parents' room, the shuffle of my father's feet on the floor as he moved from his bed. Suspended motionless in my own bed, I could trace his movements as he left the room. I heard my door shift and footsteps moving closer.

Still, my shadowy fugue continued. I was possessed with feelings I couldn't fathom, waves of fluttery convulsions in my stomach, blood rushing so fast it seemed I could implode at any moment, sucked into the center of the earth, deep into the past.

My thoughts refused to form coherent patterns. But my stomach kept jumping and my arms and chest kept vibrating. I opened my eyes and looked around me. Nothing outward had changed.

Although I made no sound at all, tears flowed down my cheeks. I was unable to stop them no matter how hard I tried. My nose ran. I could taste the salt. Yet I couldn't sniff without drawing attention to myself. Even the *shish* of a tissue slipped from my pocket would interrupt the silence.

The realization that I was about to drown in a pool of tears and runny mucus jolted me into the present. I felt like an alien in a science fiction movie who had wandered in from another dimension. I was in Meeting with a group of earnest people had no idea that I was no longer one of them. At the close of worship I rose and, without a word, walked out of the room and the building, while the rest of the community greeted each other with handshakes and hugs.

As I drove home from New Haven, fragments of thoughts whirled through my head. Stop signs, lane dividers, awareness of speed and route appeared and disappeared. Soon I found myself in my driveway, not sure how I'd arrived.

Distracted by the alternate universe I'd fallen into, I was glad to be alone. Better not to have to try to explain all this to Bill.

I left my car and hurried into the house. Fuegito bounded to greet me, as she always did. I ignored her. The hurricane I'd tried to avoid had arrived full force. I set my purse on the kitchen counter, but I kept walking.

It really could have happened.

Of course not! You're a fool.

I paced, first back and forth, then circling the kitchen island.

I'm not the person I thought I was. My life is changed forever.

You're an idiot. This is self-indulgent rot.

I stumbled into the counter. I staggered away.

My stomach jumps at just a word, the merest thought. I can't be making this all up.

It doesn't mean anything. You are a desperate twit trying to get attention.

I'm not the person I thought I was. Could that stuff with my father really have happened?

Dizzy and exhausted, I sank into a sturdy kitchen chair and hunched in on myself. Old images, seemingly at random, played nonstop inside my head—an amateur film incompetently edited, one unanticipated scene after another bombarding me. I rocked, arms wrapped tight around me so I wouldn't break apart into pieces.

Suddenly, I grasped what was happening. *My not seeing,* I thought. *That's dissociation! That's how it works! It makes you not know.* Identifying my own dissociation instantly unlocked links to hidden parts of my past. With each new piece of evidence, more tumblers clicked into place. I couldn't stop.

I struggled to comprehend for myself those things I saw so easily in my patients. Yet not only did I now understand the disconnect in my failure to recall my promise to Catherine or pay attention to my daughter and her friend, I also saw how my mother, unknowing, might have allowed bad things to happen to me.

Bad things? To me?

Once I accepted that possibility, my mind overflowed with fuzzy pictures, fragments of thoughts, fragments of body parts, powerful physical sensations I didn't understand.

You must be lying. You are a gullible, melodramatic fool!

Insults didn't stop the streaming images or calm my stomach full of fears. Yet part of me was intrigued. From somewhere separate, I observed the process. I was a meteorologist measuring velocity inside a cyclone that was blowing her away.

I moved from the kitchen to the sun room. I sat on the couch, staring, rocking. The physical sensations possessing me played on.

Thinking to harness the chaos, I decided to weed a garden Bill and I had started on a hill near the backyard shed. The space consisted of reclaimed woods that now included periwinkle, azaleas, wild flowers, and some old laurel bushes we'd moved from in front of the house. Our plants battled for dominance with an assortment of hardy weeds, including poison ivy. My task was huge. Even if I succeeded in clearing some spots, the weeds would quickly grow back. Nevertheless, I felt as though my survival depended upon making a positive impact somewhere, anywhere, and attacking weeds in a freshly opened garden seemed like a reasonable place to start.

Weeding provided structure for my frantic energy. While thoughts spun helter-skelter through my mind, the quiet, methodical process of pulling up intruding, aggressive vegetation felt somehow reassuring. I thought of the man's testimony from Meeting. *Hope? Maybe.*

Soon sweat was dripping off my chin. It ran down my arms and my chest. The blue tank top stuck to my back. My shorts were soaked. Mosquitoes interrupted me, but I scratched or slapped at them and continued on. Eventually I implored myself to stop, but I couldn't. *Just one more,* I said, the way children plead for cookies or stories at bedtime. *Just one more.* Before I knew it four, then five, then six hours had passed.

Dusk was deepening. The bugs were multiplying. I knew I had to return indoors. I had to eat dinner. I had to prepare for the week ahead. Yet, it was difficult for me to leave the haven of clearing ground cover, of making the space safe for periwinkle, and move to a new activity indoors.

You're acting like a kid who can't make transitions, twit face, I sneered.

Leave me alone. I'm doing my best.

You're a stupid crybaby. You haven't done anything today but think about yourself. The great psychologist can't deal with her own shit.

In that instant, I heard my mother's voice. I was appalled. I knew she had been a good woman, loved by many friends, but she had judged herself relentlessly, criticizing her own behavior even in the midst of a task. Whether it was taking her medicine, preparing a salad, calling a friend, or organizing an art show, she rarely acknowledged pain or forgave herself for imperfection. I'd sworn never, ever to act like that. There I stood next to the shed, hot, dirty, exhausted, and stuck between utter disappointment in myself—almost despair—and a need to prove that I was not my mother.

You can't escape this fact, I observed with bitter calm, securing the door. *You have just demonstrated how, in essential ways, you have become your mother.* Damn, I hated that.

When I sent for the records, I had expected good news. I thought they would confirm that I'd had fewer shock treatments than I'd estimated and that the hospitalizations had been a mistake. The truth proved grimmer than what I'd imagined. Although I learned that my adolescent desperation stemmed not from schizophrenia but from PTSD—childhood trauma, likely exacerbated by the 89 ECT—my dangerously disturbed behavior had nonetheless been real. How naive I'd been to assume that my journey would be simple, that by knowing my past I'd become free from those habits I disdained in my mother. Rarely was it so easy for my patients. Why would it be for me?

At last, I made my way back to the house, and as I stood

at the kitchen sink scrubbing the dirt from underneath my fingernails, I found a small interlude of peace. For the time it took to watch an owl fly from one tree to another across my backyard, I felt not dismay or fear but only sadness for my troubled mother and compassion for her little girl, me, who couldn't make her darkness go away.

Then the wind picked up, and I was blown back into the storm.

Annita Sawyer *is a clinical psychologist with a longstanding clinical practice and a writer with a more recent, but expanding, literary life. She writes about psychotherapy relationships, mental illness, shame, and healing. This essay is adapted from her first book,* Smoking Cigarettes, Eating Glass: A Psychologist's Memoir, *winner of the Santa Fe Writers Project 2013 Grand Prize in Nonfiction.*

Make It a Daisy

Joyce O'Connor

"Who ya gotta fuck to get a break in this town?"

It is 2002, and *The Producers* is a megahit on Broadway. Since we live a few blocks from the theater in New York City, a friend in the cast offers us complimentary tickets. My son Henry is nine years old. Although he doesn't speak much in life and throws autistic fits, Henry is becoming a musical-theater enthusiast. He has trouble comprehending complex meanings, but he decodes and memorizes with computer-like speed. When he was a toddler, he recited *Pinocchio* and performed all the choreography. Now he has memorized the entire soundtrack of *The Producers*. Most of the jokes go over his head, of course. At the theater, Henry laughs along with the audience, even if his giggles are a little loud and a tad later than everyone else's.

Late one afternoon and right on cue, Henry begins his regular cursing tantrum over not getting his way, so I blink through my own fatigue and diligently send him to his room for a timeout. This is our daily routine, but today, on his way angrily down the hall, I hear him repeat Nathan Lane's line: "Who ya gotta fuck to get a break in this town?"

In this moment, I am weary, so weary of parenting a nine-year-old boy with autism, and I'm angry at his fit. Still, I cannot help but laugh. I stand alone in the kitchen, wondering how I will get through another evening, but throughout his nine-minute timeout—a minute for every year, like the latest parenting book recommends—I also relish the often charming personality of my son. Later tonight I will again despair for his future and mine, but just now, for nine minutes, I am content. It is these absurd moments that save me during the long years of struggle with Henry.

"Who ya gotta fuck to get a break in this town?" Although Henry doesn't fully understand the implications of the line, he certainly knows it should be used when frustrated and up against "the man." From his perspective, I am "the man."

I know how he feels. I am also up against "the man." I have sued the Board of Education several times in order to place Henry in an appropriate special-education classroom and not a basement full of unwanteds. A constant stack of medical and therapy bills is our permanent kitchen table centerpiece. My serious and once-thriving acting career is reduced to commercials. "Who ya gotta fuck?" I wonder as well.

But just when I cannot take another moment of Henry's autistic tantrums, he says or does something ridiculous yet appropriate, and all the other stuff melts away. It is in these moments that I am absolutely smitten with whoever is inside this boy, an individual with no social filter who speaks only the truth. He is a little potty-mouthed Buddha.

Henry was diagnosed when he was three. Until that point, he was just a baby who cried like so many other babies. Around age two and a half, though, I realized he was, in many ways, not like most children. He didn't look at me. He flapped his hands and threw himself down on the floor. He screamed at the slightest noise.

After many specialists shook their heads and checked the boxes, he was diagnosed with "Pervasive Developmental Disorder—Not Otherwise Specified," which seemed a coward's way of telling me he had autism. This was in 1996, when autism seemed relevant to only a few unlucky people. I had seen the movie *Rain Man* and a television news program showing a child spinning in circles in the center of a living room as the pitiful parents, unable to communicate, sat helplessly on the sofa. I looked up autism in the dictionary and found that it was from the root word *aut*, meaning "within." That was the extent of my knowledge of the disorder. Indeed, diagnosticians and medical insurance companies were also at a loss regarding cause or intervention. It seemed I had won the reverse lottery, with a son destined for a life trapped inside of the self. Henry was someone I would never know.

My pediatrician, an old man, balked when I told him Henry had been diagnosed elsewhere as autistic. "Henry!" he yelled, and Henry looked at him, startled. "That child is not autistic!" the doctor declared.

To him, Henry did not fit the bill. He was not as affected as others who were considered autistic. Despite the pediatrician's doubts, he sent us to a developmental specialist who conducted tests with Henry. Ultimately, I left with a huge bill and a diagnosis of "infantile autism."

Soon after, I visited a school for special needs and was told by the teacher that older students with all sorts of mental disorders had once been simply labeled "retarded." When I was young, that's what we called the boy on our block who was not like us. That's what we called our janitor who had a developmental disorder. Both may have also been autistic or had other mental disorders, but "retarded" seemed to describe any kind of difference. At school, we called one another "retarded" and "queer" as the worst of all possible insults.

Alone at night, while my husband Jim was desperately making a go of his newly founded off-Broadway theater in hopes of supporting us, I wondered what I had done to curse my son. If I had caused it, then I certainly could cure it. After the news of Henry's diagnosis, other mothers in my neighborhood who had only last year been my friends swerved their strollers to the other side of the street to avoid me. Was it Henry, or could they sense my hatred of them and their strollers full of potential? If some of them approached, it was only to ask a question about choices I had made in order that they might avoid my plight.

"Did you have a Pitocin drip?"

"Was he vaccinated?"

"Did you drink when you were pregnant?"

I answered their questions with my usual kind smile while simmering in self-pity. "Why me?" I wondered.

Until he was two Henry attended a typical preschool, but as he got older, he became increasingly disruptive and anxious.

After he was diagnosed, he was sent to a special-needs pre-school. The change in routine was a transition that, like all transitions, overwhelmed him. Each morning, we waited in the lobby of our apartment for the school bus, and Henry sometimes had fits.

On one particular morning, his former preschool classmates filed into the lobby. Henry happened to be throwing a thrashing, screaming fit in the middle of the floor. His former peers just stepped around him on their way out the door. To them, Henry had become nothing more than special-needs roadkill.

Another afternoon, I took Henry and his little sister Lily swimming at our gym. I loved the time in the pool, when I could let go of so many fears and concerns and just enjoy playing with my children. Back in the locker room, I helped Henry change out of his suit and into the only other outfit he would accept: a tight green turtleneck that allowed him to feel his body in space. He was in his perseverating-with-light-switch phase and, as I helped Lily out of her bathing suit, a thin twentysomething woman angrily addressed me.

"Your son is turning off the lights!" she said, poking her head around the column of lockers.

I didn't know what she was talking about. The lights were on around me. Busy with Lily, I hadn't noticed that Henry had escaped. Just around the corner, he was quickly flipping the switch up and down, causing the lights in the other part of the locker room to flicker. I picked up Lily and rushed to extricate Henry. As I turned away from the wall, Henry unleashed his discontent in long and desperate wails. It was akin to taking the addict away from the needle. The twentysomething scowled.

Too tired to take this woman's attitude and desperate for some help, I pulled out the "A" word. "He's autistic," I explained.

"Well," she replied without pause, "then he shouldn't be out in public!"

Off she went toward the showers.

After dressing the kids, I picked up one under each arm and stopped on the way out of the locker room. I flung open the shower door, exposing the naked young woman. Surprised, she did her best to cover herself.

"Do you have children?" I asked.

Terrified of me now, she timidly answered, "No."

"Judge me when you do." I slammed the shower door and marched out with my two toddlers. It was a moment for the movie adaptation of my life, in which I am played by some attractive actress with great hair who holds two perfect versions of my kids. The applause swells triumphantly at my exit, my life taking a new and better turn.

In the real world I went back home, turned on a kids' movie, and snuck into the bathroom to cry alone.

He shouldn't be out in public. The potential truth of this statement was my secret fear. I envisioned Henry as an adult in a straitjacket in the corner of a dark institution for the insane. Nonetheless, I kept taking Henry to school and the gym, hoping one day he would be able to go out on his own. This woman had shamed me. Even as I acted like a heroine, brave and triumphant, I worried that maybe she was right. Maybe there was no place in the world for Henry.

Each evening, as Henry threw books off the shelves and tapped nonstop on the coffee table, I watched the Hudson River, two blocks to the west of our apartment. I prepared the only meal Henry would tolerate: strawberries, cucumbers, and macaroni and cheese. At my most desperate, the deathly water looked enticing. The period just before dinner was the loneliest. If Jim was even a few minutes late, I felt like I would explode. Counting every second, I gazed out at the Hudson, imagining myself running to the elevator, turning left on West Forty-Third Street and running past Tenth Avenue, then Eleventh. The Henry Hudson Highway was dangerous and I would have no choice but to stop at the traffic light, but then I could keep going all the way to the river and then—what? What would I do?

A year after the diagnosis, when Henry was four years old, I was alone with the kids in the evening. We had a one-bedroom apartment. It was just after the usual bedtime struggle. Henry had been screaming, staring, and hand-flapping all day. Nobody had given me any hope in regard to his future. That day, in fact, a kindly speech therapist had told me that Henry would most likely never say anything more than simple commands.

After the kids were finally asleep, I was sitting on the futon in the living room, trying to find something funny on TV. As I switched through channel after channel of bright images, I had an idea. I could, I thought, walk into the bedroom and quietly pick Henry up from his bed. I could wrap him in his blanket and carry him to the terrace of our thirty-seventh-floor apartment. I could open the door and climb over the rail. I could cradle him in my arms to protect him from the fall that would kill us both.

Unable to look into another's eyes, enter any room with more than a few people, engage socially with his peers, express love or compassion, Henry seemed more like an animal than a human. I learned from specialists that all these characteristics are symptomatic of autism. But autism was all I could see. To my mind, Henry wasn't a boy so much as a disorder. He loved *Pinocchio* and memorized the entire movie, including choreography. I often thought it appropriate that he identified with a wooden boy who wanted to be real.

Only when he slept could I picture Henry as the child I wanted. In sleep, he seemed to have potential.

One especially lonely night, I awakened him. In desperation, I began teaching him to parrot the phrase "I love you." Eventually he could say it, and even though I knew he didn't understand the meaning, hearing him say those words helped me see him as human. I was grieving the son I imagined while trying to accept the one I'd been given.

My new peers became the mothers I met in therapy waiting rooms. We were an intense bunch, most of us having relinquished our own lives in the hopes of saving our kids. When I brought Henry in for treatment, one therapist commented, "I'm not sure which one needs me most: you or him."

Before it was understood, autism was once blamed on "refrigerator mothers." People blamed the coldness of the mother for the child's inability to bond. I understand the confusion. Parenting a child with a mental illness leads to feelings of guilt and despair. "It's a womb issue," I told a friend. "He came from my womb, and I feel responsible for whatever good or bad he inherited."

One mother from the therapy sessions handed me a memoir written by another mother who claimed to have discovered a remedy. I threw the book away without reading it. While a part of me felt at fault for Henry's struggles, I truly knew that autism was unfixable. I had a choice: I could lose my own sanity trying to make Henry into who I wanted him to be, or I could take a look at my own needs and accept him for who he was.

I found a therapist. On my first trip to see her, I climbed the single flight of stairs out of the subway as if ascending Mount Everest. My legs would barely move. But I made it to her little office, where I began to see that Henry was not a monster; rather, he had broken free the monster hiding in me.

Henry did rounds of therapy each week: speech and language therapy to get him talking; occupational therapy to get his body developing; behavioral therapy to get him in the world and out of himself. Eventually, we added music therapy to the list.

I waited in the lobby with a few other mothers while Henry spent time with the center's co-director and angelic therapist, Carol Robbins. "Welcome to music therapy, Henry!" Carol called. Like Odysseus following the sirens, Henry went into the room with none of the usual transitional fits and without anyone dragging him.

The mothers in this room weren't the terrified autism moms I'd met in the past. These mothers seemed calm. Their daughters had Down syndrome. I sat, pretending to read an old magazine, wondering if it would be better to be a Down-syndrome mom. Maybe they were relieved of the idea of fixing their children. Then I become ashamed of my jealousy, as if any diagnosis were more tolerable than another.

I could hear the beautiful music, a piano, and Carol's flute-like voice, and was that a harp? But the loudest sound was the continuous screaming of my son. That Saturday and every Saturday thereafter, he screamed for forty-five minutes as I squirmed in my seat, pretending not to hear anything but the gentle music.

Finally, I gave up. I decided to quit. After the sweet little girls had left with their mothers, I spoke to Carol.

"Okay, I get it," I sighed. "We're done here."

She looked at me with perfect surprise. "What do you mean?"

"Oh, come on!" I said. "I can hear him through the wall. He's screaming the whole time!"

"Yes," she nodded, and then she whispered into my ear: "But have you noticed—he is screaming on key!"

This was the first positive thing any therapist or specialist or doctor or person had said about Henry since his diagnosis.

In his way, Henry was trying to communicate.

Gradually, I began to notice that whenever I accepted Henry's behavior, he seemed to sense my change of heart and responded by throwing fewer fits. Whenever I relaxed and had fun with him, he got better. This little noncommunicative nonhuman could sense my emotions, even though he did not look into my eyes.

By the time Henry was seven he was able to play alongside other children, although still not with them. One Sunday after a therapy session, I watched as he climbed around on the playground equipment. Another boy Henry's age was also playing and, after a while, his mother approached me. We exchanged pleasantries, and then she asked me where Henry went to school.

In Manhattan, this question is like asking about future earning potential. Although Henry had made some progress, he had bounced around from one special-needs school to another as principals often ended up saying, "This just isn't a right fit."

I named the current school, which, of course, the woman had never heard of.

"Oh," she said, getting to the real reason she had asked the question. "My son attends the T.A.G. Program at P.S. 31."

"What is T.A.G.?" I asked, knowing full well but wanting her to say it outright.

"Talented and Gifted," she replied. "A classroom for exceptional children."

"Oh," I said, pretending ignorance. "My son is in a special -needs program, too."

This mother appeared to swallow her tongue as she choked on her coffee and tried desperately to correct me. I walked away while she was still struggling to speak.

Almost immediately I felt bad about my interaction with this mom, who was understandably proud of her son. The truth as that everywhere I went, I was ready for a fight. Jim escaped to work in part, I knew, to get away from me. Like Henry, I threw fits all over Manhattan. As with the twentysomething in the gym locker room, this mother on the playground was a battle I could have avoided. In both cases, Henry wasn't looking for a fight. I was. I couldn't be mad at Henry, so I became angry at everyone else.

I knew I needed to find the boy inside the "ism." Jim and I took Henry on the train to Bethesda, Maryland, to visit Dr. Stanley Greenspan, a child psychologist. Greenspan had the radical idea that each child with autism was unique and could be reached not by demanding that the child come into our world but by going into his. He taught me "floor time," a method of getting down where Henry was perseverating and joining him in his actions.

When I asked Dr. Greenspan what I could do to help Henry, he replied, "The best thing you can give your son is at least one healthy parent." On the train back to New York City, I decided to change my work schedule so that I could spend more time with the kids. As the scenery whizzed by, I thought of another thing Dr. Greenspan had said. "Children don't need our love; they need our respect." I had been too busy fixing Henry to notice much about him. Could I respect him? Did I even know him?

Back home, the director of Henry's special-needs preschool heard that I had visited Greenspan. She called me into her office and warned me about Henry's future. "People will give you false hope," she said. I understood that she was trying to help, but the hope didn't seem so false as little flickers of life appeared in Henry's face. Music appealed to him, so I sang all the time. I discovered he was receptive to eye contact when swinging in the park, so I sang songs and pretended his little feet were kicking me each time he swung up toward my face.

I used the skills I'd learned in acting conservatory to appeal to Henry's inner clown. I put clay on my nose and sneezed it off. He laughed and looked for more.

"Again," he said, and I acquiesced, repeating it forever. I bounced him on my knee and made fart noises. He laughed and said, "Again." I acquiesced. I did a pratfall onto the bed. He laughed and said, "Again." I kissed his neck "a million times" and did it again when he asked for "a million kisses." Lily, unaware of Henry's differences, also blossomed in play. Because of Henry's issues she got a tense, but ultimately better, mom.

We spent whole days in Central Park riding the carousel again and again, because Henry loved it. Sitting on a wooden horse together, winding round inside the little carousel house,

I felt like any other mother with any other boy.

"You are at war," said the voice over the telephone. I was listening carefully for any sign of hope. This was a mother who had been through what I was now in the midst of. Her son was ten years older than Henry. She sounded unusually sane for an autism mom, and I was hoping for encouragement.

"You are at war," she continued, "but remember that it won't last forever. You have a limited window of time in which to influence his development, and then it will be up to him."

I kept listening, holding my breath.

"How long," I asked, "until the war is over?"

"When he's nine years old or so, you can pull back."

I started counting years in my head. Her estimate was better than eternity, which was what I had imagined.

It wasn't what she said to me, necessarily, this autism-mom-stranger on the other end of the phone line; it was the sanity in her voice that kept me hopeful. Other mothers around me were frantic and alone; most fathers stayed in denial. I had received this mother's number from someone who heard she had done a therapy in Montreal for auditory processing delay, which, of course, was something difficult with which Henry struggled.

This mother on the phone sounded okay. Her voice was another sign that Henry and I and our family might survive.

So I followed her advice and took Henry to Montreal for two weeks. There, Dr. Gerard Binet, a warm, kind, homeopathic French Canadian, performed "auditory integration training." Dr. Binet saw Henry twice a day. During these visits, Henry wore earphones and listened to strange music. Henry and I ate crepes each morning and walked through the old French squares with fountains in the center on our way to Dr. Binet's. In the afternoons, we ate more crepes and played in the park until the next therapy.

I felt alive in Montreal. I was happy for the first time since Henry's diagnosis. We were away from the therapists, the Board of Education, and the unhappy faces of the New York developmental pediatricians. Here in beautiful Montreal, I had escaped the science project that was my son. Instead, I was just a mother and he a little boy. Dr. Binet had been doing this therapy for a long while, as his gray hair attested, so one day I asked him about Henry's future.

Dr. Binet looked straight at me. "He will manage in his own way."

Oh, come on! I thought. I wanted specifics. I wanted to know details, but Dr. Binet just kept repeating the same sentence.

"Okay," I said, "but how can I make Henry better?"

Dr. Binet started repeating his sentence, and I put up my hand to stop him.

"Really!" I pleaded, leaning on the desk between us to look right into his face. "What can I do?"

"You are that powerful?" he asked.

"Yes," I replied.

He indicated the plant between us. "See this hydrangea?"

"Yes," I replied.

The hydrangea was beautiful and in full bloom.

Dr. Binet looked at me. "Make it a daisy," he said.

Our trip to Montreal coincided with the twentieth anniversary of Elvis's death. Most of the magazines in the airport stores had Elvis on the cover. So when we got to Montreal, I bought a tape of his greatest hits and played it repeatedly in our hotel room. We listened to Elvis each night after dinner, dancing and pretending to play guitar.

Until then, to my chagrin, Henry had not participated in "normal" childhood activities like dressing up for Halloween. But that year, Henry asked for a costume. Excited, I promised him any outfit. From a catalogue, he picked "Seventies Elvis," complete with a gold lamé jumpsuit split down to his belly button, a side-burned wig, aviator sunglasses, and an inflatable guitar. No other little kid wanted to be bloated seventies Elvis. Only mine. And I loved Henry as absurd little Elvis. I was thrilled that he was behaving like other kids, but more than that, I was completely charmed by his difference.

On Saturday at Central Park, a bunch of harried parents tried to keep their sons running in the right direction at special-needs soccer practice. One particularly fast kid always tore out toward the east side with his dad in pursuit. We wouldn't see either of them again until the following week. Another older kid would break from the game about ten times each week to ask me if I liked Don Johnson. Kindly, I told him to get back into the game, which he did for a few moments, until suddenly his face was right in front of mine and he was asking if I had seen *Miami Vice*.

Basketball practice was easier, because it was contained in a small gym and the kids had nowhere to run. There wasn't much competition in special-needs sports. We had no pride as we yelled to our sons, "Wrong hoop! Run to the other one!"

But once a dad told me as we watched on the sidelines that his kid had Asperger's, not autism, and some of these kids were not a challenging play date for his son.

How desperate we were to move our kids up on the ladder, even if it was only one small step. Another friend refused to get her child diagnosed with special needs because she didn't want him "labeled." But she was the one who didn't want to be labeled. I know. At first, I wanted to keep Henry in a typical school because I felt a special-needs classroom would mean I had "given up" on him. A teacher asked me, "Is this for you or for him?" It was then that I understood how attached my ego was to his label.

One flustered day, while taking Henry to his soccer game, I forgot to take his little scooter out of the trunk of the cab. Henry, of course, threw a fit right on the sidewalk on the way into the park, so I promised to get him a new scooter after the game. I would do anything just to get home with my raving son. After soccer, although I could not afford it, I bought him a new scooter, but Henry still wanted his old one and couldn't understand why he couldn't get it back. A week later, he was still harping on the old scooter.

"Henry," I finally said, "I can't get it back because I didn't get a receipt, so I don't know the identification number of the cab!"

I was expecting this to end the conversation, but Henry replied, "I remember it," and proceeded to recite the number.

This was the moment I realized my little boy had memorized the identification numbers to every cab we have ever been inside. "We took this one last month to the orthodontist," he told me one day as he read the numbers on the back of the cab's front seat.

Henry has recently acquired a fascination with cursing. He says words he doesn't understand but knows are bad, just to see what I'll do.

"I just took a big shit!" he will announce, coming out of the bathroom.

When I ignore him, he says, "Yes, I just took a big crap!"

I will correct him. It goes on and on like this with every new curse word he discovers.

Last week, in a crowded elevator, Henry said, "Excuse me. I farted." Last month, he came out of his bedroom after listening to music and stood before the couch, pausing to get my full attention. "All humans love the Beatles," he announced. Then silently, he returned to his room.

Today I am standing in my apartment kitchen. Although I am looking out onto the Hudson River, I no longer have fantasies of running toward it.

"You can come out now, Henry," I call to him when the timer goes off, signaling that his nine-minute timeout is over. Each day something makes me wonder, "Who is this boy, and why is he mine?" I am still frightened for his future, but he feels *more* than human to me now.

I hear him padding down the hall. The more he comes out, the less I want to fix him.

Joyce O'Connor *was a professional actress on Broadway, off-Broadway, and television in New York City when her son was diagnosed with autism. She holds an MFA in theater and has been involved in the Signature Theater since its inception. She lives in New York City with her husband and daughter and is currently completing a memoir of essays. Her son, Henry, works at the American Museum of Natural History, performs in community musical theater, has a girlfriend, and lives independently.*

A Day in the Life with Bipolar Illness— and Nine Years Later

Madeline Strong Diehl

2006
Tuesday, 7:15 A.M.

"Mom, you promised you'd make me oatmeal today."

I wake up to find Amelia, my eleven-year-old daughter, standing over my bed. Three alarm clocks strategically placed around my bedroom have been buzzing for fifteen minutes, and I have slept right through them. Amelia is staring at me with a look of guarded hope. But I can barely keep my eyes open because I am so heavily medicated and still only got two hours of sleep. Because I dread its side effects, I waited too long before finally taking trazodone, my sleep medication of last resort.

Trazodone takes no prisoners. I affectionately call it "the sledgehammer." It will be hours before the trazodone and two other sleeping medications work their way out of my bloodstream enough for me to be fully conscious and functional. I'll be lucky if I can wake up when Amelia comes home from school. But I am now on the third day of almost no sleep—a day that is pivotal to my battle to stay out of the hospital while my husband is away for two weeks on one of his frequent international business trips.

Amelia's face falls before I even tell her; this has happened too many times. "I'm sorry, honey," I say, and a lump forms in my throat. "I've got to sleep more, or I'll get that mean, old crabby sickness again. Come up and give me a hug before you leave. And I'll be wide awake and ready for fun things when you come home."

"You'll be here when I come home from school? You promise?" Amelia asks.

"I promise," I say and add silently: *God willing*. Because I am currently suffering from mixed states and rapid cycling—some of the most difficult forms of bipolar to treat—I can go from giddy elation to deepest despair within a few hours and end up in the hospital with little or no warning. I can experience, within a day, a range and intensity of moods and emotions that most people do not experience over the course of their entire lives. Imagine scaling the slopes of Mt. Everest and achieving the sublime view from the summit, then, hours later, finding yourself plummeting headlong into the deepest, darkest part of the sea—without an oxygen tank. It is uncomfortable, to say the least. Not surprisingly, it can be fatal.

The fact that this illness can be deadly—in fact, very deadly —is little understood among the general public, but those of us who have it know the stakes are often high. According to the National Institute of Mental Health, as many as 15 percent of people with bipolar die of suicide. That doesn't include the unintentional deaths that come from driving while overmedicated or getting into dangerous situations while feeling lost or disoriented. Those suffering from mania can die unintentionally from classic symptoms such as recklessness, delusions of grandeur, and lack of judgement.

I close my eyes until I hear Amelia leave my room. A hot tear rolls down my face and into my ear, and I just let it stay there. The forbidden thoughts started yesterday and I hadn't reported them to my doctor because I knew I might end up in the hospital, away from my kids. I need to be with them right now—they are the only thing that feels real to me anymore, and they give me reason to fight for my life. But I know I am slowly losing that battle; I am so tired I no longer feel in control of my thoughts. I am entering the period when that can be very, very dangerous. I have to somehow get through this day without the illness overtaking me. This day and then nine more before my husband gets home, and I'm safe.

Amelia and her brother Bob are eating breakfast downstairs and I try to join them, but the drugs send my mind reeling and I fall back in bed. Then the Accuser enters my room, just as she did yesterday. *You are a worthless, lazy mother, she says. You cannot even get up with your children when they go to school.* My hands break into a sweat. The intense anxiety that comes with my depression has begun.

I hear the door close as my children leave for school, and I have not even hugged them goodbye. I am a terrible mother.

Never one to miss a beat, the Accuser recognizes her opening. She repeats the instructions she has perfected over all these years. *Go to the river. Tonight, while the children are asleep. Take a water bottle, like we planned, and all your pills. Call one friend and let her know. It will be just like sleeping. It won't hurt anymore. You will float.*

10:30 A.M.

I wake in a panic. Am I missing an important meeting? I jump out of bed so fast that the room spins. I check my schedule. No meetings, but I see I have a grant proposal due in two days. My hands are sweating again, and I start shaking. My self-accusations and loathing build in fierceness and intensity: *What a loser. I should be fired. I can't even make oatmeal for my children.* I must meditate to gain control over my thoughts. I sit on my meditation pillow, often the only place in the entire house that feels uncluttered and orderly. On days like this, just breathing, just showing up for life seems like a major accomplishment. After ten minutes, I find the wise internal voice that tells me to stay home. I must devote the next twenty-four hours to getting better. I know from past experience that if I just keep making good choices from moment to moment, I can turn things around; I can beat this illness. If I rest and take care of my illness today, I will be in much better shape to do my work tomorrow. *Everyone gets sick. Why is this any different from a bad cold or virus? Why don't I just call in sick without all this self-flagellation, self-judgement, shame, fear, panic?*

Just as I hoped, my boss doesn't demand an explanation. Even though I don't have to go to the office, my anxiety is building; the stakes feel too high. This is Day 3 of almost no sleep, and my caregivers and I have come to believe, based on past experience, that Day 3 often determines the outcome of an episode: if I can start slowing down the mania and get more and better sleep, most of the time I can pull out of a downward spiral. I am at risk of hospitalization or worse if I don't get improved sleep during Night 3.

Through some stroke of undeserved luck, I receive wonderful health care. If I am having a crisis, my therapist will fit me in on a few hours' notice (though she never admits she is giving up her lunch). I also enjoy similarly generous and warm relationships with my primary care physician, my psychiatrist, and my polarity therapist, all of whom also appreciate the need for an urgent response if I am having a serious episode.

The day before yesterday, when I started my rapid decline, my therapist and my psychiatrist met with me and decided there was nothing they could do in terms of medication changes, since my mood was cycling so rapidly. During these times, when I feel I am alone in the wilderness, my therapist, Claire, indulges me in what we have come to call "therapy by email." Since childhood, writing has been a form of therapy for me, and if I am feeling shaky it is not uncommon for me to send Claire daily emails for reassurance; sometimes I even send her several a day. Often the number and length of these emails provide a good indicator of whether I am manic or not. Usually I try to make them as witty and entertaining as possible because I know she cannot possibly get paid enough to read them all. But today, all I can manage is this email:

Dear Claire: Are you still there?

She would probably fit me in again today if I called and said it was urgent. But what can she do at this point? Who can do anything except me? My husband certainly can't help: he's 3,000 miles and an ocean away. Why should I make him worry? It's time to look the illness straight in the eye and tell it who's boss.

I eat a healthy breakfast and take my morning medications. Then, even though I am shaking, I force myself to go out into the world and notice everything in it. The great seduction of depression is that it causes us to believe that our suffering is singular and unique—the worst suffering anyone has ever experienced in the history of all humankind. This is how we get mired deeper and deeper into the illness—this arrogant notion that no one else could possibly understand our pain. In fact, everyone feels alone, everyone's heart aches. When I can notice the pain in the eyes of strangers and recognize it as my own, I know I have begun to overcome my illness.

Noon

I visit the library and every book seems connected to the next and the next. A fire is kindled in my mind; it is as if words, not blood, circulate through my body and my heart is pumping ideas faster than I can write them down. It feels like if I don't record my thoughts, my skin will burst and there will be no membrane separating me from the rest of the world. My heart, my mind, my spirit seem to empty out into the room through my eyes; I can see the "why" of things, the secret interconnections, the inanimate and animate love. I begin furiously writing notes on the little scraps of card-catalogue paper. I use a series of strips in quick succession to capture the stampede of ideas pressing against the walls of my brain. Unable to keep up, I am madly scribbling snatches of rhyme, words linked with phrases linked with titles linked with authors linked with messages to myself to look at later—messages I know I will probably never understand again.

This is the other great seduction of bipolar: while I am in this manic state, I believe I can go home and transform some of these scraps into transcendent writings which might speak to many people. I believe I can channel this fire into essays, poems, plays, stories so effortlessly that it will feel like typing, not creating. Some of these writings might even win awards, make me famous. All my writing professors and editors have said that I am remarkably talented, that I have the "gift." But at forty-four, after seven years with this diagnosis, I know the "gift" can often be a Trojan horse, containing within it the means of my destruction. I know to be suspicious. I know that, especially today, I cannot afford to play with fire.

No. *No*, I tell my gift, my illness, my genius. *You must wait, maybe my whole life.* I am the wife of Ed, the mother of Bob and Amelia, and they are worth more than the Pulitzer Prize.

I crumple up all the profound, foolish scraps and throw

them away.

2:00 P.M.

Uh-oh. I see a fire in the azalea bush: the brilliant red-purple leaves are burning to ash in the wind. Maybe that's the fire Moses saw? Or maybe Moses was psychotic. Or maybe I am?

No, I am just manic, seeing inside to the living essence of things. I am in love with the world and everything in it. I begin crying uncontrollably and my emotions are at cross purposes with each other. I experience myself as a mind-body. My mind can no longer process or understand what I am feeling or what is happening. A familiar pattern unfolds: I lose sensation in my body because it is trying to flee the grinding pain in my mind. First I lose my feet. I have learned this early-warning system after years of study with a meditation teacher and a polarity therapist. Once I lose my feet, I will lose control over my mind. So I take off my shoes, sit cross-legged on the sidewalk, and squeeze my feet between my hands. I see the heels and the toes, but they seem to belong to someone else. I stomp down the sidewalk, ignoring the stares. I try to force sensation into my feet; if I can get them healthy again, they will pull groundedness from the earth up through my body.

Instead, the numbness creeps up and up until I feel that I am no longer contained. I am flying in the sky and then beyond, through the earth's atmosphere and into space. "Great," I say. "Now I am manic again." Initially, I feel annoyed that I have become manic, knowing what a mess that always makes of my life. But soon I feel blissfully light and free—free from the pain in my body, my mind—free even from the Accuser, who is too weak to threaten such an amazing person like me, who can fly.

For a few moments I experience profound harmony with the universe, watching the earth from outer space with total understanding. But almost simultaneously, I become filled with pain, longing, and a growing sense of foreboding—being up this high without a parachute cannot end well. Just as I am figuring out how to get back to Earth and to my children, I am hit head-on by a solar flare. I feel like I am being burned alive. The equivalent of 160 billion megatons of TNT burns away every molecule of my psyche; the small orb of living matter that is me no longer has any layers of atmosphere to protect me from the void.

Now the Accuser finds me at my weakest moment. *You were willing to leave your kids for a cheap thrill, a ride in space. You don't deserve to be their mother. I'll show you your way back to the river. We'll do it tonight while the children are asleep. I'll carry your water bottle, like we planned. You bring all the pills. Call one friend and let her know. The kids won't have to find you. It will be just like going to sleep. You'd like that, wouldn't you? You're so tired. You need sleep. You won't hurt your children with your illness anymore, your not-being-there, your lazy sleeping in. They'll be free.*

2:30 P.M.

Water puts out fire, I remind myself after a timeless stretch of emotions that seem to change by the moment. I have no idea how I got back to my house. Over the span of an hour, all my emotions have become as compressed and toxic as the fuel in a nuclear reactor. I've only had one episode like this, and there's no mistaking it: it's rapid cycling AND a mixed episode at the same time. I know I should probably go to the hospital. I cannot come back into my body. I'm in so much pain that suicide has become a real option. This illness may never stabilize enough so that I can live a normal life. Why not just remove myself so my husband can marry someone who's not sick all the time and my kids can have a real mother? If I chose to die today it would be for them, but could they ever understand that? I'm a good writer. I can write them a note to explain it.

My hands are shaking so bad, all I can write is: *I am leaving because I love you. I want you to have a normal life with a normal mother. And I will never be a normal mother. I am sorry. And Ed, I am so very sorry.*

As I think of each of them—my kind, gentle, devoted, loving husband, my two trusting kids—I can see their faces through the fog of my pain, and they're beautiful, the most beautiful things I have ever seen. How could I leave a world with such beautiful faces in it? For a blissful moment the pain loosens its grip, and I sense there's some terrible lie inside the idea that I can choose to leave the world. My brain tries to figure it out: *What is the lie in the middle of the pain?* But when the pain hits hard again, questions return: *What is the right thing to do? To stay or to leave? What is best for Ed and our children?*

I realize the voice of the Accuser is slowly winning. It's now louder than my voice, and that's how people die.

Water puts out fire. Some wise speaker returns to break up the fight. I go to the pool and I swim. People are definitely looking at me like they are afraid, even though I don't say anything. I swim as if my life depends on it—and on a day like today, it does. I meditate while I swim, mindful of the movement and rhythm of my body, trying to shake the fire out of my limbs. Slowly, I begin to feel my body again.

I swim until I am so physically exhausted that I can hardly move. Back at home I find an email from my therapist.

Dear Madeline, it says.

I am still here.

Claire

I am still alone in the wilderness, but at least someone knows I'm there.

I could page Claire and she would talk with me, but she would know just from my voice that I am suicidal. (It's not hard since, like a loon, I'm laughing and crying at the same time.) Then she would put me in the hospital, where, granted, I probably belong.

For seven years, I have lived under the false belief that Claire is so powerful that she can keep me from dying. Now I realize that, ultimately, I'm the only person who can save myself—and that's terrifying, given my present state of mind.

I could go to the hospital right now. I already have people lined up to care for the kids if and when I need them. But going to the hospital feels like admitting defeat; once there, I give up my self-determination, my freedom.

Even as that thought flits through my mind, there's a dark place inside me that has chosen to die tonight and get it over with. I'd rather die one death than the thousand deaths this illness no doubt plans for me.

One last time, I think of calling Claire. I pick up the phone, put it back. No. This is my decision, and I haven't finished making it.

3:30 P.M.

I have lost my faith. I am weeping uncontrollably in the minutes before my children come home; when I hear them open the door, I try to freshen up my face. But they are mirrors of my emotions, always have been, and the moment they see me their mouths turn down. I must look awful. I am not going to make it.

"How was school?" I ask, and I make them popcorn and grilled cheese. But my mind is not there and they know it. My mind is thinking about how much better they would be with a different mother, how much better they would be without me.

9:00 P.M.

Somehow I have gotten through it: the part of the day when I have to "perform." I have managed a decent though uninspired dinner, and now the children are in bed. Now no one is watching and I am left alone with my thoughts. This is the most dangerous time of the day. I begin to eat large amounts of gorgonzola cheese. Luckily (and perhaps it is strange that I say "luckily"), I get a call from Beth, a close friend who, it turns out, is suicidal. Of course I feel sad and upset that she's suicidal, but I also know that, by calling on me for help, Beth is giving me an opportunity to get out of my own solipsistic, narcissistic self-absorption and return to the real world. If I can help Beth, I can help myself. I have to stop thinking of suicide and such nonsense and remember my responsibilities—which are to take care of the people I love, the people who need me. I have to be strong. So many people have told me they see me as living proof that a person with mental illness can contribute to her community, be married, have kids, a job—I can't let these people down by killing myself. I owe it to them to stay alive. So I tell Beth in no uncertain terms that suicide is not an option. When we get off the phone, I write her an email.

"Dearest Beth," I write:

> *The secret is to stay in the game. Stay alive. Just breathe. That's all anyone expects of you right now. Ride it out; it's a bucking bronco. It sucks. But also, Beth, when we're happy, there's a good chance we feel happier than most people ever do. Scientists can't measure that, but*

*that's what they think is true about this illness. I believe
we are here for a reason. We are here to teach people how
to be really, really alive. We're passionate, and we are
profoundly connected to all that is most beautiful and
sublime in this world. Living with and mastering this
gift is a lifetime process, but there are many teachers all
around us who can help us, if we only seek them out, or
just notice them and listen. And it's not just other people that can teach us. I mean other creatures, too, and
trees—the wind. Everything here in this world can teach
us, if we just listen.*

As always, I convince myself with my own brave words. That's
how writing has always been for me: it's not just a gift from
me to others. It's a gift to me. Now I feel stupid and mad at
myself. Why didn't I give *myself* that same pep talk sooner?

Because I am so tired. So tired.

But maybe if I just get a good night's sleep, I can turn this
thing around.

11:00 P.M.

I take my nighttime medications, but I'm becoming more anxious. If I don't get control over my thoughts, I am going to give
myself insomnia just from being terrified of insomnia. Then
I'll end up in the hospital for sure.

What's the worst that can happen? I take out my emergency list—a phone-tree system I designed. If I ever have to
go to the hospital while my husband is gone, all I have to do
is call one person on the list to come and stay with the kids;
then that person can call one or more of ten other people to set
everything else in motion. I haven't ever had to use the list,
but just having it helps me get to sleep.

As I look at each name, I remember how lucky I am to know
such fine people. I hold each person close to my heart. I feel
them holding me.

My sleeping medicine is working. It starts taking me out to
sea. I feel light; I can almost float. But there's also some huge
eye inside my brain still fighting to stay awake, so it can stay
in control. It's the part of me that believes if I stay in control,
I will never get sick—and ironically, it's keeping me sick. It's

making it impossible for me to let go—the one thing that can help me get better.

If I don't relax, the effects of the medicine will be undermined by my growing anxiety. I say this prayer:

> *Dear God. Please help me let go. Please help me trust myself to this darkness, this night, to the mysterious ways our spirit communicates to us through things that look like illness and hardship but are really divine grace.*

Yes, my life depends on the help and support of a lot of people, and I'm thankful for that. Why should I feel ashamed that I love and am loved? For everything that is given to me this day, I will give back and then some—in lasagna, in laughter, in love. Unfortunately, I know that my friends will know times of hardship, too, and I will be there for them just as they are here for me now. We live in community. We are connected. We love.

Now I understand the lie in the middle of the pain. My life doesn't belong to me; it's not mine to throw away. My life belongs to all the people who love and need me.

Wednesday, 6:30 A.M.
The alarm clock rings. Three of them, in fact. I jump out of bed before my children even wake up. I run downstairs to make oatmeal. It is going to be a good day.

Summer 2015
I wrote this piece nine years ago, when my moods were so volatile and unpredictable that I didn't know how I was ever going to survive my illness. I chose not to publish the essay then because I decided it would be a liability—the stigma might affect my professional or personal life.

I no longer suffer from the kinds of mood fluctuations portrayed here. Now that I have stabilized, I want to tell my story and offer hope to others who may feel like their lives will never be normal again. I will experience ups and downs the rest of my life—just like everyone else. However, I have developed strategies to prevent more serious episodes. The most powerful is reaching out to others for support, just as anyone else would have to do. So many people with bipolar illness feel they can't ask for help because they're too afraid to let others know about their diagnosis and struggles, causing them to be isolated and therefore at even higher risk for suicide. About 2.6 percent of Americans have bipolar, and they die at their own hands more often than people with any other diagnosed mental illness. In my opinion, they are dying because of the stigma, not because of the illness. Many also cannot afford treatment or treatment is not available in their area.

The only reason I am still here is because I refused to give in to the stigma—the message that told me my illness was shameful, something I should never reveal to anyone. My abnormal behavior wasn't the result of a medical condition; it was evidence that my mind and body were polluted by the stain of insanity, the result of degenerate genes. I suffered from an irreversible curse. I was damned.

The most dangerous stage of a bipolar episode occurs when the mind of a sufferer forms a "suicidal intent"—a plan for how and when she will kill herself. To reach this stage, she must be in tremendous psychic pain, fueled by a level of self-hatred that has become impossible to contain. When I have been in this stage, it feels like there is a murderer constantly following me—and yet, at the same time, that murderer is me. The illness has pushed me right up to the riverbank, and the stigma would have been more than happy to push me all the way in, if I listened to its poisonous words.

Luckily, I knew I couldn't resist the voice of the Accuser on my own—I needed to create a circle of love that could protect me from my illness and self-hate. I feel incredibly fortunate that I found friends and supporters who were not afraid of my illness or my behavior when I was ill. They reflected back to me that I am a beautiful child of God and that the pain of my episodes would pass—that my sense that I was always sick was an illusion. Over the past decade, as I stabilized, I have had the honor to support them through many hardships as well.

Lately, I have begun to appreciate the irony that the disease management my bipolar requires may even give me a higher quality of life. I have to stay physically, mentally, emotionally, and psychologically healthy. I must keep to a serious routine. Swimming at least half a mile a day is at least as important as taking my medicine. So are love and maintaining meaningful connections with family, friends, the natural environment, and the community where I live. I must faithfully follow a spiritual practice—not one that demands rigid beliefs, but one that is flexible enough to help me find meaning in all my own life experiences.

Instead of seeing bipolar as a battle, I have learned to live peacefully with my illness. After completing a cognitive behavioral therapy program, I no longer need medicine to sleep. For the past six years I have flourished as a freelance writer. My husband and I have begun composing songs together. Our two children, who at times did not get oatmeal growing up, are thriving in college. I feel so relieved that I did not leave them when my illness felt so overwhelmingly painful.

Madeline Strong Diehl *has worked as a magazine journalist, editor, and grant writer for almost thirty years. She has won the T.S. Eliot Poetry Prize from the University of Kent at Canterbury and published a book of poetry entitled* Wrestling with Angels *(2013). Her comedies have been produced off-Broadway and around the Midwest and she has published many humorous essays, believe it or not.*

A Blessing

Leslie Smith Townsend

I pulled off my parka as I watched Dad rifle through the hall closet. My eyes stung from the cold, and my chin was numb. "What are you doing?" I asked.

He went into the bathroom and began rooting through the vanity: Crest toothpaste; aftershave; Mennen deodorant; Dad's small black comb; his razor; and phenobarbital and Dilantin, medications I'd taken since my seizure when I was twelve.

"I'm cleaning out the medicine cabinets," he said. "The doctor said Mom's been taking too many pills. He told me to get rid of them."

He removed two bottles from the drawer and plopped them into a paper sack that was half-full already.

"That's ridiculous," I protested, following him from the bathroom to the kitchen. "What did Mom say?"

"She denied it," he said, scrounging through the cabinets. He pushed a large Tupperware container of candy aside and uncovered three more bottles of pills mixed in with Hadley mugs and saucers.

"If Mom said she doesn't, then she doesn't," I said.

Dad's thinning black hair revealed a bald spot just below the crown of his head. He wore a burgundy knit shirt with a collar, a scuffed-up belt, and wide-wale corduroys. Something about the slope of his shoulders spelled defeat. He smelled like Aqua Velva and sweat.

153

When he didn't answer, I marched down the hall to my room, slammed the door, and flung myself onto the bed. My room was pink, not because I liked the color but because Mom did. Striped curtains hung from the windows in bright, cheery colors—red, fuchsia, yellow, and lime green. There was a bureau in one corner and a white secretary's desk in another, with a bookcase in between. There were no posters or mementos. The room represented my mother's tastes, not mine. I was not a girlie girl. I liked trees, rocks, creeks, and weather. I hated those cheery curtains.

Mom wouldn't lie.

But neither would Dad.

Why would Mom take pills she doesn't need? I flipped onto my back and stared at the ceiling. *If she were taking pills, wouldn't I know?* For the first time, it occurred to me that Mom might have secrets, her own double life.

The next day, I came home from school and she was gone. "Where's Mom?" I asked.

Dad sat on the green plaid sofa in the family room with his feet propped on the coffee table. "She's been admitted to Our Lady of Peace," he said.

He flipped through the pages of *TIME* magazine. A picture of General Johnson, Army chief of staff, adorned the cover. The tagline read, "The battlefield is a lonely place."

"It's a psychiatric hospital," he added, momentarily shifting his gaze to me.

I stared. I had never known anyone who had been psychiatrically hospitalized. In 1966, I had not heard the term "nervous breakdown," and movies such as *One Flew Over the Cuckoo's Nest* and *Girl, Interrupted* had not yet been made. I'd just turned fourteen and had no template to help me understand what was happening to my mother.

My older brother, Bruce, and I were carted off to friends' or church members' houses. No one mentioned our mother's absence. It was as if she'd drifted off the earth's surface, a victim of antigravity.

Mom had been in the hospital a couple of weeks when Dad took me to visit her for the first and only time. It was the week before Christmas. Either Bruce didn't want to go or Dad was afraid he would be disruptive. Bruce had severe learning disabilities with hyperactivity. Though I didn't know it at the time, Mom was undergoing electroconvulsive therapy. She must have been suffering from drug withdrawal as well. Bruce and I were told nothing.

We entered a brick building that looked more like a prison than a hospital. An orderly ushered us through a heavy metallic door and locked it behind us. Our footsteps echoed as Dad and I walked down the hall to Mom's room. "You wait here," Dad instructed. "I'll be out in a few minutes."

I waited in the hallway with my ukulele strapped over one shoulder. A woman shuffled past me in a pale blue bathrobe, mumbling something unintelligible, her expression wooden, arms weighted against her side. Another woman, older, hair springing off her pale scalp in white tufts, rocked back and forth in her wheelchair in front of the nurse's station. "Oh Lizzie," she whined, pulling against the straitjacket that tied her to the chair. "Oh Lizzie," she wailed, over and over, until her voice became a high-pitched screech.

My heart battered in my chest. In an effort to control my rising panic, I stared at the floor and counted—315, 316, 317, 318. There was nowhere to sit. In the middle of the hallway, I was stranded between worlds.

Finally, Dad appeared. "You can go in now," he said.

He waited in the hallway while I went into Mom's room, eager for proof she didn't belong in this place. She was lying in bed so still she seemed lifeless, like her spirit had left and only its carcass remained. She looked tiny. She reminded me of an old rag doll that had been abandoned. How could this person be my mother?

"Hi, Mom," I said. The room was bare except for a bed, wooden dresser, sink, and closet.

"Hi, honey," she whispered. Her eyes glazed as if looking at something far away. She didn't move.

I didn't know what to do. I was used to my mother being in charge. She told Dad, Bruce, and me what to do. Dad was supposed to fix us breakfast; Bruce was supposed to take out the trash; I was supposed to set the table. Even my feelings were dictated by her tastes. I felt sad when she thought I should feel sad. I got upset about things she thought should upset me. Suddenly I felt lost and hugely self-conscious, as if a familiar connection had been severed. My head hurt and it was hard to breathe. "Want me to play you a Christmas carol on my ukulele?"

"Sure, that would be nice."

I heaved a sigh of relief. I played "Away in a Manger," singing in my best voice. When she failed to respond, I played "The First Noel" and "O Come All Ye Faithful."

"Play 'Silent Night,'" she requested.

"Mom, I can't. I don't remember."

"I want to hear 'Silent Night,'" she said. "It's Christmastime. Surely you remember 'Silent Night.'"

"I left my book at home. I don't have the chords." My mouth went dry and I could hardly swallow. *Why was she acting like this? What was wrong with her?*

Her eyes snapped into focus. "Then figure them out. I want to hear 'Silent Night.'"

My face flushed. I stared at the fretboard. I rearranged the fingers of my left hand to form a C chord as I strummed with my right. My shoulders hunched up around my ears. "Si-lent night," I sang, but the note was too high, and my voice faltered. "I'm sorry, Mom. I can't do it." I hiccupped a sob and fled from the room.

Mom was discharged from the hospital a couple weeks later on her birthday, January 8, 1967. Dad, Bruce, and I picked her up in the morning and by dinnertime, she was still in her flannel nightgown. She was all bones and hollow, like a bird that could be crushed in your fist. She sat without moving on the couch and waited for each gift to be placed in her hands. Through floor-to-ceiling windows, oaks, poplars, and maples—stripped of their leaves—stood like silent sentries against a sullen sky.

After all the presents were unwrapped, she gazed at me and asked, "Is that all?" She looked like a child, dumbstruck with disappointment.

I couldn't speak. I wanted my mother back, the one who wore clothes and fixed dinner and took me to doctor's appointments and stopped for ice cream at Fairmeade's Pharmacy.

"We didn't have a lot of time to shop," I explained. "Here," I said, placing my gift in her lap. "I made this for you. Don't you like it?" I'd handstitched an address-book cover in crewel embroidery.

She barely glanced at it and began to cry. In the flutter of a sparrow's wing, my mother and I had changed places.

This is what I thought: It was my fault my mother was depressed. I'd disobeyed her the previous year by swinging on a rope from a cliff and had almost died. Mom said it was the stress of my accident that put her over the edge. She would never outright blame me. Still, she seemed like one person before my fall and another person after. In the wake of that realization, as she entered and left the hospital less and less the mother I remembered, I put it together that it must be up to me to make her whole.

Over the next few months, family life returned to normal, which is to say my mother and brother fought constantly while Dad buried his nose in the newspaper or stared at the TV. "Fuck you," my brother would yell. "Goddamn it, I'm not going to mow the fucking lawn."

I'd hide in my room or find solace against a giant sycamore down by the creek. I felt sorry for Bruce, who hadn't stood a chance since being diagnosed as perceptually handicapped in first grade. Though he could pass for normal in superficial social contexts, he was always failing at school. Kids made fun of him. He channeled their harassment into bullying Mom and me at home. She was overpowered. At the same time, she had a way of making him feel small when he asked for help. "Don't bother with that assignment," she'd say. "You can't do it." She claimed she was protecting Bruce. I claimed she was destroying the little confidence he still possessed. Dad sat unmoving on the couch.

As their battles waged with greater and greater intensity, I'd scream, "Will you all please shut up," then hate myself for losing my cool. It was up to me to make things right, yet the harder I tried, the more I screwed up.

By spring of my senior year in high school, I couldn't face another day. I thought about running away. I could buy a ticket to Boston to stay with my grandparents, but they'd just send me home.

There was nowhere I could run.

I thought about killing myself.

The thought rose like mist on a hidden lake—unexamined and undefiled. Suicide so thoroughly captured me, lifted me, floated in me that suddenly all sensation fell away and we were one. No other thoughts existed. No more voices circled like vultures: *Stupid idiot! You think you can save the world? You can't even save your family. You're a failure—a hypocrite—a joke.* Peace at last. Who would have thought resolution could come so easily?

The rest was pure mechanics. In the bathroom with faux-leather wallpaper and blue towels, I took the bottles of phenobarbital and Dilantin from the medicine cabinet. I lined the pills up next to the sink. I filled a Dixie cup with water and swallowed the red-and-white capsules first. By the time I moved on to the plain white tablets, I could barely choke them down. I placed the empty pill containers back on the shelf and shut the door of the medicine cabinet till I heard the magnets click. Then I retraced my steps and climbed into the maple bed that used to be my grandmother's. Not a single thought passed through my mind. It was finished. No regrets; no second thoughts. I waited for oblivion.

I was hospitalized in the same facility where I'd visited my mother. The first morning, I awakened groggy and dazed to the painfully cheery voice of a nurse who said, "Get dressed. It's time for coffee hour in occupational therapy." She tugged the covers off me. As I rose reluctantly from the coma of sleep, she asked, "What made you want to kill yourself?"

I turned away from her, pulled on my jeans, fastened my bra, and slipped a sweater over my head. The nurse continued observing me as I leaned down to tie my shoes. I looked up, hoping she'd forgotten her question.

She regarded me patiently.

As daylight filtered through the iron bars, I whispered, "I don't know."

I hadn't planned on having to explain myself or figure out my life post–suicide attempt. I'd planned on being dead. I'd planned on sparing my family any more pain. In my suicide note, I'd written, "The world will be better off without me."

More than anything I had wanted to be different from my mother, but I was following in her footsteps. Like her, I had my own psychiatrist and psychiatric file. Like her, I underwent shock treatments and, for a time, lost the essential threads that constituted me. When my friend Moose came to visit I sat like a zombie, subdued and unresponsive until he stood to leave. "Why haven't you visited me until today?" I asked. After he left, my mother explained that he had visited every single day.

In the hospital, I met other teenagers bent on self-destruction. I earned privileges and was eventually moved from a locked ward. The other kids and I hung out in the stairwells, jamming on guitars and harmonicas and comparing stories on how to off ourselves.

Thus began a seven-year stint of treatment programs, attempted overdoses, binging and purging, cutting, and codependent relationships with young men.

Yet life went on. I graduated from high school and enrolled in college. I made As and was introduced to cocaine by a professor who called it "the love drug." I also hid behind bulimia and dead-end relationships.

Fortunately, I didn't hide well enough, and some of my professors found me and helped me find myself. Dr. Barbour, my philosophy professor, asked me back to his office after the first exam. He picked a volume off his bookshelf and asked me—a sophomore taking my first philosophy class—what I thought of Spinoza and Kant. Another professor, Dr. Akers, asked me to write a student version of *Our Bodies, Ourselves* under her direction as an independent study. Little by little, such attention made small positive notches in my self-esteem.

By the second half of my junior year, my life was beginning to level out. I still took unreasonable risks, like the time I took mescaline with a guy I barely knew way out in the boonies and had to find my way home when I couldn't keep track of space or time.

But the proportions changed. The desperate acts of despair, when I binged and purged or cut myself, gradually diminished. I got a part in a rock opera. I went camping in Red River Gorge. I ran off with friends to Gulf Shores, Alabama, on a lark in the middle of the semester. In the end, I graduated.

Within months of finishing college, I landed a job working second shift as a residential aide at a juvenile center for girls. These girls were tough, hard, cold, and unpredictable. Any illusion that I could save them ended abruptly the night they staged a sit-in at the end of the dorm hall. A wide-eyed, auburn-haired seventeen-year-old bit me on the shoulder and left a bruise that took an entire year to heal.

One afternoon, Bess, a coworker, invited me to a picnic on a country farm. "There'll be lots of people there," she said. "It's a Christian group."

"I don't know," I said, stirring a tureen of cabbage on the stove in the residence-hall kitchen. I'd given up on Christianity not long after the night of my first suicide attempt. Where was God when I'd taken the overdose? My faith had become dismantled, not so much through acts of intention, as through attrition. Life was full of suffering; the secret was to learn not to attach to desire.

Bess checked the ham and began setting the table for the girls' dinner. The odor of sour cabbage mingled with the scent of salted pork and a hint of cinnamon. "No one will pressure you," she promised. "It'll be fun."

The farm was nestled among rolling hills at the end of a gravel lane. Dark green cedars and white-barked sycamores lined a dry, rocky creek bed. Brown and white cows flicked flies away with their tails as they stood ankle deep in a muddy farm pond. The air smelled pungent with the mingled scent of new spring grass and manure.

Bess drove us up the narrow road until we reached a two-story brick house with an open porch at the top of a hill. Groups of people dressed in shorts and jeans clustered on the lawn, laughing and chatting as they ate hot dogs and potato salad.

Not long after lunch was packed away, someone started singing. Another joined and another until clusters of folk, more than a hundred scattered across a half-acre of land, raised their arms to heaven and sang, "This is the day that the Lord hath made; We will rejoice and be glad in it."

The chorus continued, gaining momentum. Harmonies blended and rose to a crescendo. Bodies swayed and quieted with the commonality of a single organism. Gradually, the singing subsided until the final round was murmured barely above a whisper. Laughter bubbled up among the crowd. Self-consciousness disappeared. My heart lurched in recognition. In that moment, I knew exactly what I wanted. I wanted joy.

Worshippers opened their eyes and hugged one another. I was grasped in the arms of first one, then another, as if I were one of them. Their warmth was infectious. It was as if we had all participated in a life-transforming event. We'd been plucked from the roiling surf and deposited on dry land together. What a marvel to be alive! What a festival of love and gladness!

They belonged to one another, and I could belong to them. Had I ever belonged anywhere or to anyone? My parents had grown weary of me. I hadn't had a friendship last for more than a year or two. What would it be like to inhabit a world where joy, purpose, and friendship commingled?

For a little more than a year, I delighted in my newfound faith at New Blessings Fellowship, but as time passed, the boat that had rescued me and placed me on solid ground began to leak and take on water. I started to ask questions: Why weren't we supposed to talk about our struggles with daily living or, especially, with doubt? If the Bible said, "Ask and you shall receive," why didn't we receive what we asked for more often? If God had created us with the potential to sin, how could we be blamed for messing up?

My questions upset the fellowship leaders. Still, I couldn't help challenging the absolute male authority. I squirmed at the dictates of female submission and the total discouragement of independent thought and action. I couldn't envision a future in which I would marry someone approved by the male hierarchy, have children, keep house, and remain under the authority of my husband. I tried to bully myself into submission—*Leslie, what's wrong with you? Why can't you accept the fellowship teachings like everyone else? Surely, you can't be right while all these good people are wrong*—but it didn't work. I began to fall from favor. I rocked the boat until it began to sink.

Weeks later, I left the community. I continued my spiritual journey—the quest to find a place where it was acceptable to ask questions. I kept looking for truth *and* freedom. I needed to believe in the unconditional love of God and in myself as part of God's good creation. I no longer wanted answers. I wanted transformation.

At age twenty-six, I entered seminary, where I made friends and found other professors who affirmed and encouraged me. My first semester, I interned as a chaplain at a physical rehabilitation center. Instead of disqualifying me, my personal experiences with anxiety and depression helped me understand patients who'd suffered strokes, amputations, or spinal cord injuries. There was something therapeutic about getting out of my own head—the constant cycle of obsessive self-examination—and being drawn through empathy into others' stories.

Early in my tenure, as I was sitting in the chaplain's office writing up my notes, I remembered that Lena, a woman I'd been visiting with spinal cord cancer, was being discharged. I debated whether it would matter to her if I said goodbye. Yes, I'd visited her daily, but what had I said or done that was so significant?

I set the notes aside and walked to her room. She wasn't there. I walked two flights of stairs down to physical therapy, but she wasn't there either. Thinking we might have passed each other en route, I headed upstairs again. As I rounded the bend in the stairwell and emerged at the far end of the lobby, I saw Lena being wheeled out on a stretcher. Flat on her back, she threw her arms into the air and cried, "I knew you'd come. I knew you'd come." I took one of her hands, gripped it tightly, and offered a brief prayer. She met my eyes. Tears streamed down her cheeks and mine.

Only then did I realize I mattered—that I was important and had something to offer as a unique human being. At the same time, I understood that if I failed to value myself or take myself seriously, I would fail others—as I had nearly failed Lena.

Months later, I was offered a position as a staff chaplain, something unheard of for one with less than six months of training. My supervisor asked me to job-share. Here was my first female role model, and she believed in me. My life wasn't wasted. I myself wasn't a waste; I wasn't worthless or, worse, a blight upon the world. It was like gazing up through the trees at an intensely blue sky and seeing eternity instead of some giant smudge smeared across my sorry self. I felt whole. I felt alive. I felt a sense of the possible.

Years passed. In January 2001, my brother died of alcoholism. Three years later, Dad died of Parkinson's disease. Mom thrived during the first few years following Dad's death. Her social calendar was full of outings to restaurants, trips to Spring Mill State Park in Indiana, and midwinter jaunts to Florida. Before long, however, her health began slipping, first from a stroke and then from an accumulation of problems. As her health declined, she became intermittently depressed and cranky. She developed a dependence on codeine, which she added to a full repertoire of other sedatives. She tried to quit smoking to no avail. Trips to the emergency room became more and more frequent.

On Tuesday of Holy Week in 2010, my mother called and asked if I would drop by her condo. I was fifty-seven years old, remarried with young adult children and working as a psychotherapist. When I arrived, Tina, my mother's housekeeper, met me at the door. "Your mother fell last night," she said. "She tried to kill herself. She took almost an entire bottle of sleeping pills."

Over the next few days, I found myself reacting from so many different age levels that my head spun. I looked at my mother and remembered watching my father comb through cabinets. I was fourteen with my ukulele strapped across my shoulder, visiting her in a psych hospital. I was a senior in high school, writing my suicide note.

Yes, I understood what it was like to be so depressed that nothing and no one mattered, but I wasn't able to let my mother off the hook. I felt so bereft, so wounded in the face of her plans, that I couldn't see her behavior as anything less than selfish and willful.

The following week, after I took my mother to her psychiatric appointment, we stopped for lunch. As she ate her roast-beef-and-provolone sandwich, I observed her. She was a painfully slow eater because of problems with her dentures. Otherwise, she was in remarkably good shape for a woman of her age and habits, not to mention the events of the last week. Today, though, she looked paler than usual and the brightness was gone from her blue eyes.

Tension stretched between us. My neck ached. All the words of tenderness and longing we might have expressed went unsaid. We were moored on separate islands of heartbreak. She wanted me to understand without judging her; I wanted her to say she was sorry.

As she took a sip of her milkshake, I asked, "Are you glad you survived?" Even as I asked the question, I knew I was being stupid. What kind of answer did I honestly expect? As a therapist, I knew I was setting myself up. As a daughter, I knew nothing other than my overwhelming need for reassurance—my need to hear my mother say, "I made a mistake. I love you. I would never hurt you or want to leave you."

She avoided the question, shuffling crusts of bread around on her plate.

"Are you glad you survived?" I asked again. The muscles in my jaw strained as I waited for her response.

Mom took another sip. It seemed like she was making a point of taking her time.

With a final slurp, she released the straw and looked up. "If I'd died, you would have coped," she said. "You would have coped, wouldn't you? You might have been upset initially, but you would have come through it. You would have coped."

I felt heat rise in my cheeks, as if I'd been slapped. My breath caught in my throat. "Yes," I admitted. "I would have coped, but the legacy of suicide is very different from that of a natural death."

She dipped her head, avoiding my eyes. "I know," she said.

How I hated her for making me admit that I would cope, for using my competence as an excuse to think only of her needs, as if "coping" was the ultimate betrayal and negated any requirement on her part to be responsible. I was sick of coping. I was sick of feeling guilty for the cardinal sin of competence.

Later, as I rehearsed the restaurant scene over and over in my mind, I realized something that changed all my hard-fought assumptions about myself. For years, I'd struggled with survivor guilt—the guilt, not so much of surviving my brother but of surpassing him—the guilt of being the one who was spared intellectual disability. I'd assumed this guilt drove me to despair and suicidal behavior. But as I thought of my mother's words, an alternative version of reality presented itself. It wasn't Bruce alone whom I'd betrayed by surviving (or thriving), but my mother. I was not supposed to survive her. As she suffered, I was meant to suffer. As she aged, I should age. As her life diminished, so should mine. My survival guilt was tied to my mother, not just to my brother.

Two years later, my mother died. Her death was precipitated by an overdose. As I rifled through letters and drawers in the aftermath of her passing, I discovered that she had tried to kill herself at least four times. Though I'd forgiven myself in stages throughout the years, I forgave myself more fully then—for not being able to make her whole, for all the grief I caused her, for not giving up my life to take care of her. I understood that I'd needed something from my mother that she couldn't give: the security of constancy.

I think back to the day when I asked my mother if she was glad she survived. I'd been so angry, so certain her words were intended as an accusation, but what if I was wrong? What if, instead, she was expressing her grief—her deep, abiding sadness that our lives were moving in opposite directions? She needed me, and I didn't appear to need her. She would leave me, whether at the time of her Holy Week overdose or soon thereafter.

On another level, she could have been acknowledging that she'd done her job as a mother. She had faith in me. She knew she was not the cornerstone of my life. I had a host of other loved ones to whom I was committed. She knew I'd be all right. She'd raised a competent daughter. Maybe her words—"You'd cope, wouldn't you"—were not so much a curse as a blessing. My mother had blessed me with competence and tenacity, gifts she'd believed she was lacking. At whose hands other than hers would I have received such blessings?

And so I cope.

I more than cope. I am sixty-two years old, happily married, the mother of four children and six grandchildren. There are days when I still struggle to be kind to myself. It is in my nature to doubt myself, but here is the crucial difference: I am surrounded by people who love and believe in me, thus enabling me to love and believe in myself. Those qualities that once incited self-hatred—jealousy, competitiveness, envy, greed, temper, guilt—I now recognize as human qualities with which we all struggle.

As a psychotherapist, these are the same truths I try to impart to my clients:

You are loved.
You are important.
You have a unique contribution to make to the world, and—
I believe in you.

Leslie Smith Townsend *is a licensed marriage and family therapist in private practice. Her essays and poetry have been published in the* Louisville Review, Arable, New Southerner, *the* Christian Science Monitor, *and the* Louisville Eccentric Observer. *"A Blessing" is an excerpt from Townsend's mem-oir-in-progress,* Blame.

The Pain that Tore in You an Ocean

Chloë Mattingly

I.

I come to consciousness the way mud slides from a glass: slowly, thickly, grudgingly. There's a thudding pain behind my brow and a dull fog clouding my senses. For a few moments, there's nothing beyond the rhythmic pulse of blood in my temple—I do not exist outside this swilling mind—but slowly my awareness spreads beyond the realm of ache, and I realize I am lying in a bed. My bed.

That's okay. That's right.

The room is awash in yellow as light streams through the curtains. They hang ten feet high, stiff pillars of Cotenza cotton. The retailer described them as "citron," but in fact, they are more the color of radioactive mustard. I had been going for a Joan-Didion-in-New-York aesthetic; the reaching ceilings of my new apartment demanded a certain sense of drama, I thought. It is my first place to myself and I love it. I love the old Victorian-styled building, new apartments tucked into old rooms along the halls. I love the high ceilings and crown molding and scratched hardwood floors. I love the ornate mantel next to built-in shelves from the seventies. I love the feel of histories lost here, the way my bed sits on the tiled hearth of a long-removed fireplace, could-be coal dust still grimy in its grout. I love it, even with the blaring yellow light like an alarm.

I fumble across swells of bed linen and grasp my phone.

I pull it to me and squinting, I examine the screen. It's two o'clock in the afternoon. A Sunday.

I groan. I reach for my glasses, but they aren't where they should be, perched on the edge of my dresser, a hand's breadth from the bed. I assume I knocked them off in my sleep and struggle to rouse myself for the blind-eyed search across the floor. I have the eyesight of empty blackboards, of waggled fingers inches from faces, colors of flesh fading into blurs of nothing.

A striking bolt of pain stops me midway, twisting feet from sheets, touching the floor. My head pounds the primal drumbeat of an unknown fear: something isn't right.

I notice through my bleary, blinded gaze that I'm wearing jeans. I never fall asleep in my clothes, particularly not jeans. I hate them, their stiffness, the way they pinch at the waist. I didn't discover yoga pants until I graduated from college, but now I am morally opposed to legwear that doesn't come in spandex.

The pain persists as I force myself to kneel and feel around the floor for the missing glasses. I locate them, an inch under the bed, and the world reconfigures itself from behind corrective lenses.

I perch back on the edge of the mattress and delicately assess the source of the pain. The mirror on the door slantwise reflects me. There are marks on my neck—one, two, three— little impressions of I'm-not-sure-what. I peel my shirt off over my head and watch as it falls to the floor. Nothing unusual here. I unzip my jeans, the tight ones, the ones I've had since college that no longer fit right but that I refuse to get rid of because jeans aren't cheap, and yes, I'm now a gainfully employed college graduate, but this new apartment is expensive and so is that beautiful new couch I just ordered.

Tenderly, I strip away the jeans like pulling petals, and then I see. Along my thighs are blossoming bruises: purple and blue and black as memory.

A wave of something resembling nausea overtakes me, and I rush through the mirrored door, fall to my knees by the toilet, and empty myself into its basin.

I don't know how long I crouch there, sobbing and hiccuping and spitting and retching, but eventually there is no more, and I stop. I can feel it now.

The emptiness.

There are things to be done. Doctors to call, tests to take. Preventative measures. Obligations.

I do none of these things. I stand up. I brush my teeth. I vomit again. I crawl back into bed and let the sheets gather me up in their folds. I sleep.

Time is swift . . . and sluggish. It bottles me up and I am swallowed into its darkness. It moves like oceans, and I bob along inside my bottle. The waves carry me as the moments tick on and on and on and on, and I sleep. Hours, then days, weeks, and I sleep. Seasons rise and seasons fall, and time goes on, and I sleep. Centuries pass and civilizations die, and when I finally wake up, I am standing at the kitchen sink, scalding water pouring onto my hands, and I stare at them as if they aren't mine. As if they never were.

"What am I doing?"

"You're making tea."

A friend looks at me from across the room and I think I feel love. Is that a thing I can feel? I don't remember. She's come to stay with me, to help me. I'd forgotten she was here, but she is beautiful, and good, and kind, and she loves me, and I am making tea.

II.

I stand at rail-edge, looking out at what I know to be the ocean, but all I can see is impenetrable blackness. There is no horizon at night. I love this moment. I am wearing a dress, flower blue and white. Its skirt is wide and billowing, and I feel like Grace Kelly. The briny wind wrecks havoc upon my hair, and salt-slicked tresses fall back against my brow.

Out here, it's quiet, and I am alone. For just this moment.

I am on holiday with my sister and her husband. They live in Florida, so the monolithic ships of Royal Caribbean are just a drive away. Despite my near-phobic fear of swimming or water sports of any kind, I love being on this ship. I could stand here staring at the dark blur of sea and sky for hours. Crests of waves are barely visible in the black. There's a silence to oceans when you get out far enough, the squall of gulls a land-bound memory from days before. The swish of waves, of swell and froth, fades out to a sort of white noise, and all that's left is the coolness of air, the sticking of salt, the clutch of cold bars along the deck's railing. You can close your eyes and the view doesn't change much. They say the vast nothingness of the ocean has driven men mad, but I have never seen anything so comforting.

Inside the ship's gut, people mill about. There's music and lights and drunken giggles, and spills are blamed on sea waves, and couples snug a little closer.

Party lights, in all this nothing.

Our room is a pocket with a porthole. My sister is getting dressed for dinner tonight. I cram my way into the mirror-space and scowl. A mountainous zit has appeared on my chin; my skin rebels. I add it to the list of ways my body is failing me.

"I'm breaking out like mad," I complain. My sister suggests it may be the salty ocean air, but I say no, it's stress. She asks why, and months from now, when I remember my answer—was it a lie?—a sad smile will tug at my lips.

"I was with this guy," I tell her, "and it was okay, but then it got really bad."

Oh, to rewrite my history so cleanly.

"But it's okay. I'm fine."

Yes, a lie.

We are leaving dinner; the ship churns beneath our feet. The weather shifted last night and all day the sea has spun us about, great growling bursts of waves that stagger feet and clatter the cutlery. Stepping out from the dining room, a man and his wife pass to my right and for whatever reason—a wave, a drink—he knocks against me.

"Sorry!" he says. And then he places a hand on my arm in apology, fingers wrapped around like rope, and squeezes. "Sorry about that." He continues on.

I walk several paces, but my insides are churning like the fitful sea beneath me. I tell my sister and her husband I need to sit for a moment. "A little seasick."

No, stop —
His fingers, behind my ears and around my neck.
I'm too —
His fingers, grasping, pushing into my arm.
Stop —

Somewhere inside me, I hear an inaudible shatter, quiet as the snuffing of candles, but it's there. It's there . . . and crumpling. I hear it.

I don't want to hurt you.

III.

Swallowed up in sheets that lace like serpents around my limbs, I wake. It's a sudden waking: an exhalation of hot breath from nostrils, lids snapping up above eyes that dart around the darkness. The body doesn't move, frozen in the habitual trap of terror and sleep paralysis, a sort of rigor mortis for the allegedly still alive.

The room is hot and sticky despite it being winter and about twelve degrees outside. I have no control over heating in my apartment, and the landlord keeps it cranked to sauna-like levels. A deep breath and I clench fingertips to palms, squeezing my knuckles in a sort of release. *You're awake. Move.*

My muscles relent and I twist about painfully in my hurry to confirm: keys, phone, knife.

Okay.

I squint at the time on my phone. Just after three o'clock in the morning. *Oh, come on.* I roll over in bed, pressing palms to the sockets of my eyes. Dancing phosphenes glimmer against the black of lids and I watch them, the little constellations of light, images where there should be none. I open my eyes and they are gone; all I see is the shadow of flesh. If only the images of nightmares would fade so cleanly. Perhaps then I'd get some sleep.

But I am awake. There's no getting around that; never mind that I only shut my eyes two hours ago. To go back to sleep now would be to invite the nightmare again, and I feel lucky to have made it this far unscathed. Some nights are worse than others. Some nights—most nights—I awake screaming, slashing, sobbing, ripping at the sheets that hold me hostage. Some nights, the terror doesn't end upon waking; the dam of dreams bursts through with oneiric horrors, with memory, with pain—real, thrashing, burning pain.

It's the pain that scares me the most. How can he still hurt me? Invade my nights with terrors, my days with memories—fine. But how can I wake and feel the same pain that once made me cry out in a dank room that was not my own? That pain I won't soon forget; my body won't let me. It obsesses in echoes. The pain that creaks in the bits between your bones, places you didn't know you could hurt. The pain that cripples, that torments, that disturbs, the pain that tore in you an ocean, and you drown, sinking, squirming, inside the skin of your own sea. The waves that send you spluttering, that crash against your chest, that steal away the breath from your lungs: they are your own, your very own.

I dream of whales that will swallow me whole.

Time heals all wounds. People like to say this. There's comfort in the thought of this man-created deity, the slow religion of the tick-tock clock. Time heals all wounds.

It's a lie.

Some wounds heal with time, sure. Blood congeals, scabs grow like lichen across skin. Even splintered bone can mend. Some wounds heal, but others . . . others become dislodged from time—looping and skipping and spinning—sticking to misbegotten memories like dew on a web.

My memories have fallen out of time, out of order. I don't know when they began to refile themselves in my brain, but I've lost close to a month, I calculate. I know that month happened because I see pictures of myself on Facebook. I smile. I see comments I've made and posts I've liked, and I have no recollection. That time is gone, those memories are lost—lost in the dark swells of an unknown sea.

Sometimes they come back to me, little messages in a bottle. The storm draws them in.

There are fingers clutching at my throat.

No. I don't remember that. It didn't happen like that. It couldn't have happened like that. But it's always in the dream, the dream that haunts my every night. Over and over and over and over. Fingers—ripping out my throat.

He said, *I don't want to hurt you.*

Still in bed, I curl into myself like a question and reach for the pocketknife I always keep in close proximity. Holding the small red switchblade in my hand, I rub my thumb gently over its plastic case. It's a foolish thing, like walking through the streets with keys pressed through knuckles. A tonic for your terror, a useless way to say you tried.

Did I try?

Stop that.

It's too early for that.

I need tea.

My apartment is split in two. On one end, a bedroom with a tiny bathroom tucked in the corner. On the other, a living room and kitchen, stuffed in the old walls of an old house. Between these two halves, a public hall leads to the other apartment at the end of the building. Occasionally the two girls who live there cross by, but it's not as weird as it sounds. I have two locks on each door.

I slink from sheets into slippers; grab my keys, my phone, and my knife; unbolt the door; unhook the chain; and step out into the bright light of the public hall. Its carpet is the color of rust, its walls an aging off-white. Spidery cracks trail from the ceiling. I shut the door quietly behind me. I lock it. Three steps across and I'm at the other half of my home. Holding the knife and phone in one hand, I unlock door number two and step into my living room. I bolt the door. I hook the chain. I go to the kitchen, put on the kettle, and wait for the hours to slide by.

Perhaps I will go into work early. I've been doing that a lot lately, getting in before everyone else. Then I can actually get something done. I have a good job at a good university with good people. I—I used to be good at it. But lately, I've been finding it hard to function when there are other people around me. At work, there are always other people around me. So I'll go in early.

173

I gather my things—keys, phone, knife—unbolt the door, unhook the chain, exit, lock the door, cross the hall, unlock the door, enter, bolt the door, and hook the chain. I walk to the cramped little bathroom, the toilet shoved under the slope of a staircase, the shower just barely a cubby. I peel off my pajamas, step into the shower, and let the hot water engulf me. Steam fills up the room, clouding mirrors, fogging minds.

My memory is a groove in the record; the needle scratches, and skipping, skipping—I spin.

I don't know where I am—I don't know—no, wait. I'm here. Here. In his room. In his swamp of a bed. And he's here too, oh God, oh God, oh God . . . but he's sleeping. I have to get out of here. I'm going to throw up.

I grab at the first T-shirt I find—it's his; it smells like him— and I feel my way to the bathroom. It's a tiny bathroom, the tub almost touches the toilet. I sit on the edge of the tub, poised to vomit if necessary, and begin to shake. It must be 3:00 A.M. I'm miles from my apartment. I can't walk home like this; I can barely stand. Oh God, what did I do? What did I do?

I can't go back in there. I'll just sit here, with my head in my hands, till morning. No—you can't sit here, you idiot. He has fucking roommates. What's wrong with you?

Roommates. Will they help me?

Oh please. No one's going to help you, you miserable little slut. You did this to yourself. What the fuck were you thinking? That he was your friend? That he wouldn't hurt you? For fuck's sake. Grow up.

I can't sit here forever.

He's your friend.

Okay. Okay. Okay.

I stand up with a shuddering breath and creep back into the room like a ghost. Can't be more than a few hours till dawn, right? I lower myself back onto the bed and curl my body along its edge, barely a bone on the mattress. I will lay here, eyes wide and open and awake until the sun comes up, until my legs stop shaking, until I can control my body again. Then I will get the fuck out of here.

I guess I fight it, the way sleep sinks into your skin, tugging your eyelids down, pushing from inside your head. I guess I fight it, the way the darkness slinks in like fog, blurring, blending, erasing. I guess I fight it.

Or maybe I don't. Maybe I don't want to fight anymore.

When I wake up, it's two o'clock in the afternoon, and I'm in my bed, my own bed, in jeans, with a throbbing pain along my thighs.

When I wake up, it's a month later, and I'm standing at the kitchen sink, scalding water pouring onto my hands, and I don't recognize them as my own.

When I wake up, I'm sitting with my head in my hands on a storm-battered cruise ship, feigning seasickness, my sister asking if I feel any better yet.

When I wake up, I'm curled on the floor of the shower, and the water pummeling my back is cold as a christening. There's a metallic taste in my mouth and, after a moment, I realize I have bit my lip so hard it burst. I drag myself up, slipping slightly on the linoleum, and step out onto the sodden bathmat. The mirror is fogged, so I can't see my reflection, but looking down at myself, I examine a sprawling map of angry, welting scars along my skin, up and down legs and arms and stomach. An intricate web of agonies. Skin under my claws.

I wrap a towel around my body, trying to steady my feet. Coming back is never easy. I'm shaken but not too surprised. These days, violence haunts me. I file my nails with teeth. I bully my skin raw. I step out into the bedroom. The scars will fade—they're just scratches; they always fade—but I'd better wear long sleeves today anyway. I glance at the clock. 9:00 A.M.

I'm thirty minutes late for work.

"Fuck," I say. "Fuck, fuck, fuck!"

I grab my phone and text my co-worker: OMG I just woke up, my alarm didn't go off. Can you let everyone know I'll be there in a half hour? I'm SO sorry.

I hesitate over this lie for a moment, but what else can I say? Sorry I'm late. I was unconsciously beating the shit out of myself in the shower. Sorry I'm late. I was time-traveling and just got back.

Please.

I throw on clothes—a yellow pencil skirt from J.Crew, tights, a turtleneck sweater, a pearl-string necklace. My go-to when I need to look put together in a rush. I tie my wet hair up in a ponytail—it'll look awful but never mind. Now to do something about the lip. I examine it in the small magnifying mirror I keep on my desk. The bottom lip is just barely swollen, a blistering gash of bright red against pink. Never mind. A smudge of lipstick, and you can barely tell. The rest—foundation, eyeliner, mascara—I'll have to do without. It's best not to look too put together on days you're late anyway.

I throw on a heavy coat and hat and boots. Unhook the chain, unbolt the door, step out, turn, lock, trudge down the hall, out the house, and marching numbly, I begin the walk to work.

I am a golem of myself, dusty words in the shape of a girl. Do my bidding. Go.

IV.

The doctor's room is cold, bright, and sterile. It's been eight months—eight months since I woke up bruised and bleary. Eight months since my memory went spinning into the void. But time has passed, and the realization of—my memories of—well, they're mine again. I think.

Eight months. I'm so tired.

The doctor says not to worry. Just a few tests. Everything will be okay.

Lying in a paper gown on her table, I scream. The lights in my mind flash and it is dark, and there are fingers, fingers at my throat, and I scream. The room is brightly lit, but I lie in shadow as he rapes me, again and again—how many times must I do this? How many times? Again and again—I am dying, why doesn't she stop? Don't let him! Again and again. Stop, I scream, stop! Oh God, oh God, oh God, oh God, oh God…

She turns off the lights and tells me to lie in the dark and concentrate on my breathing.

Oh God, oh God, oh God, oh God…

She takes my hand and then thinks of better of it. I can still feel the brevity of her clammy touch.

Oh God, oh God, oh God…

Post-traumatic stress disorder. The words are handed to me like a prize. Look, you have a name, they say; you have a box. Look, you aren't losing your mind. You just have post-traumatic stress disorder.

The words conjure images of desert-dressed soldiers and dust-covered caravans. IEDs and blasted bones and blood, blood, blood. Snapshots of presidents shaking hands with grim-faced vets, of yellow ribbons on SUVs. The tiny ways we deign to help.

These images do not fit. I have no ribbon. My bombs are fingers, my blasts the mere brutality of flesh. The war is in me, my skin, my body, my soul—ticking, ticking, a bomb in the brain.

The doctor says I have been so strong.

Strong.

I loathe the word strong. It feels false; it feels like a cliché. I don't deserve it. How can you call me strong? I tremble at the knock of a stranger. I quake at the brush of a friend's hand. The flash of a moment on television has me locked in the bathroom, crouching on mildewed linoleum, a sweater stuffed between my teeth so no one will hear the images wrenching me apart. Do not call me strong. I can't sleep without a knife under my pillow. I clutch my keys, ready to run, run, run away—from ghosts, from ghosts that haunt me still. What good is a knife against ghosts?

Words defeat me. I fumble my phrases, I trap myself—I start a line and lose the track—and I ache, I ache, I ache for it to end. I ache to end it.

How can you call me strong?

It feels like a command. Be strong, or be nothing.

But oh, I crave the nothing.

Don't tell me I am strong for climbing out of the sea, don't tell me I am brave for clinging to your raft. I want none of this—I don't want the medicine, I don't want the memories. I want to slip back under the waves, back to the dark. I want to sink down, down, down into the murky depths of forgetting, until the glimmer of your sky is but another memory I've lost. I don't want to be brave, I don't want to fight. Find yourself another warrior, another bright-eyed heroine who makes poetry of her pain and let me go back to sleep, please.

I'm so tired.

Let me fall back into my sea.

Please.

The doctor says this is the hard part.

V.

My apartment is empty. I hollowed it out, sold my furniture, and dispersed my possessions to friends, scattering the debris of this life like shells on distant shores. The gray velvet couch is gone. The coffee table. The chairs. The ornate mantel looks naked over the fireplace, and the shelves are bare of the teacups and cake stands and candlesticks that once cluttered them. In the middle of the room, a still life: two suitcases and a backpack, stuffed to strained seams. The things I'll carry with me. The things I won't leave behind.

The lofty ceilings of my apartment feel cavernous now, and the clack of shoes on rough hardwood echoes with each step. There's no furniture left, so I sink to the floor and sit against the wall. I've got time to kill, waiting for the cab to take me to the airport. Morning light fans through uncovered windows and snowflakes tick against the glass. It is winter again, and it amazes me. A year gone swirling by. What happened to spring? To summer? To fall? The day in and day out of the year that led to this? It's not that they're forgotten—the way other memories had been forgotten—just . . . muddled.

A year in fragments. I collect shards of scenes: the glint of this moment with a therapist, the sharp edge of that day at the doctor's. A mosaic of sertraline and citalopram and sleeping pills that did nothing to cull the nightmares.

Time heals all wounds.
Time heals.
Time wounds.

I quit my job. Broke the lease on my apartment. Bought a plane ticket to Thailand on the vague promise of a teaching gig. If time cannot save me, then it is space I choose.

There was some concern among friends when I announced I was getting rid of nearly everything I owned. That's a warning sign, isn't it? But I talked about fresh starts, the punishing practicality of the matter, the costs of a moving van. I didn't know how to explain that my apartment had become a minefield of memory, that every item was a tiny trigger, a sleeper agent waging war on my ability to cope. So I did what I'd become so good at doing: I lied.

"I'm going minimalist. I don't need any of this stuff, anyway. They're just things."

I did keep some of it. The birthday presents and books I couldn't abandon. The breakable, pretty fixtures that mean so little and so much. I packed them in boxes and shipped them off to my parents' basement, sealed away where they couldn't hurt me.

Just things.

We burn our clothes after a plague that we may be clean. So too I'll burn this life and hope the ash blows the other way. Perhaps it is wishful thinking. Perhaps this gaping ocean will always swill inside me, spitting salt into old wounds. But I won't know unless I try.

My phone rings, a startling reverberation in the apartment's echoing silence. The cab is here. I push myself up. I leave the keys on the empty counter. I tuck my phone into my pocket. I've lost track of my knife in the chaos of packing and purging. I slip the backpack over my shoulders and clutch a suitcase in each fist. I hesitate by the door. Down the hall, I hear the garbled talk of neighbors. Above, the familiar creak of footsteps on stairs.

I will leave this place, this home, and carry with me only a hodgepodge of possessions and a patchwork of fragmented memories. One day, I will unpack those boxes and sort through this shipwreck year. With time—or space—I will remember the good things that happened here, too: the late nights with friends, the cups of tea, the bowls of matzo-ball soup. The love that buoyed me, even at my lowest ebb. The friends who kept me alive.

But for now, it is enough to close this door. I don't know what comes next. I don't really know where I'm going, what I'll find when I get there, which way the current will pull me, but I'm strangely calm as I drag my bags across the dusty carpet of the public hall. You can call me strong, you can call me brave, you can call me whatever you want. I'll be okay. Because you know what?

This was the hard part.

Chloë Mattingly *received her bachelor's degree in creative non-fiction from the University of Pittsburgh. She has lived many places but currently resides in Tennessee. She writes essays and stories and sometimes emails.*

There's a Name for That?
Living with Trichotillomania

Alison Townsend

It seems ordinary at first, this biscuit-colored brush that always works its way down to the bottom of my bag, its shiny bristles clogged with strands of my own reddish-brown hair and dusted with that mysterious lint that seems to sift down to the bottoms of women's purses. If it were not my own, it would even be faintly repulsive, repellent in the way of objects that come into contact with other people's bodies—toothbrushes, razors, pumice stones. It isn't unpleasant, however, because it is mine, smelling (when I lift it to my nostrils) faintly of expensive Aveda hair care products—Blue Malva shampoo, Elixir leave-on conditioner, and witch hazel hairspray commingled into a faint powdery scent not unlike the flowery one that greets me when I bury my nose in my cat's fur.

The brush is made of wood, something you don't see much anymore in this day of mass-produced, plastic throwaway objects. The wood is blonde, slightly lighter and less red than oak. Ash, I would say, if I had to hazard a guess, though it has an interesting grain in the handle (for it is a ladies' brush) that catches in the light and looks almost like bird's-eye maple. Stained with some sort of clear natural finish, the wood is darker in places—the handle and spots where the sides of it touch my head as I draw it through my hair—marked with oils from my own skin, which have permeated it over the thirty years it has been in my possession.

I've had the brush for over half my life, though I never think of it that way, running its familiar shape through my hair every morning, fluffing my bobbed tresses neatly around the scarf or headband I have arranged carefully over the places that are bare or thin or growing back in, places that, like Hester Prynne's scarlet letter, mark my shame. I am artful about this, with scarves that either match or contrast every outfit, scarves that fly out behind me as if they were hair, scarves one of my students says seem a symbol of what she mistakenly calls my "free spirit." I am not free. The brush is my faithful accomplice.

The bristles of the brush are natural too. "Pure boar bristle," I remember the package said. "Good for your hair." My vegetarian heart hesitated for a moment, but I went ahead. I plunked down twenty-five dollars (a lot to pay for a hairbrush, in 1975 or now), surrendering to the superstitious hope that a new brush, a really good brush, like the kind I remembered my mother brandishing in my childhood as she braided my waist-length hair, might be the solution to my "problem" (for which I had no name in 1975). Like the magical objects that appear in fairy tales, the new brush might transform me, stimulating not only my scalp (as the package also promised) but me into some new mode of behavior, one where I didn't fall back on my body for solace when I was anxious or scared, one where I stopped pulling my hair out, one where—like the Rapunzel I sometimes pretended to be as a girl, hanging my long hair over the edge of my four-poster bed—I could, literally and metaphorically, let my hair down again, not to a prince but to some lost self with whom I had lost contact.

If the brush could speak, what stories would it whisper? More than half my life has been groomed by its scratchy caress. If my brush could speak, would it write the autobiography of my hair in the air around my head like a flaming aura? Would it explain things, finding out the reason behind this bizarre disorder, this affliction called trichotillomania, this biochemical misfiring in the brain, this internal itch (like bees hived inside the body) that compels people to pull at their hair?

Would it say how I have gone on living with the chronic and hidden thing, this condition that ebbs and flows over the course of a lifetime, disappearing at times like those fires that burn underground for years, only to flare up again worse than ever? Would it say how, despite everything (stress, anxiety, compulsion, secrecy, and shame), I have not only survived but prevailed, arranging myself to face a new day in the bright headgear I am known for with this simple object guarding my secret, hiding it, hiding me, even as it strokes me into being? Wise companion, what might it tell me that I do not know I know? Would it sing lament or praise-song? Would it remember every hair? I run my fingers over its bristles. I sniff at it again. I lift it to my head and begin brushing, the rustle and skritch of it through my hair taking me back to the place where all my stories begin.

Trichotillomania (also referred to as TTM or "trich") is a disorder defined by the uncontrollable urge to pull one's hair—from the scalp, eyelashes, eyebrows, pubic area, underarms, beard, chest, legs or other parts of the body, resulting in noticeable hair loss. First given its name in 1889 by a French dermatologist named François Hallopeau, it is a combination of three Greek words: *trich* (hair), *tillo* (pull), and *mania* (which has obvious, unfortunate, and incorrect connotations, since hair pullers are neither manic nor psychotic). Trichotillomania is now classified by the American Psychiatric Association's *Diagnostic and Statistical Manual of Mental Disorders-5* as a category of obsessive-compulsive disorder. TTM is characterized by recurrent body-focused repetitive behavior (sometimes abbreviated BFRB) and persistent (but often unsuccessful) attempts to lessen or stop the behavior. The *DSM-5* criteria for trichotillomania include:

- Recurrent pulling out of one's hair, resulting in hair loss.
- Repeated attempts to decrease or stop the hair-pulling behavior.
- The hair pulling causes clinically significant distress or impairment in social, occupational, or other areas of functioning.
- The hair loss cannot be attributed to another medical condition (e.g., a dermatological condition).
- The hair pulling is not better explained by the symptoms of another mental disorder (e.g., attempts to improve

a perceived defect or flaw in appearance, such as may be observed in body dysmorphic disorder).

People with trichotillomania often describe experiencing tension before pulling their hair and claim feelings of relief afterward. But because of the compulsive nature of the disorder, relief is fleeting, vanishing almost instantly in the face of what they have done. Sufferers live on a hamster wheel of discontent, running from the disorder even as it appears before them. It is with them daily, inescapable, inexplicable.

Each day when I come home from work, the tabby cat has pulled out more of her own fur. I find it around the house in tufts and clumps that are tipped with sable and gold at the roots. She pulls out down too, like a mother bird building a nest from her body. The vet can't say why she does this and we can't seem to stop it, though we try cortisone, more bulk in her diet, and time away from the other cats, who make her nervous.

Sometimes she even pulls at night. I recognize the sound by the way her tags clink as she clamps down and rips, shaking the fur from her mouth afterward, as if to rid herself of something crazy inside. I recognize it because it is the juicy, popping sound my own hair makes when I tear it out, flinging it away from me, exactly like the cat. But she cannot tell me the source of her trouble. And I cannot name the meaning of my own as I rub the bony knobs of her back, avoiding the bald spots, touching her body to keep from touching mine.

No one really knows why people pull out their hair. As an informational handout from the Massachusetts General Hospital TTM Clinic notes that many theories have been cited (often with little documenting data) to explain this peculiar and disturbing behavior, ranging from problems in parental bonding, psychosexual development, dysregulation of grooming behaviors, or merely a bad habit (like nail biting or skin picking). The most promising explanation seems to lie in the link between TTM and OCD, where similarities in clinical symptomatology and treatment response have been observed, implicating the serotonergic neurotransmitter system. As someone who also suffers from depression, another serotonergic glitch, this makes sense to me. However, just as many factors and aspects of brain neurochemistry are responsible for this disorder, it's also likely that a number of different factors may account for its onset and duration (which is lifelong, though it can wax and wane significantly over time, following a transit all its own like some errant planet).

TTM often begins in childhood or adolescence, sometimes during a period of stress or tension. As a girl with long braids all through early childhood, I can remember picking or digging at my head when my mother first became ill with breast cancer and then died when I was nine. But I did not actively pull my hair until I was in junior high. One day, the boy who sat behind me in history class was playing with my long hair, running it through his fingers. A few months later, while writing an in-class essay, I paused briefly while thinking and ran my fingers through my hair. As I did, I noticed an odd, wiry hair among my otherwise straight, silken strands. I pulled it through my fingers again and again, my skin stimulated by the touch of the hair, each whorl tingling. Then, just as suddenly as I had touched the hair, I was filled with the uncontrollable urge to pull it out. I did so, fascinated by the globule of follicular matter on the end (which I mistook for the root and thought had something "wrong" with it). I rubbed the root-end of the hair across my lip, stroking it back and forth, like the smallest sable watercolor brush. It was cool and wet, a tiny tongue, licking me into submission. Then, horrified by what had happened, I flung the hair away from me.

And so it began, this condition that, with undulating strength, has affected the rest of my life, this affliction I didn't even know was a disorder until I was thirty-three and being treated for an episode of clinical depression. "You know, there's a name for that," my psychiatrist said when I cautiously brought up the hair pulling, wondering if it had any connection to the anxiety that peppered my depression like a line of gunpowder dots. His words broke the lock on the box where I kept my worst secret. But they didn't really change anything. I was still afraid of wind and rain, going swimming, standing before a room full of people, or just being looked at too closely—anything that might reveal my secret. I hadn't had a professional haircut in a decade, and when I finally mustered up the courage to do so, I lied to my hairdresser for years, telling her I had a thyroid disorder.

Hair pulling is not painful (and it is not, as some people think, related to disorders like cutting, which numb overwhelming emotions). It brings paradoxical relief to a physical and psychological system that I have come to see is so finely tuned that the world just pours in, flooding me with overwhelming sensation. Pulling feels like a primitive attempt to cope, a focus that is soothing, even pleasurable, for the few moments that I am held in its concentrated beam, my fingers trolling my scalp in search of a hair that feels as if it is "wrong" or "bad" and thus the right one to be pulled. But any feelings of relief are short-lived. After pulling, I am filled with shame, guilt, and sadness. How can I have given in to it again? Though I do not, like some pullers, experience feelings of altered consciousness while pulling, I do watch myself, feeling vaguely unreal, in a trance, or as if it is not happening to me but someone else. But afterward? Afterward I am filled with remorse, despair, hopelessness.

Every evening after my husband drifts off, I lie awake, unable to sleep, tearing my hair out. I do not mean this metaphorically. I know not to do this. I understand how to interrupt the impulse, how to distract myself. I have played with finger toys, taken drugs, learned self-hypnosis, and memorized every intricate dance step of habit-reversal training, cognitive behavioral therapy, and acceptance and commitment therapy (these last methods said to be the best, modalities that make not pulling stick). But that is not enough, just as knowing that this is not me but what they call my brain biochemistry is not enough to make me stop or forgive myself for turning to this weird solace as if it were food, nicotine, a drug.

Nothing is enough. No matter what I do, I can't get at the root of the problem but can only pluck it out, the feeling a hair makes when it is torn from the body all that soothes me as I search for what I cannot find, trying to rid myself of the bad thing. I thread worry through the golden needle lost in the stack of strands I have pulled in my life—hair jewelry I might have woven if I'd saved it all, making something of it, mourning the mystery of this strange disorder.

The Massachusetts General Hospital TTM Clinic estimates that five to ten million Americans are affected by this disorder. One study of college students indicated that six in every one thousand individuals might develop trichotillomania. The condition appears to be more common among women, who may be affected at five to ten times the rate of men when the onset occurs during puberty (which suggests some sort of hormonal connection). Its prevalence is almost certainly underestimated. Professionals don't always ask or even know about it, and patients (me included) are so ashamed they hide it from family, friends, lovers, spouses. I suffered in silence for many years, deflecting occasional gibes—a stepbrother who teased me at the beach, asking, "Are you balding?" and a college boyfriend who accused me of being a freak—all the while wondering what was wrong with me. Mired in a mix of shame, fear, and grief, I felt even more walled off from the world than I did when depressed. Nothing has ever made me feel as isolated. The stress of hiding the condition and the strain of keeping a secret are exhausting. To this day, no one in my family knows I have this disorder, let alone the power it holds or the pain it has caused me. I cannot risk their scorn or misunderstanding. I have, with trepidation, shared it with my husband and a few of my closest friends, all of whom have been supportive. And of course, as a writer, I have explored the subject.

Each day for a year now, I've tied a beautiful silk scarf around my head like a bandage, knotting it securely at the nape of my neck. Turquoise or lavender or chartreuse, matched to my outfit, it covers my shame, and I pretend I am concealing the bare spots. So that I can get up each day. So that I can keep going, though the spots get bigger and harder to hide. People think it is an element of my style. I'm a writer, after all, a bohemian. Now I look like one.

I tear myself apart, strand by auburn strand, because I am not perfect, the stubborn root there (though I restrain myself in the presence of others), even as I bend over the white page, helping my student build a word-house from her pain. I am good at this. I am getting an A. I fool everyone with my long skirts, my dangling earrings, my silk scarves that trail behind me like I am a rare tropical bird.

I wear my armor. I step out bravely into the world, teaching, giving readings, spending time with friends. My life is rich. I have a good job, where I am a beloved professor esteemed by her colleagues. I have published two books and have a wonderful husband, a house in the country that nurtures my soul, a circle of dear friends. But I live in a state of perpetual rawness, as if I have no skin. Even the light on spring evenings goes through me, polishing the lake I can see from my back hill into one, smooth line. I look at it, running my hands over my head, trying to gentle myself the way I have read one can gentle horses, the way I calmed the girl in my office, listening as she read, her words a frail dam she said helped her not to purge.

I listened. And listened, my bald spots covered and my own hands folded, still as a nun's in the empty church of my lap.

I wish I could say I had answers about trich. In many ways, despite the pain I have experienced as a result of this disorder, I have been lucky. I've had understanding psychiatrists and spectacular therapists. I joined the Trichotillomania Learning Center for several years and attended its conference and retreat, where I was able to learn more about the disorder and how to cope with it from experts in the field. I've explored a variety of treatment approaches, learning behavior modification techniques and self-hypnosis. I know that when I exercise regularly and remain consistent in my mindfulness meditation practice, the urge goes down, which suggests that there could be a need for self-calming when I am in a pulling frenzy. The most effective treatment I've ever found was when I was part of a ten-week study at the University of Wisconsin-Milwaukee, where I participated in acceptance and commitment therapy, a modality that, while I was unable to maintain it on my own, enabled me to stop pulling completely for many months. But there are still times when the disorder overruns me. Other times I make what feels like a bodily decision to stop, and I do. In those moments, it feels as if a switch in my head has been flicked, my neurochemical circuitry actually altered in some way. Perhaps it has. I feel like a different woman then, more the person I really want to be and sometimes even am, my long hair streaming behind me in the wind.

There is much that is still unknown about this disorder

and how it progresses. When diagnosed at an early age, there is, it appears, the greatest possibility for complete recovery. But for most people it is chronic, a condition that, like hot, humid weather in midsummer, can be depended upon to return. It recurs with what Mass General calls "exacerbations and remissions," then stops for no apparent reason. Then, just as inexplicably, it begins again, along with the feeling that I am falling down a rabbit hole of despair I find difficult to articulate. As Emily Dickinson once wrote, "Pain has an element of blank." Writing about trich has helped because it names and contains it, and as Isak Dinesen says, "All pain can be borne if it can be put into a story." I was even brave enough to include a poem about it in my second book, *Persephone in America*, in the section about the underworld, because trich, for me, is a kind of descent, a return implicit even in darkness. I try hard to get to know it, to befriend the monster inside me that, it turns out, is not a monster after all, but a wounded part of the self who only wants comfort and consolation. As Kat Duff says, "There is an untold story behind every symptom, an entire human drama surrounding every illness, and only the person who is sick can find that story." Trichotillomania is mine.

I also try to remember something my therapist once told me—that the person, the part of me that pulls my hair, "thinks she's helping you"—which has enabled me to be more tender toward that part of myself. As Albert Kreinheder suggests, "The greatest treasure comes out of the most despised and secret places. . . . This place of greatest vulnerability is also a holy place, a place of healing." My disorder reminds me that, much as I want to be, I am not in control. As much as I despise trich, would do anything not to have it, does it not also teach me something, instruct me in compassion, remind me that we are all bigger than we think we are, that sometimes the best one can do each day is begin again? In my better moments, I believe this and try to live with it as a process taking me some place (I know not where) on my spiritual path. Beneath the symptoms, something or someone (a lost part of me, tiny as a newborn kitten, desperate as a child banging on a locked door), wants all of my attention. How can I not attend to her?

At the trichotillomania support group, no one has hair. Not a full head of it, at least, though we hide the disorder well, piling our curls up in saucy poufs over the bare spots, folding gypsy scarves into bright headbands people mistake for a trademark style or wearing partial "falls" that clip on with a snap and are dyed to match so closely no one can tell the difference.

I can, though, as I watch the others covertly, the jumbled brain chemistry we have in common a sentence to secrecy, subterfuge, stealth. I'd recognize another sufferer anywhere—the girl at Walmart with scabs on her head or the woman at the post office with her hair teased ineffectually over the bare spots. Our facilitator is a sufferer too, though she's "in remission," as I myself have been, sometimes for many years. My hair grows long and, in a breeze, swirls around me like a veil. But the weird alchemy of illness is as fickle as the wind that blows, the wind that, like an enemy, reveals all the hidden bare spots.

We're supposed to reveal things here, but I flinch from stories too much like my own, of sleeplessness and plucking to soothe a system so high-strung it cannot calm down without translating stress back into the known world of the body. I will learn that it's called a body-focused repetitive disorder when I attend a conference and retreat sponsored by the Trichotillomania Learning Center, TLC for short—tender loving care, something we all need.

At first, hearing about others' pulling is like finding a hair in my food, and I don't want to be like them, these "trichster" women who laugh and cry like anyone would. I don't want to watch a movie called Bad Hair Life, log self-acceptance, or track impulses to pull on a form Xeroxed from Mass General's psych ward. I certainly don't want to believe that "trich" (as we call it here) is "a gift," the facilitator's words like a self-help cross-stitch I pick apart in my head, thread by shining thread, the trapdoor of artifice falling open beneath me as I work my way backward through this disorder to the root.

Genetics or brain chemistry, trauma or karma? It doesn't really matter what it's called—after all, no one really knows for sure what causes this affliction—except that it ends. Can I stop doing this? Am I even able? The bees trapped inside my body buzz and whir, needling my nerve endings with delicate stings. At least it's not so bad I have to wear a wig, I think. Or a jaunty red baseball cap like the one the young woman across the room wears, turned backward on her head so she looks like a kid. I toss the tails of my scarf back over my shoulders like the hair I sometimes have. I do not want to be one of these women, part of this "family." But I am one of them. I am.

Despite my reluctance to be part of the support group, I listen, I talk, I share. When I go home, I take the old, wooden brush from my purse and slowly, gently, as if it is all I ever need to do in the world, begin to brush my hair. As the soft, worn bristles rustle through the strands, I remember my mother brushing my hair every morning before plaiting it into tight braids that reached nearly to my waist. Wielding the brush, she lifted and stroked, lifted and stroked, my hair rising and falling with a rhythm like surf that rocked me briefly back against her body before releasing me again. It was hypnotic, one of the most comforting experiences I have ever known. Elemental in its care and tenderness, it was also radically ordinary, a daily occurrence from a time before the pain of this mysterious and recalcitrant disorder ever began to haunt me. *That's the real beginning,* I think to myself as I brush. *That's the self I need to find, braided into my being as deeply and inseparably as this thing I call trich—my light, my bright angel, my blessing.*

Alison Townsend *is the author of two books of poetry,* Persephone in America *and* The Blue Dress, *and two chapbooks,* And Still the Music *and* What the Body Knows. *Her poetry and essays appear widely, in journals such as* Chautauqua, Feminist Studies, Parabola, Quarter After Eight, Southern Review, *and* Zone Three, *and she has won many awards, including a Pushcart Prize, a Wisconsin Arts Board Fellowship, and the University of Wisconsin-Whitewater Chancellor's Award for Regional Literature. Emerita Professor of English at the University of Wisconsin—Whitewater, she is completing a collection of essays,* The Name for Woman Is River: Essaying the Geography of Home.

Playing Catch

Terri Sherrill

The ringer volume on my phone is set just below "wake the dead," and oddly enough, my husband is able to sleep through it. I am not so lucky. It's well after midnight, and I don't have to check caller ID to know that it's my sister. At this time of night, it's almost always Jerri. Or about Jerri. My heart starts thumping right on cue.

Her voice is excited and the words tumble out. "I just woke up on the floor in my bedroom completely naked! I don't know what happened. I must've blacked out. The last thing I remember is taking a shower. Not sure how I got to my room... I think maybe I had a seizure."

I rise up on one elbow, turning away from Stan and trying to keep my voice low. "How do you feel now?"

Okay, she thinks. Maybe a little sore. She might have hit her head on the floor, but she's not sure. Her words sound a little slurred, but coherent.

She reminds me that she's had seizures before, years ago, after a car accident. Those seizures were the result of a head injury.

She doesn't want to call an ambulance. The last time she did, the two paramedics checked her vital signs and asked some basic questions, but when she started listing her medications, they made eye contact over her head and began packing up their gear. Since she brought it up, I ask, "Has

193

anything changed with your medications? Did you take them all today?" I'm a marketing director at a pharmaceutical company, so drugs are my comfort zone.

Nothing in her answer implies that medication is a factor. Still, knowing her history, I hesitate to rule it out.

We decide she needs to see a neurologist. She promises to make an appointment in the morning, and to try to get some sleep. Staring at the ceiling after her call, I wish I could promise the same.

I'm a competent person, but Jerri overwhelms me. For one thing, I live too far away to support her at the level she needs. I mean, someone ought to be with her right now, but it's not like I can jump in the car and get there in ten minutes. She lives in Winston-Salem, which is a hundred miles from my house. Besides, it's now 2:00 A.M., and I've got meetings in the morning.

Mom and Dad could get there in ten minutes, if only they were an option. Mom doesn't believe my sister is sick. She believes Jerri takes prescription meds she doesn't need. If I were to call Mom right now, she'd say, "Your sister's just messed up on her medicine again." Helping Jerri, Mom says, is only enabling her. Most of the time, Dad goes along with Mom. It's just easier.

Outside my bedroom window, the cicadas are chanting. The ceiling fan whirls and somewhere in the living room Max scratches, jangling the tags on his collar. I roll onto my side.

I'm really all Jerri's got. The weight of this knowledge settles in the darkness.

The last time Jerri called at 2:00 A.M., she wanted help getting rid of a neighbor who refused to go home—another problem I couldn't solve long-distance.

"Which neighbor?" I asked.

"Third." (With a degree of narcissism equal only to that of George Foreman, Third's father named all of his sons after himself. To keep them straight, the family simply calls them by the appropriate suffix.)

"Have you *asked* him to leave?"

"Yeah," Jerri said. "But he won't go."

"Well, why not?"

"He won't say."

That didn't seem normal. Kind of like the time Jerri woke up to find Phoebe, Prue, and Piper, the witch sisters from *Charmed*, in her bedroom. They weren't really there, of course, but the only way Jerri could tell was by tossing a pack of Marlboros. In my sister's world, you can't be sure people are real until they play catch with you. The sisters didn't.

Remembering the sisters, I'd asked, "Are you sure Third is really there, Jerri?"

"Yeah, I already thought of that," she said, using her I'm-not-stupid voice. "I threw my lighter and he caught it."

To this day, I'm not sure how she eventually got rid of Third or why he was there in the first place.

When most people hear about hallucinations, they think *schizophrenia*, but Jerri has bipolar disorder. She was diagnosed when she was almost thirty years old. The disease—or, more accurately, brain disorder—causes unusual mood swings which make daily functioning difficult. Sometimes Jerri goes into a deep depression and can't get out of bed for days or do even the most basic task, like taking her medicine or brushing her teeth. Other times she's manic and may go an entire week without sleeping. Her mind races and she talks extremely fast, trying to get her thoughts out before they escape. She gets paranoid and thinks, for example, that Third's parents are running a child-pornography ring. They know that she knows, and therefore they must kill her. She's most likely to hallucinate when in a manic state. She's been seeing people who aren't really there for most of her life.

Technically, Jerri has a dual diagnosis: bipolar disorder and substance abuse. The symptoms of the two are virtually the same and it can be difficult to tell them apart. When people use cocaine, they feel euphoric, like they can do anything. They have an overwhelming amount of energy and don't sleep. They may experience delusions, hallucinations, and paranoia. Their judgment is impaired and they may do things they wouldn't normally do. The same is true for someone in the manic phase of bipolar disorder. Then, as cocaine wears off, depression typically follows, mirroring the depressive phase of bipolar.

Jerri's bipolar diagnosis came after she had wrestled for more than a decade with cocaine and all that goes with addiction. She lied and stole to support her habit. She couldn't hold down a job. She formed relationships based entirely on shared drug use and then watched as four children were, one by one, removed from her care.

A felony charge and the terms of her probation eventually forced Jerri into Prodigal's Community, a residential drug-treatment program in Winston-Salem. After Jerri was clean and had the urine tests to prove it, her symptoms didn't go away. That's when she was diagnosed with bipolar.

Research conducted by Duke University suggests that as many as 60 percent of people with bipolar will have a substance-abuse issue at some point in their lifetime. Brain chemistry might explain the link, according to a report by the National Institute on Drug Abuse. Serotonin, dopamine, and norepinephrine are chemicals in the brain that affect mood and emotions. People with bipolar often have abnormal levels of these chemicals, and drugs and alcohol influence the way the brain processes them. People with undiagnosed or untreated bipolar disorder may start drinking or using drugs in an unconscious effort to stabilize their moods and ease the distress caused by their symptoms. Instead, the substance use tends to make symptoms worse.

The similarities between bipolar symptoms and substance abuse are part of the reason my parents don't believe Jerri is sick. Jerri says Mom accused her of abusing drugs long before she ever actually did. At the time Jerri was a teenager; given the friends she hung out with, it seemed the most likely explanation for her odd behavior. But Jerri had symptoms of mania as early as elementary school, long before drugs were in the picture.

When I was about eight and Jerri was nine, she started seeing a raven-haired woman perched on her dresser at night.

"She's the ghost of an Indian buried under our house," Jerri confided over bowls of Campbell's soup. (She had tomato, while mine was chicken and stars. Rule number seventeen in the sibling-rivalry handbook states that sisters should never agree on anything.)

"Our house is built on a sacred burial ground," Jerri explained. "So now we're being haunted."

"You mean, *you're* being haunted," I said. "No one else has seen her besides you."

Jerri shrugged and spooned an oyster cracker around her bowl. "She's got black hair that's really long and straight. It hangs down below her waist."

That conjured a picture of Cher singing "I Got You, Babe" and sweeping her glossy hair over her bare shoulders. In my mind, I dressed the woman in suede with fringe, moccasins, and a beaded headband for good measure, just like the Indians on *Wild, Wild West*.

Jerri said the woman on her dresser wore a filmy white gown that wafted around her.

"Indians don't wear gowns," I told her. "They wear buffalo."

"Not after they're dead," Jerri said.

It had been hard for me to argue with that. At the time, I thought she was making the whole thing up anyway, so I did what little sisters do best: I told on her.

"Your sister just has a vivid imagination," Mom said. "Now go clean up your room, and tell Jerri to come empty the dishwasher."

As an adult, Jerri still says Indian Cher wasn't a dream or someone she made up to scare me. I've reminded my parents about Indian Cher and emailed articles from the National Institute of Mental Health website confirming that hallucinations can accompany severe episodes of mania or depression. My parents won't budge. As far as they are concerned, the only thing that causes hallucinations is substance abuse. Jerri is an addict, pure and simple, a substance abuser who converted from cocaine to prescription psych meds when she discovered Medicare would pay for them.

The closest Mom has ever come to acknowledging mental illness was when she said, "Well, if Jerri *is* bipolar, she brought it on herself with all those chemicals she put in her body." "Chemicals" is Mom-speak for cocaine. As much as I hate that idea, even the mental health community hasn't completely ruled out the possibility that substance abuse might trigger mental illness.

It's your basic causality dilemma. Which came first, the drugs or the disorder? Mental health professionals say it doesn't matter—that addiction, itself, is a mental illness since it changes the brain in fundamental ways and weakens the brain's ability to control impulses. For my family, however, it's still a quandary. The answer shouldn't matter, but it does.

For Mom, it's about blame. If the drugs came first, then it's Jerri's fault. The rest of us need to let her experience the consequences of her decisions. It's *tough love* time. We need to *stop enabling* her so she can *reach rock bottom*. This version of reality helps Mom and Dad resolve the dissonance between being good parents and distancing themselves as much as possible from their own daughter.

But if the disorder came first, Jerri really can't be held responsible for her actions. Even in court, you can plead not guilty by reason of insanity. So, then, who is responsible?

Mom's generation tends to blame mental illness on the mother. If Jerri isn't at fault, then Mom must be. She must have smoked or drank or taken over-the-counter medications when she was pregnant. Perhaps she has undiagnosed mental illness and passed along the bad genes. Maybe she was such a terrible parent, she drove Jerri mad. That, I suspect, is where the rubber meets the road for my mother. Jerri can't have a mental illness because Mom can't bear the responsibility.

I keep coming back to Indian Cher. She is ground zero, the point where Jerri began to unravel. After Indian Cher, Jerri wasn't the same.

I remember that, in fourth grade, I also had a bizarre nocturnal encounter. Mom had decided to move my bedroom across the hall to the room formerly known as the den. During my first night in the new space, I woke to find a shabby, gray man standing by my bed. I tried to cry out but couldn't make a sound, so I sat up and pounded on the wall of my parents' room. There was no response from the other side. The only escape route was blocked, since Gray Man was standing between me and the door. There was nothing I could do except burrow deep beneath the covers and pray he'd go away.

When I told my family the next morning, Jerri was absolutely giddy. Now Mom and Dad would have to believe her because I was seeing *them* too.

Mom explored my room and discovered a window had been left slightly open. We decided what I'd actually seen was a sheer, white curtain lifting in the breeze. The explanation made sense because I wore glasses. Without them and in the dark, I had the visual acuity of a mole. The curtains could explain Indian Cher, too. Jerri, also nearsighted, had the exact same curtains in her room, and if you squinted just right they could easily pass for a filmy white gown.

For me, Gray Man happened, Mom explained him, and it was over. (Though I still made Mom move me back into my original room.) But for Jerri, Indian Cher kept coming back. Jerri didn't want to sleep in the room with her. She became terrified of the dark and refused to sleep alone. As much as she despised me—not only for the Gray Man incident but also for simply breathing the same air—at night I became her best friend.

"Scoot over!" she'd whisper, crawling into my twin bed and scrunching me against the wall. A foot fight would ensue, and if luck was on my side, she'd plummet to the floor. Undaunted, she'd drag her sleeping bag into my room. Other nights, she dragged it down the hall to our parents' room.

Mom and Dad told themselves this was normal. After all, what kid *isn't* afraid of the dark? They stuck to this story even when they had to lock their bedroom door to keep Jerri out, even when she camped outside, wailing and pleading for them to let her in.

"It's a phase," Mom said. "She'll grow out of it." But at sixteen, Jerri was still rolling out her sleeping bag on their bedroom floor.

Looking back, I sometimes grapple with why Mom never discussed Jerri's childhood issues with a doctor. True, we were kids in the sixties, and our pediatrician probably wouldn't have pinpointed mental illness. Still, I've wondered at our family's ability to explain away the oddest things as "that's just Jerri."

There's an old wives' tale that says if you put a frog in a pot of cold water and raise the temperature ever so slowly, the frog won't perceive the danger and will be cooked to death. I don't know the first thing about thermal relations and the physiology of amphibians, but I do know that when it comes to my family, the metaphor fits. Mental illness crept in gradually, and we just kept adapting.

My parents did eventually check Jerri into Mandala, a residential behavioral-health facility for troubled teens, but not until after she had started using drugs. Mandala had "straightened out" Connie, the daughter of one of my mom's friends. Jerri was about fifteen at the time, the same age as Connie. The therapist at Mandala eventually diagnosed

Jerri with borderline personality disorder. When the diagnosis was shared with our parents, they packed up Jerri's stuff and drove her home.

"She doesn't have that," Mom said. "She's just acting out."

In my mother's mind, Jerri was in control of what was happening to her. If the therapists couldn't see that, Mandala wasn't credible.

Bipolar disorder gets worse if left untreated, and clinicians believe that early detection may help prevent subsequent substance abuse problems. If Indian Cher was in fact an early manifestation of the disease, Jerri went untreated for over twenty years. Just thinking about this makes me ill. Her life might have been totally different if we, her family, hadn't been such frogs.

Today, Jerri doesn't talk about the-people-who-aren't-really-there with anyone except me, although I've tried to get her to tell her psychiatrist, the one person who might actually be able to help by adjusting her medication.

"You don't understand," she says. "Hallucinations are psychotic episodes, and that makes me bipolar I. That's the bad bipolar. Right now I'm only bipolar II. You don't want to be I. People treat you like you're schizophrenic. I'm not schizophrenic. I'm not like that."

I've learned that even people with mental illness have stigmas about mental illness.

Jerri also hates being labeled a substance abuser. As soon as that notation gets into her medical chart, healthcare professionals assume that no matter what symptoms she presents with, drugs are the culprit. She changes doctors frequently, trying to outrun the distinction she considers inaccurate and unfair. From her perspective, she's gone to great lengths to break the cycle of addiction; she doesn't think the label should follow her around for the rest of her life.

I can't disagree that she's gone to great lengths. She completed the Prodigal's Community program and also stayed on with the nonprofit, working as an administrative assistant. She joined Narcotics Anonymous and got a sponsor. But then Norman, her boss and the founder of Prodigal's Community, died from AIDS. He was one of the few people in Jerri's life who had ever believed in her, and Jerri was devastated.

Her depression and her cocaine cravings returned with a vengeance. Not knowing what else to do, she checked herself into a mental health facility, where she agreed to seventeen sessions of electroconvulsive therapy (ECT).

With ECT, electric currents are applied to the brain, causing small seizures that appear to change brain chemistry. Despite its wide acceptance, the procedure seems positively medieval. A quick Google search uncovers countless patient stories of what the Mayo Clinic terms side effects but that, to a layperson, sound more like brain damage. Jerri says that she hasn't craved cocaine since ECT and that her depression has been much less severe. She also says it took a solid year to teach herself how to read again after the treatment.

If Jerri is right and she's had a seizure, maybe ECT is a factor. I'm not sure how, though. It's been decades since the ECT. We should still mention it to her neurologist.

It's more likely that Adderall is involved. Adderall is an amphetamine used to treat attention deficit hyperactivity disorder (ADHD). It's a Schedule II controlled substance, the same level as cocaine, and the prescribing information includes a black-box warning which states, "Amphetamines have a high potential for abuse; prolonged administration may lead to dependence." For obvious reasons, Adderall is contraindicated for people with a history of drug abuse. Why a psychiatrist would ever prescribe this product to my sister is beyond me, and yet there it is, part of her current regimen.

The prescribing information contains a warning regarding bipolar illness: "Particular care should be taken in using stimulants to treat ADHD patients with comorbid bipolar disorder because of concern for possible induction of mixed/manic episodes in such patients." In essence, Adderall can cause one of the main symptoms we are trying to treat.

There's also clinical evidence that stimulants can cause seizures in some patients.

We argue a lot about Adderall because I want Jerri to stop taking it.

"I *need* it," she says. "I can't concentrate at all without it. I can't read or crochet or get anything done."

She's extremely protective of the drug. She counts and recounts it obsessively. Pills are missing; she's sure of it. She suspects Third is taking them. Or she tells me she's out of the prescription only three days after filling it. She didn't like the way it made her feel, so she flushed it. Of course, these are exactly the sorts of things an addict might say. And how can you tell when an addict is lying? That's easy—her lips are moving.

This is probably my biggest issue related to Jerri's dual diagnosis. I never know what to believe. It doesn't matter which came first, the disorder or the drug abuse. What matters is which one is in play at the moment, and I can't always tell.

Adderall is not the only medication concern when it comes to seizures. Once, the pharmacist at Daymark, Jerri's mental health provider, filled a "10 mg twice daily" prescription for Lexapro with the 20 mg pill. Jerri didn't notice. After only three days of the doubled dose she was disconnected, slurring her words and blacking out. I asked to see her medicine bottles, to check if the remaining pills matched the fill dates and dosage instructions, and that's when I discovered the error. In a panic, I phoned a pharmacist colleague, then Poison Control. It took Jerri almost a week to recover.

Jerri's life seems to revolve around medicine. She constantly adjusts her doses. She asks her psychiatrist to discontinue one product or add another. She believes there's a magic cocktail and if only she can find it, she'll feel normal again. Because of my job, I know we should worry about drug-to-drug interactions. I wonder how her doctor can possibly keep track of it all.

"If you're going to experiment with your medication, then go to pharmacy school," I've told Jerri. "At least then you'll know what you're doing."

"I don't experiment. I always take my medicine like I'm supposed to," she retorts, but she also admits to finding pills here and there all over her apartment. It's as if she sets them down on her way to the kitchen for water and forgets them. She suspects that Spider, her dachshund, finds pills on the floor. According to Jerri, he's also having seizures.

Hours pass before I finally drift off to sleep. I have to pump myself with coffee in order to function the next morning. It takes Jerri a few weeks to get an appointment with the neurologist, and then she calls to say he has scheduled an MRI. She wants to be sedated during the procedure, so would I be willing to drive her?

On the day of her appointment, I rearrange my work schedule so I can take the afternoon off. Her apartment is on the second floor of a building that's part of a series of two-story brown brick rectangles connected by steel staircases. The Regency Apartments complex is outdated but conveniently located, and the property manager, Sheena, is a psych major. Sheena keeps an eye out and calls me when Jerri needs help.

When I arrive, Jerri is wearing a neon-green tee with overall shorts in a shade best described as road-construction orange. It brings out the highlights in her recently dyed hair. She's had it trimmed, and her ears stick out, making her look like Despereaux the mouse. She probably weighs ninety pounds soaking wet.

I've come directly from work and am wearing a conservative black suit. "You're not actually going to wear that to your appointment, are you?"

"Well, I thought I would," Jerri answers. "Why? You don't like it?" Jerri looks down at herself. "I think I look cute," she says.

"You do look cute. If we were going to Oz, the Munchkins would be all over you."

She rolls her eyes and pulls out two alternate outfits. I pick one, and she changes.

At the hospital, the nurse administers Valium to help Jerri relax for the MRI. The nurse says someone needs to stay overnight with her while the drug is in her system, so she doesn't do anything nutty. Somehow, I manage to maintain a straight face.

Afterward, we grab dinner at Golden Corral.

"You don't have to stay with me," Jerri says. "I'm perfectly fine. They didn't give me enough Valium to even feel it. In fact, I asked the nurse when she was going to give me the Valium, and she said she'd already done it. It was in the IV. I didn't feel a thing. Nothing at all."

She says this last part as if she's disappointed.

I decide not to spend the night. She does seem fine, better than I've seen her in a long time. Maybe Valium should be added to her magic drug cocktail.

We talk about Mom and Dad and about things that happened twenty-five years ago, things Mom seems unable to forgive. We talk about the time Jerri moved back home after she totaled her car and suffered the head injury.

Melanie, Jerri's dealer, had visited, and when Jerri returned from a trip to the bathroom, she found Melanie had disappeared along with Mom's jewelry. The Mikimoto pearls were quite valuable, and the rest was sentimental including our grandmother's engagement ring. Mom claims Jerri was in on it and had given Melanie the jewelry in exchange for drugs.

Jerri sits across from me and swears she had nothing to do with it. She was just naive. Yeah, Melanie was a crack hound, but Jerri never imagined she would steal to support her habit. Jerri herself wasn't so badly addicted at that point that she'd have done *anything* for a fix. It never occurred to her that Melanie would.

As she talks she strains forward, and the vein on the right side of her neck bulges. Her eyes plead with me. Tears start to pool along the lower rim of her eyelids. She is so vehement and so lucid. I believe her—God help me—I do.

"Why won't Mom forgive me? Why can't she just let it go?" She looks away and wipes her face with the back of her hand.

A mixture of frustration and anger wash over me. I hate this. I hate all of it. Mom and Dad believe Jerri is responsible for all our family has suffered, but I know the responsibility is ours. We weren't there for her. I wasn't there for her. She needed me in her court to convince our parents she was really sick.

I feel guilty about what's happened. I feel heartsick for all Jerri has lost. I feel terrified she may never be well again. But most of all, I feel alone. It's just me and Jerri waging war against this disease that has devastated her and divided our family—a disease that has forced me to take sides. And the side I have taken is here, sitting across from me, at the Golden Corral.

Back at her apartment, Jerri drops onto the couch and lights up a cigarette. Spider jumps up and nestles against her. I remain standing while we finish our conversation. It's a long way home, it's getting late, and I need to get on the road.

"Thanks for coming." She takes a drag from her cigarette and exhales. I make a face and a big deal about waving the smoke away. She smiles.

It's not always like this for us, the honest conversation, the teasing. It's been a good day for us—surprisingly good.

She picks up her lighter and fiddles with it, flipping it end over end. Unexpectedly, she tosses, and I catch it. She seems relieved.

Author's Note: Some time has passed since the events detailed in this piece, and Jerri's disorder is currently well managed. She hasn't been hospitalized or had any visitors who won't play catch in over two years. (The MRI, by the way, was not particularly helpful, and the neurologist could not determine if Jerri had experienced a seizure.) I credit Jerri's recovery to a number of factors. First and foremost, Jerri moved to Durham, where I live, and I am better able to support her. She is now working with an Assertive Community Treatment Team (ACTT), which provides comprehensive services including psychiatric treatment, medication management, housing support, and case management. She is no longer taking Adderall and even grudgingly admits that it worsened her disorder. She is also being treated for hypothyroidism, and the treatment seems to help with her depression.

Terri Sherrill *is a program manager at a multinational pharmaceutical company. Her writing has appeared in blogs and venues such as* To the Bone, HomeLife, *and the* Durham Herald Sun. *She lives in Durham, North Carolina, with her husband, Stan, and their canine kids, Max and Tucker.*

Another Trail of Breadcrumbs

Peg Quinn

I'm baking date-nut bread for my daughter's three boyfriends. She's sleeping with two of them; the other has vowed to keep their relationship platonic. Perverted? Irresponsible? Crazy? Once upon a time, I'd have thought so.

Actually, even I am shocked by the adjustments I've made simply in order to survive each day after my daughter was diagnosed with a mental illness.

I wouldn't have considered myself naive. I was thirty-four when Bebe was born and had learned some tough lessons about life and given some thought to how I'd been raised. I intended to do better and was so washed in waves of love and joy and thankfulness when I first held Bebe in my arms that I knew I would sacrifice anything, anytime, for the privilege of being her mom.

As a child, I'd been devoted to my younger brother, who had Down syndrome. His treatment by the majority of adults in our lives instilled in me an awareness of hypocrisy and prejudice before I knew there were words to describe such attitudes. But his life also taught me that people and circumstances don't need to be perfectly conventional in order to inspire compassion, commitment, good times, and optimism. He was my sibling of choice. I invented ways to teach him skills, like how to walk without holding someone's hand and how to ride a bike. His observations on life made me laugh. Our grandfather, the most optimistic man I've known, was just as enthusiastic about Kenny, showing me that one man's goodness can override a world of negativity.

Kenny died suddenly from leukemia when we were teenagers. I believed I'd suffered as much emotional pain and loss as was possible.

I was wrong.

It was difficult for me to find my identity after his passing. I'd assumed he would be dependent on me his entire life, and so I planned accordingly. When I started dating, I introduced every lucky guy to Kenny in order to observe his reaction. If he seemed uncomfortable, the evening and the relationship came to a screeching halt. If the guy took Kenny in stride, my interest spiked. Unconsciously, I assumed that marrying me would be a package deal that included my brother.

Several years passed before I realized my mistakes. Kenny deserved as much independence as possible, and it was unfair of me to stifle his autonomy. I was blindly meeting my own needs as much as his. His death forced me to question what else I might not be seeing.

I'm learning now that life is complex and nuanced. I'm learning to take nothing for granted. As the poet Theodore Roethke wrote, "This shaking keeps me steady."

Currently, I'm the art specialist at an elementary school. It's been two years and one day since I grabbed the "dinner" I'd packed from the teacher's lounge and fairly trotted to my car. It was four o'clock. I'd be eating as I drove to Cal State Fullerton. Bebe, a junior there after two years at our local community college, would be singing a solo in a choir concert. I wouldn't miss it.

Under perfect conditions I faced a two-hour drive, but it was Friday, and I'd be heading into L.A.'s rush hour. The concert began at 8:00 P.M., so I thought I had some wiggle room. Within ten minutes, traffic was crawling, bumper to bumper. Four hours later, I tore into the concert hall a wreck but was told I had five minutes before Bebe's solo in the final song of the evening.

I met her and her boyfriend in the parking lot afterward, chatted a few minutes, then got back in my car and drove home. The freeway was wide open, a full moon beaming as I reveled in the utter beauty of my daughter's powerful voice, the success she was enjoying, and her exciting future, not knowing I'd just heard the grand finale of a dream I'd been living.

Saturday night at 9:30 P.M., Bebe's younger brother Owen, pleasantly exhausted from a middle-school camping trip, was already asleep. The phone rang. I lifted the receiver, and, as if the phone were a horrendous explosion, our lives disappeared.

Through the gurgling wet sounds, all I recognized was a muffled, "Mommy."

"Bebe?" I listened to her sobbing. "Sweetie—what's wrong?" I mentally shuffled through a deck of possibilities: car accident, romantic breakup, dropping out of school, self-righteous roommates?

She tried again but broke down. Fear had me by the throat.

"Honey, take a deep breath. Listen to me. Take a deep breath, then tell me what's going on."

"I don't know what's happening. I hear voices. They want me to do something, but I don't know what." Then in a whisper, "They want me to hurt myself."

I wanted to grab her as our world blew away, but we were separated by 160 miles, with only this thin line holding us together.

The monsters responsible were allowing her a phone call, but I was afraid to speak, afraid of the language of monsters and how I might upset them. Intuition said to keep her talking, but what could I say? Should I leave her brother alone and start driving?

"Have you—have you hurt yourself?" I had no idea what hurting herself might mean. "Where are your roommates?"

"No! No! Nobody's here! It doesn't matter!" she snapped. Then her tone changed. "I'm scared. I think they're in the room, in the corner of the ceiling." She was panting. "They want me to kill myself."

With that, I didn't want to be a mom anymore. This called for judgment, wisdom, and a form of courage I didn't possess. Couldn't imagine. This was the moment we crossed the divide from twenty years of taken-for-granted mother-daughter conversation to my pretending I knew what I was doing.

Starting now, and for many dark months to come, I would pretend order amid chaos. I would create the calm eye of the storm, a mechanism born of pure, simple desperation.

She needed help, but I didn't want to create a spectacle of police sirens, flashing lights, and a crowd of curious gawkers, so I chanced a question. "What would you think if I called the suicide hotline—maybe they can help—and then I'll call you back?"

Sobbing, she agreed.

I lowered the receiver, knowing I might never hear from her again. Knowing I'd possibly abandoned her to the voices in the corner; knowing she might kill herself while I was on the phone. I searched for the number of the suicide hotline with the deliberation of a sniper. I could feel this or I could function—but not both.

So with an eerie calm, I found the number, placed the call, and arranged a connection between a counselor and Bebe. Then I waited.

A lamp was on above my desk. The house rested in a deep, dark quiet. I felt nothing. I sat on the sofa and stared at the floor across the room. Abandoned by gods or guardians, I was seduced by what could be a deadly sin: denial. For a time, my emotional survival would depend on my creating a version of Bebe that increasingly denied reality.

Forty-seven minutes passed before the phone rang and Bebe, sounding weary but calm, assured me that the counselor had helped. She'd promised to go to Student Health to talk to a psychologist in the morning.

"Do you want me to come get you?" (How serious could this be if one phone call had calmed her down? Was this the stress of finals? Exhaustion? Complications from being away at school for the first time? If she could hold on until the holidays, she'd have a month at home to relax. I'd lie religiously to make her seem whole.)

"No, it's okay, Mom. I really want to go to sleep."

Monday, Bebe called me at work, confused. The school psychologist wanted her hospitalized. I sped home, leaving a trail of voicemail for anyone I could think of who might be able to explain what was happening.

Finally, a call came from the psychologist. Bebe was suicidal and needed to be watched. A psychiatric hospital was the best place for her. Jesus. I appreciated her concern. I did. And her involvement. But I thought twenty years as Bebe's mother trumped her one hour of analysis. Bebe sounded fine. I suspected the psychologist of overreacting but assured her I'd connect Bebe with a psychiatrist.

For the next five months, we patched and pasted Bebe's life together even as it continued to crumble. She'd phone, furious with her roommates, demanding I find her another place. This kind of drama was new to her personality, so, trusting the judgment of the Bebe I knew, I assumed there were serious problems that needed to be addressed. The next day, through work and after-school sports with Owen, I was mentally scrambling, trying to figure out what to do. Then Bebe called, laughing, talking about the fun she'd had playing UNO with her roommates.

Slightly confused, I dropped her request for new living arrangements from my to-do list. But there were many mounting variations on these radical swings in her behavior. I was a little irritated at the stress she was creating for me but thought maybe this often happened when a child stretched her wings in search of independence. I remembered how I'd clung to Kenny, and I tried to give Bebe her space.

Six weeks before the end of the semester, her psychiatrist phoned. Bebe was curled up on the floor of his office. He was going to have her committed.

I contacted her father, who agreed to drive down and get her. The three of us sat speechless in the emergency room of the local hospital, watching people with dog bites, broken bones, and minor burns from their barbeques come and go. Tears alternately ran down Bebe's face and mine until 3:00 A.M., when she was admitted into the psych ward.

Like an animal being led to slaughter, she was systematically stripped of belts and shoestrings and searched for any objects a person might use to end his or her life. I tried to open the blinds, only to discover there were no cords. Across her breakfast menu in red letters was printed, PLASTIC UTENSILS ONLY. They actually thought my daughter, my little Bebe Jean—competitive swimmer, jazz alto, choir soprano, lover of cats and drawing and journals and books and movies and the Hanson Brothers and Dave Matthews Band—was going to kill herself.

Someone at the desk informed us that insurance companies

generally covered a three-day stay, so she'd be home by the weekend.

Heavily medicated, she was released two weeks later with instructions to seek psychiatric counseling and a brochure on local mental-health organizations—but no diagnosis.

She moved back home. She slept. Somehow, she developed a network of friends she'd met in the psych ward. I felt I was living with a stranger, a young woman whose moral and ethical compass had lost its stabilizing direction. Her emotional highs were punctuated by exhilarating, trivial passions, reckless ideas, and friends so oddly pierced and tattooed I was afraid when they were in my home. I was afraid to have them around Owen. I felt guilty, judging them by their appearance.

She went goth—colored her hair, lips, and nails black; tried to conjure up some cleavage; bought ridiculous boots that came up to her knees, with multiple buckles running up each side; started the process of dreadlocks; wore fingerless, rainbow-patterned gloves to her elbows, even though it was summer.

When we walked downtown together, everyone stared. I wanted to run. But trying to be conversational, wanting to portray an image of normalcy, I asked, "Why the gloves?" She peeled one back. "To hide the razor cuts."

This person was not my daughter. I never knew who she would be from one moment to the next and couldn't have managed without my bulwark of denial.

I did not want to be this person's mom. But what were my options? My daughter was gone, vanished, but there had been no funeral, no ritual of support to mark the loss before moving toward recovery. I bounced hard between fear and emptiness.

I scrutinized every aspect of her childhood, looking for clues I couldn't find. Bebe had sung almost as soon as she could talk. After every Disney musical we watched, I'd sew costumes. Bebe assumed the role of leading lady, and Owen eagerly played all the other parts. They'd refine their performance until the next Disney release. These were delightful, hilarious times.

I reread my copy of little Bebe's eighty-seven suggestions in her version of *Life's Little Instruction Book*, written when she was nine. Number twenty-one: *Write a long true story.* Number thirty-one: *Make sure your kisses are dry.* Number

thirty-two: *Don't waste time, money, energy, erasers, or paper.*
Number thirty-six: *Own a rabbit.* Number fifty: *Go to the zoo
once a month.* Number fifty-seven: *Be happy on the phone.*

At ten, Bebe had started swimming competitively; she
played on the water-polo team in high school. An A student,
she could draw well and spent hours writing and illustrating
stories. She was shy, but so am I. She always had a friend. She
played piano.

We did own a rabbit, and a cat and a goldfish. We lived near
a small stream where neighborhood kids would try to catch
frogs and tadpoles. The land bordered a horse barn and riding
stables; all this, I thought, would keep the children connected
to nature.

I'd quit working when Bebe was born and didn't return until Owen started first grade ten years later. Though we never
recovered financially, today I am exceedingly grateful they
weren't in daycare, freeing me from wondering, worrying that
she had, in some way, been damaged.

When the children were nine and fourteen, I divorced their
father, but there was never trauma or drama to our marriage.
It was a problem of oppressive indifference. Having felt my
own foundation buckle from under me when my parents divorced, I vowed that I'd never, ever, do that to my children. But
I'd compromised myself almost out of existence trying to make
my marriage work. I sought counseling and eventually decided
that divorce was better than modeling this hollow alternative.
Their father and I remained friendly and cooperative.

But does any of this matter now? Yesterday, I took Bebe to
the Social Security office to apply for Supplemental Security
Income. I should have taken her months ago, but this is the
first time I've had the emotional strength to walk up to an
entry-level government clerk without emotion (or a baseball
bat) and ask if my daughter, diagnosed with a mental illness,
living at home, medicated and overweight, qualifies.

The petite young clerk glanced up at Bebe's dyed-black
dreadlocks (which seemed particularly dreadful), nodded, and
set up an interview for next week. While this is just one of
many responsibilities before me, it is the first appalling step
in what feels like admitting this nightmare is true. I feel revul-
sion—as if we've been randomly persecuted, then sentenced to

life without the possibility of being anything but being feared, avoided, and mocked.

I enrolled in a twelve-week class called Parent-to-Parent, organized by a mental health association. It was run by two women who had children with mental illnesses, and everyone around the table was asked to explain why we were there.

A couple I knew fairly well from my kids' elementary-school days were sitting together. They had donated a great deal of time, money, and talent to the school. Their son had been Bebe's first boyfriend when the kids were in fourth grade. During Owen's sixth-grade graduation ceremony, the mom had whispered in my ear, "I think I have a crush on your son!" They seemed a perfect Baptist family, so I assumed they had a problematic niece or nephew who had motivated them to come to the meeting. When it was their turn to speak, the wife stared at the edge of the table while the husband explained that their middle daughter had been hospitalized three times for attempted suicide and was living at a facility in Nevada.

I knew nothing about mental illness, but here I was among perfectly normal, successful, attractive, intelligent people, and each one of their stories broke my heart. Each one of their stories terrified me. I wanted to lay my head on the table and sob. Later, we were told that most caretakers of the mentally ill end up on medication themselves. That helped explain all the silent parents who spent the evenings staring at the table.

Each psychiatrist we visited offered a different diagnosis. I'd watch these men in their three-piece suits while disbelieving that Bebe would open up to them about group sex, drugs, or rock concerts. I was right. She never wanted to return, so we continued shopping. One day, we walked into the office of a smiling guy in a Hawaiian shirt with pictures of the Buddha on the wall. His sense of humor gave me hope and Bebe settled in, seeing him once or twice a week, depending on how she was feeling. He suggested she had borderline personality disorder (BPD).

Earlier today, as we shopped for baking ingredients, Bebe and I talked about mental illness, specifically hers, and her male relationships. Rather, I shopped while she talked, much like I wrote the grocery list at home, sorting through cupboards while she talked.

In the spice aisle, she described her relationships with the date-nut bread recipients. Mark knows her well but is depressing to be around. Ken, the platonic friend, is adorable but caught up in the drug culture. Then there's Clark, to whom she can't entirely open up. For example, she says, "I can't tell him about the night Ed and Ken and I stayed up all night cutting each other. It was so psychotic, and Clark couldn't handle it."

With this, the store spun sideways for a few seconds and I wanted to throw up.

But my emotions are a luxury we can't afford. So I mentally congratulated myself on how well I masked my reaction and carried on the conversation, agreeing there are some things so out of the ordinary that people with less experience might be shocked or burdened or threatened by the information. We have to consider what we're willing to reveal about ourselves. I added that some of her problems exist because she's young. Ten years from now, everything will seem easier. Like relationships with men. But who am I kidding?

Currently in a manic phase, Bebe is obsessed with Renaissance music. She sings in two city college choirs and reads music theory and history for fun. She'll join a church choir over winter break in order to keep singing. These are wonderfully constructive interests, but I'm concerned for her passion, given the eventual comedown from her elated state—the dropping out, the withdrawing, the disappointment. Again.

During intermission at last Sunday's concert, her dad announced to a friend that Bebe was "absolutely normal!" Poor guy. He refuses to do his homework, read an article, or find a support group. I've learned that she—and we—will ride a roller coaster of mania, depression, and normalcy her entire life. The friend later sent me an email suggesting, sympathetically, that Bebe's dad is in denial in order to protect himself. True. But I'm furious that his lack of awareness garners protection.

Her mood swings could level out with age, too, but I listen to her talk about Mark and Clark and recognize one of the symptoms of borderline personality disorder. She fails to learn from experience. She's unable to take lessons from one situation and apply them to another. With no core identity, no storehouse of cause and effect, she is perpetually thrashing in the moment. She relies on the person, place, or thing her mania has latched onto for self-definition, but it's an unsustainable fixation, making failure inevitable.

Because of this, the suicide rate for BPD is high. The victim, unable to cope with the mania-depression cycle and the inability to make the kind of social and emotional progress that gives life meaning and value, ends the torment.

This second anniversary of her breakdown passed without comment. We continued shopping while she described the different states of mental illness she's experienced, suicidal being worst, the creative high of the manic state the best.

We pass a young man I vaguely recognize from her elementary-school days. He too is with his mother, passionately explaining states of transcendental awareness as she reads the back of a box. I hurry past, trying to find similarities in our circumstances to mask the dark, divergent road my daughter travels. I dread the awkward, superficial conversations with near-strangers as they look at Bebe, unable to mask their shock. Her once-athletic body is now doughy, the new glasses awry, the darting eyes too bright, the dull, tortured hair.

Trying not to feel suicidal myself, I hold up my end of our conversation, telling her I'd read about the early use of pharmaceuticals and how patients would stop taking them because they missed the manic high. They were willing to risk depression rather than exist in a medically induced numbness.

Bebe nods enthusiastically. She knows. She's philosophically opposed to the medications she takes and worries that the side effects, which impair her weight, vision, memory, and concentration, will prevent her from getting a degree and a job. She gets frustrated when she has to justify their use to her friends.

I nod back. Everyone seems to agree that current medications are less than ideal, but for now, they're the best science has to offer. Privately, I fear the consequences should she decide to go off hers.

On the elevator ride down from the Social Security office, she asked if we'd ridden the elevator up. *Yes, remember this brushed stainless steel?* I rubbed the wall I'd admired. "You know, if I were undermedicated or overmedicated," she laughed, "that pattern would start moving!"

I looked away and choked on tears.

In line at the store, we talk about last week's concerts, how there was an afterparty at the director's house but she didn't go, doesn't feel she fits in, isn't sure they want her around. Mostly, she's self-conscious of being much younger than most of the singers. Then she gives a thoughtful critique of the vocal relationships she has with the other first sopranos. I'm confused as to why she can't apply the same kind of reasoning to her boyfriends.

One of the sopranos is a mother of two preschoolers, the other a wealthy, middle-aged housewife. What they have in common is a musical bond that transcends their differences. One keeps them from going flat. The other sight-reads well, and Bebe, who also sings jazz, encourages them to be fearless when facing Middle C.

I've noticed the singers casting sly grins at each other while they perform. Bebe admits their interdependence is so strong that when they come through for each other, it shines on their faces. I know how she feels. I'm reminded of jogging alongside Kenny as he struggled to ride his bike, how we smiled when all he needed was my hand on the back of the seat.

How fortunate for Bebe to have such talent and be well enough, for now, to share it. What a godsend that the director, who knew her before her breakdown, continues to value her contribution.

As we leave the store, Bebe tells me she has a favorite quote relative to her illness, though she doesn't know who said it: "Those who mind don't matter, and those who matter don't mind."

I reciprocate with a favorite of mine by Carl Jung: "Life is an experiment in consciousness that most people fail."

Kenny's passing made me painfully aware of life's complexities. Slowly rebuilding after his death and again after Bebe's diagnosis, I began to see the positives. Hitting ground zero created an open space where everything could be reconsidered: friends, family, organizations, social expectations, institutions.

I toss out the dross. I sniff out the poetry in the experience of daily living. I feel gratitude for the intense experience of trying to stay balanced, though shaking, on the tightrope of life.

Realizing I can't control my circumstances moves me to ask what practical contributions I can make through the attitudes I express and the values I hold. This awareness helps keep me in the moment and leads to growth and, maybe, a kind of experiment in consciousness I don't want to fail.

It's something I think about while baking bread for the boyfriends.

Peg Quinn's *poetry has been published in numerous journals and anthologies and twice nominated for the Pushcart Prize. She paints murals and theatrical sets and teaches art at a private elementary school.*

Like a Scratch on Vinyl

Beazie Griffin

When I was seven years old, I climbed up on a wooden step-stool in my backyard and contemplated suicide for the first time. I concentrated so hard on the looped clothesline that I didn't see my sister standing nearby, watching me. As I took the loop in my hand, she broke my trance. "What d'ya you think you're doing?" she asked, and I immediately knew from her tone that what I was about to do was really, really bad.

I begged my sister not to tell on me, but she did, of course. My mother, a devout Catholic, reacted with shock and anger. As she circled from stove to pantry and back again, (this was the early seventies and she had to get supper started) she kept asking, "Do you know what you almost did? Do you realize what almost happened?"

Yeah, I kind of did know, but I also knew that any justification I gave for wanting to kill myself—like the simple desire to just stop feeling bad—wasn't going to be the answer she wanted to hear; besides, if my mother had already started supper, that meant that in less than an hour, my father was due to walk through our kitchen door.

In Cicero—a quaint, working-class village slightly west of Chicago—my family survived by adapting itself to meet the needs of each individual's expression of dysfunction. For my father, the adjustment meant making space for his Irish temper, a character trait known well within the immediate family, the extended family, the neighborhood, and, arguably, the entire South Side.

I can't say if my mother told him what I'd done before or after he'd had his nightly shot of Jim Beam. I know that the last thing I expected was gentle acceptance, but that's what I got. He didn't get mad or yell at me. He didn't seem shocked or outraged. Instead, he reacted with a kind of sad recognition, as if the idea of wanting to end your own life wasn't beyond the bounds of his experience. As an adult, I learned more about his emotional struggles; I believe that if depression is a genetic disease, I inherited it from him, a legacy he described "as a cross you just have to learn to bear."

He took off his cap and sat down, so we could be at the same level. Then, with his ever-present Pall Mall Red in one hand, he began to pat my back with the other while speaking in gentle, soft tones. "Don't worry," he said. "Everything is going to be okay. You're all right. You're gonna be all right."

While his reaction did comfort me, it did nothing for my mother. She was still upset. She wanted to take me to see someone (maybe a doctor, maybe a priest), but that was the last thing I wanted.

"She didn't know what she was doing," he countered. "She didn't really mean it." I knew my father could overrule my mother at any time (again: see early seventies), so if I lied and agreed with him, it would mean this whole horrible afternoon would be over and I would never have to talk about it again.

"I didn't know what I was doing, Ma."

"See," he said. And that was that.

But not quite, because I have proof of a time when I didn't only "feel bad," when, in fact, I felt quite happy. My evidence is a Polaroid taken of me at three years of age. I'm standing in the middle of our back porch, facing the camera with my arms thrown open, welcoming the attention. Although I remember the cluttered porch, the stacks of board games behind me, and the sewing machine in the corner, I have no memory of being that smiling little girl in the picture, and I have always wondered what happened to her.

Only recently have neurobiologists been able to shed any light on the interval of cognitive development that exists between consciousness and self-awareness, the interlude between knowing "I am" and knowing "I am me." With the development of functional magnetic resonance imaging (fMRI), researchers can now observe the area of the brain that manages executive decision making, the prefrontal cortex (PFC), as it reacts to emotional stimuli.

During early childhood, the PFC is at its most malleable. Each new experience makes a slight impression, a new pattern of connectivity; repeated experiences make grooves, their correlated patterns given a priority and an influence over the interpretation of future events.

For example, if a happy four-year-old develops a serious viral infection in her left eye, serious enough to warrant a year of daily eye drops, weekly doctor visits, and innumerable hours waiting in waiting rooms, it's possible that over time her brain will adapt to these experiences by making apprehension the normative outlook and anxiety the preferred means of interpretation. Instead of feeling relaxed, I became pensive; instead of being self-confident, I began to feel self-conscious; instead of proudly facing the world with a smile, I shamefully tried to hide my bandaged face by dragging it along the wall.

During my year of convalescence, my mother and I traveled as a set, like binary suns. Our days revolved around my treatments. She provided the transportation to Saint Anne's Hospital in Chicago, where we sat on old, cracked vinyl chairs and waited for my name to be called. I slid under a protective arm, her faux-leopard coat scratching at my cheek, her Estée Lauder Youth Dew perfume giving me a headache. She always had a stick of Wrigley's Doublemint gum and a child-sized deck of cards at the ready, so we could play crazy eights or double solitaire. As a treat, she would buy a ninety-nine cent book from the Woolworth's with an adventure starring either Bugs Bunny or Daffy Duck. Each page had a line drawing of the protagonist in the upper-right corner, so when my mother finished the story, she'd flip the pages and I would watch it play out over and over again.

My mother became my safe harbor and my sole confidante, the only person I trusted enough to share my obsessions or, as I called them back then, the bad thoughts that stuck.

The earliest bad thought, so early that I needed to confirm

the memory with my mother, occurred in the checkout line at the Jewel supermarket on Cermak Road and Central Avenue. I asked my mother if I could have some candy. She said yes, and I walked up the line to get closer to the candy display. Checking out was a young mother with a baby sitting in the grocery cart. When I stood up with my candy, my head grazed the baby's shoe. The mother didn't say anything, the baby didn't notice, and I returned to my mother in line. No harm, no foul.

But I had learned that a baby has a soft spot on her head, so when you hold a baby you always have to be extra gentle; from these simple facts, disturbing ideas began to fester. What if, even though I had only grazed the baby's foot with my head, I still had somehow hurt it? And what if, even though everyone around me was behaving as if nothing was wrong, the baby eventually showed signs of having been harmed? What if, someday, the mother would remember me hitting her baby's foot, know that I was responsible for the injury, and come looking for me? I couldn't stop thinking about it. It was as if my mind was a needle stuck in a scratch on a record—or as if my way of thinking was programmed as an infinite loop, a computer code that insists on endless repetition with no instructions to stop.

By the time we got home, I couldn't stop crying. I was so ashamed that I might be responsible for hurting a baby that it took hours for my mother to coax a confession from me. After she heard me out, she tried to reassure me that I hadn't hurt the baby even if my head had tapped the baby's foot. I had, in fact, done nothing wrong, and I should stop crying and put the silly idea out of my head.

I didn't know how to explain to her that I would have loved nothing more than to put the silly idea out of my head, but the bad thought was like a tiny hook that caught in my mind and wouldn't let me go. The knowledge that I had done nothing wrong but still felt as though I had only deepened my anguish. What was wrong with me? How could I know one thing but feel another?

Articles published in the neuroscience journals *Neuron and Neuroscience* and *Biobehavioral Reviews* in 2001 and 2002, respectively, describe decision-making as taking place in three interactive subregions of the prefrontal cortex: the dorsolateral prefrontal cortex (DLPFC), the orbitofrontal cortex (OFC), and the anterior cingulate cortex (ACC). Faced with a question, the DLPFC deliberates the facts at hand; the OFC considers the possible emotional outcomes, both positive and negative; and the ACC tells the body how to respond. A moment of uncertainty attends every decision, and in a healthy brain the moment is so slight and quick that it's barely conscious. But in a brain with obsessive-compulsive disorder (OCD), a brain that gives priority to negative emotional references over positive ones, potential outcomes aren't positive or negative but negative and even more negative; the permutations of possible outcomes aren't contained to the immediate scenario but spiral out to include the ramifications of every possible scenario. Every decision becomes as weighted as whether to cut the red or black wire to disarm a bomb.

In a relatively short time, the carefree little girl was replaced with a brooding, anxious child. I remember my first day of kindergarten, showing up like a pint-sized Ancient Mariner, wearing an eye patch instead of an albatross and feeling like a complete freak. I remember shielding myself from the view of other people by walking so close behind my sister that I saw the world through the bend at her elbow.

My eccentric behavior may have been cause for alarm, but my struggle was primarily silent. It was all happening in my mind, so it didn't draw the kind of attention of the noisier, flashier problems—like the alcoholism, arguments, and fights that hogged the family spotlight. Considering everything else, a child being a "little too shy" wasn't that big a deal. Before sending me away for a week's vacation with my Aunt Lorraine and Uncle Joe, my mother told them, "It's okay if she doesn't say anything. She's quiet."

When I was young, my mother listened to my litany of concerns with understanding and kindness, but when I was a teen and adult, her patience began to wear thin. She began to point out that my thinking was illogical and that I needed to stop being so foolish, forget about it, and move on. She kept listening, though, even when I told her I had the bad thought that she was a bitch. (Yes, passive aggression is one of the colors you'll find flying in the Griffin family banner.)

I realize my behavior must have been as baffling to my mother as her indomitable will was inexplicable to me. "If I don't want to think about something, I just put it out of my mind," she'd say, and she meant it. Another saying she lived out loud: "If you don't have fun at a party, it's your own fault." She had a beautiful voice. I can't remember a wedding reception or big family party where she wasn't called up to the stage and asked to sing, and she reveled in every minute of it. Ma was a star.

In an effort, perhaps, to affect change from the outside in, she tried to talk me into wearing bright, colorful clothes instead of my usual black or grey. "Get a perm," she'd say. "I'll pay for it." If she gave me a gift of clothing or jewelry, it always had to have bling. One of the last things she bought me was a pair of dangling Betty Boop earrings. I had no words.

My mother wasn't the only one losing patience with me; I was losing patience with me. I knew that there was something wrong and illogical with the way I thought. I existed at the center of a very fragile paradox: it was my brain that was making me sick, but it was only my brain that could make me better.

When I began therapy in my early twenties, I expected to find the cure to what ailed me in the most obvious of places: my family. Every week for the first seven years of treatment, I sobbed my head off, describing the drinking, the arguments, and the trauma. I revealed some pretty ugly stuff and expressed my anger and confusion at the fact that the trauma had come at the hands of the people I loved most in the world. Undeniably, talk therapy and Xanax improved the quality of my life. I enrolled in college, earned my bachelor's degree, and started on my career.

But there was a problem. Even though talk therapy eased the symptoms of my OCD, it couldn't cure it. I remember being so frustrated that I asked the doctor if I should be trying to unearth a traumatic event or repressed memory, something that would break my recursive thinking. He said no, just keep talking, but after seven years of weekly sessions I had run out of things to say. Maybe my way of thinking wasn't a problem that could be fixed; maybe my way of thinking was me and, as my father suggested, I would just have to learn to endure it. My sessions with the psychiatrist became less frequent. I only went in to see him at times of extreme stress. After my therapist retired, my general physician began writing Xanax scripts for me. If I needed someone to talk to when I felt stressed, I always had my mother.

In 2007, the real-estate bubble burst, leaving me with a two-bedroom, two-bath condo on the West Side of Chicago that was decreasing in value on a daily if not hourly basis. I was underwater financially as well as emotionally. I couldn't sell the condo because it wasn't worth what I owed; if I walked away, I would destroy my credit and risk being sued by the bank. Disaster loomed everywhere and every decision, no matter how trivial, felt like it was one degree removed from catastrophe. When I picture myself at this time I see an overexposed image, insubstantial, spectral.

Every morning I had to follow the same routine before I allowed myself to leave for work. With coat on, I would stand in the hallway facing the back door, my left hand on the light switch and my right hand holding the house keys. Out loud, I would say *off-off-off-off-off* as I checked the faucet and each oven burner. Then I'd flip the light switch and walk out the back door as quickly as possible. If I made it to my car without an image of a fire catching from the stove or a leak of water cascading down the building, I could turn the ignition and drive out of the parking lot. If I couldn't keep my mind blank, if an image caught, I would have to go back to the light switch and start all over again. It was like I was trapped in my own flipbook and someone else was turning the pages.

In 2012, when my mother told me I should just move out, I did. While continuing to pay the mortgage on the condo, I moved into an apartment in her building. At that point, as far as I was concerned, I was done with my tedious joke of a life, but I couldn't do anything while my mother was alive. If I felt sad when I thought of suicide, it wasn't because I would die but because I would die feeling I had never lived.

About a year after I moved into the apartment, my mother's left arm began to swell. When my phone rang and I saw it was her on the caller ID, I knew she had seen her doctor for tests. In an effort to soften her news, she delayed saying the worst until the end. By the time she said the words "my breast cancer has returned," she was only confirming what I already knew. She continued, describing the kind of chemotherapy she would receive and her schedule of treatments. Her voice trembled only once. I'm ashamed to say that after we hung up, I burst into tears not out of concern for her, but for myself. I was terrified, but I was also determined not to be a drain on her.

My mother and I had come full circle, but this time we were on divergent paths. While my mother visited her oncologist and received chemotherapy, I saw my psychiatrist and received prescriptions for antidepressants; while her doctor reviewed her white cell count, my doctor reevaluated my dosage; while my mother's body began breaking down, my mind began to heal.

An antidepressant drug interacts with the neural activity of an OCD patient by leveling the perception of negative and positive stimuli, allowing the brain to recognize and consider the potential of a positive outcome as much as a negative one. I bristle when I hear people describe antidepressants as "happy pills." If they're to be named for the effects they help produce, they should be called "not-constantly-feeling-overwhelmed pills." Besides, antidepressants have given me something much more profound than anything that could be described by that small, anemic adjective "happy." They gave me freedom.

In addition to the pills, I began to use cognitive behavioral techniques to strengthen patterns of thinking that had atrophied from lack of use. I learned how to recognize and breathe through my body's reactions to stress—tight chest, increased heart rate, sweaty palms. I was able to slow down my thinking and, in turn, break one overwhelming fear into many smaller, more manageable thoughts.

For example, one of my biggest concerns was the condo. I knew that before I could rent it I'd have to go and clear my things out, but every time I imagined opening the front door, all I could see on the other side were water-stained walls, warped floorboards, and damaged ceilings. I started breaking that image apart by first visualizing myself getting into my car and driving to the condo. I could do that without feeling doomed. Then I imagined driving my car down the block toward my condo—still good, no doom. Next, I stepped out of the car and stood at the front gate—not good, slight doom. For the first few months of therapy, I had to stop there, but eventually, with practice and the antidepressant kicking in, I made it inside the building, up the three flights of stairs, and past the front door both in thought and in body. I was rewarded by being reminded that it really was a nice condo. I hired a management company and began to rent the unit out.

In the first week of September 2014, my mother's oncologist told her that the chemo and radiation treatments had stopped working. Her regular bed was replaced with a hospice bed and my mother began to officially die. For the next five weeks, she was never alone. Children, grandchildren, nieces and nephews, grandnieces and grandnephews, cousins, and neighbors rotated in and out of her room. She played trivia games, shared laughs, and talked. When she said, "I really thought I was going to beat it, Beazie," I believed her.

My aunt, my niece, and I became her primary caretakers: Team Gram. This time I handed her sticks of Doublemint gum. We changed her diaper, took turns administering morphine during the day (I took the night shift), and, when she could no longer swallow, soaked pink foam swabs in water for her to suck on. In the past, the thought of each action would have paralyzed me, but I kept going.

By the middle of October, she had begun losing control of her verbal skills. First her sentences became elliptical, missing a noun or a verb. Then, as she weakened, her speech dissolved into a string of sounds, her intent becoming completely open to interpretation. Due to weakened blood circulation, her breathing became erratic. At times she didn't breathe for up to thirty seconds. Twice, her hospice nurse estimated that she would die within seventy-two hours.

Her insistence on living took on dramatic overtones for me. Was there something she wanted to tell me? Was there something she wanted me to do? Did she need something? Sitting alone with her, an idea occurred to me. "Ma," I said. "Are you afraid?"

She responded with a guttural sound I interpreted as yes.

"Do you," I asked, "want me to go with you?"

She responded with the same sound, another yes.

I couldn't speak. I couldn't say anything. I knew that I had no intention of accompanying her in death, but before I could consider a reply, my aunt walked into the room. The intimacy that the conversation demanded was lost. The moment had passed, so I remained silent. That night my mother died in her sleep.

Nine months later, I did something that, for me, was extraordinary. I packed all the belongings I could fit in my Jeep, stowed my two cats in the back, and drove across the country by myself.

My journey loosely followed Route 66 and took eight nights and nine days. Every night I'd unpack the cats, my overnight case, and stay in the hotel I had booked that afternoon; every morning I'd pack everything up again and strike out into the unknown.

Along the way, during moments of doubt, I tugged on my Betty Boop earrings and remembered my mother's strength and sense of adventure. I believe that, having passed her own moment of fear, she would have encouraged me along my chosen path. I imagined her with me, giving me a smile and a wink. "Don't worry," I could hear her say. "Everything is going to be all right." Ma would've loved L.A.

During the journey, I had the time to take the temperature of my own thoughts and emotions, and I discovered that I now revel in achieving the goal I attempted at seven but only recently attained: the sensation of simply not feeling bad. I won't be greedy and dare for hope; the absence of dread is enough to put a smile on my face. I relish the most mundane encounters of life—the joy of a boring lunch, the relief of a light switched off and forgotten. I acknowledge the time that I've lost living in my own head, but I don't dwell on it. Now, once I consider a thought and dismiss it, I can put it out of my mind. Like my mother, I've learned to move on.

Beazie Griffin *received her master's degree in writing and publishing from DePaul University in 2014. She currently resides in Long Beach, California.*

Sequelae: The Inner War

Beth Wiles

The Greek historian Herodotus wrote about an Athenian soldier who, in 490 B.C.E., suffered no injury from war but became permanently blind after witnessing the death of a fellow soldier in the Battle of Marathon.

In the early 1800s, soldiers were often diagnosed with "exhaustion" after the stress of battle. The only treatment for this "exhaustion," which was characterized by mental shutdown, was to bring the soldier to the back of the battlefield for a while. Soldiers returning home forever changed by their experiences in the Civil War were diagnosed with "soldier's heart," named for a racing heartbeat that seemed to have no physiological cause.

During times of intense and repeated stress, fatigue is the body's natural reaction to fear and shock. What occurs in soldiers' parasympathetic nervous systems, as well as in their brains, has been called by many different names over the years: shell shock, battle fatigue, exhaustion, soldier's heart, battle-weariness, and traumatic hysteria. Today, the condition is called post-traumatic stress disorder, although to call it a disorder is misleading. PTSD is actually an injury—a psychic wound that can paralyze, devastate, and, in its immeasurable complications, even prove fatal to the person with PTSD—and to people nearby.

I am looking at a photo of Marine Corps Staff Sgt. Travis Twiggs standing with President Bush in front of the White

House, smiling broadly. He has a Marine Corps haircut, bulky shoulders, and a solid body. His teeth look slightly bucked, and if you look at the picture for a while, you begin to see what Twiggs looked like as a little boy; it's still there in his face.

President Bush has his arm around Travis's upper shoulder and is squeezing his trapezius muscle. The president has his usual guffaw-smile, which makes him look confused or senile or slightly drunk. President Bush signed the photo for Travis, who, in six years of service, had done one tour of duty in Afghanistan and four tours in Iraq. According to an embedded writer who went on patrol with Twiggs in Iraq, Twiggs was "regarded in the US military as one of the best combat trackers alive."

There is a lot to be said for being a good tracker, the animal sniffer in us born again: Locate, identify, pursue; follow and interpret signs; notice if any signs have been left in the dirt—a footprint, rocks overturned; turn on your senses full throttle—smell the air, hear beyond sound.

And you—are you a good tracker yourself, these days? Can you decipher the enemy?

President Bush was cropped out of the photo when it was later used for a wanted poster of Travis.

I have in my hand the book *The Boy Who Was Raised as a Dog And Other Stories from a Child Psychiatrist's Notebook: What Traumatized Children Can Teach Us About Loss, Love and Healing* and the journal article "Neurobiological Sequelae of Childhood Trauma: Post-Traumatic Stress Disorders in Children." Both the book and the article are by Bruce D. Perry, M.D., Ph.D., who is an adjunct professor of psychiatry and behavioral sciences at the Feinberg School of Medicine of Northwestern University in Chicago. (The book is co-authored by Maia Szalavitz.) I highly recommend both.

I'm looking at a paragraph, for example, which states that the symptoms of PTSD tend to fall into three clusters: 1) recurring intrusive recollection of the traumatic event, such as dreams and "flashbacks"; 2) persistent avoidance of stimuli associated with the trauma or numbing of general responsiveness; and 3) persistent symptoms of increased arousal characterized by hyper-vigilance, increased startle response, sleep difficulties, irritability, anxiety and physiological hyper-reactivity.

Perry goes on to say that while PTSD was originally described in combat veterans, "a high percentage of rape victims, sexual abuse victims, survivors of natural or manmade disasters and witnesses to violence also experience symptoms of PTSD."

"The largest group of victims of these traumatic events," Dr. Perry writes, "is children."

Children who live in abusive households, children who have been physically or sexually abused or have been witness to violence, have, essentially, the same experiences as soldiers in combat and thus suffer the same effects.

The recurring dream has been with me for nearly twenty-five years. In it, I am the owner of a large, square metal shovel with a wooden handle, the kind you find in a horse stable or on the back of an asphalt truck. The handle is the gray color that wood turns from frequent use. The blade is rusty. I am alone in streets and neighborhoods I don't recognize. My senses are at superpower level: I can see 360 degrees; I can hear everything people are saying; my skin vibrates and tingles with awareness. I am the wrong kind of Wonder Woman. In this dream, I feel life-or-death threatened. People in groups especially make me unbearably paranoid. I walk by a group of people and hear someone say something critical about me. Or maybe they don't; maybe I just imagine it. I spin around and, in one economical movement, smash the back of the shovel into a girl's nose. She screams out in pain. Blood runs everywhere. Her friends huddle around her. Some yell at me, and I glare back as I stand there, puffed out to three times my normal circumference. No one dares come near me. I am brandishing this shovel and I am shaking with rage.

Later in the dream, I see the girl again. Her nose is bandaged and she is wearing glasses. Her face is bruised all over. She is sitting at a table with her friends. Seeing her enrages me. I walk past her and they yell out that I am crazy and a loser and an animal. I turn the shovel sideways in my hand and, in one ultraswift movement, using the power of my hips and pushing off one foot like a pitcher throwing a fastball, I stab the shovel toward her, smashing the blade right between her eyes, into the already cut and broken cartilage. Her scream breaks the sky. I pull the shovel back and now I must run—as fast as I can—because men, her friends, are coming after me.

I am fast. Faster than they are. They don't have my heart, which is pounding with the hot crystal meth of adrenaline.

I am running toward the end of the street, where there is a painted scene. The scene is from the musical *South Pacific*, the part when they are in Tahiti. If I can just make it there, I can burst through the canvas. I fall into a black oblivion, from which I wake up unable to tell if the dream happened or not, my heart pounding and my eyes wide with terror. Usually I get up and let my little dog out of her crate and bring her into bed with me. She wags her tail and licks my face and wiggles because she isn't usually allowed to sleep in the bed. If I am sleeping beside my partner, I don't wake her. I'm too ashamed.

When Travis Twigg met President Bush in late April of 2008, he bear-hugged the president. "Sir, I've served over there many times, and I would serve for you anytime," he said. Travis's wife, Kellee, told *New Yorker* reporter William Finnegan that if you cut Travis, "he bled green," such was his devotion to the Marine Corps. Three weeks after Travis left the White House, he was in Arizona in a stolen car, with the police in pursuit and a helicopter overhead. He pulled out his .38 and shot his older brother, Will, who idolized him, in the left temple, killing him instantly, and then he shot himself under the chin. The bullet ricocheted out his cheek, so he fired again into his own right temple. His nervous system was finally at rest.

Neurobiological: Pertaining to the biology of the nervous system.

Sequela: A condition that is the consequence of a previous disease or injury.

Trauma: A deeply distressing or disturbing experience; an emotional shock that sometimes leads to long-term neurosis.

Four months before he killed himself, Travis wrote an article about his struggle, titled "PTSD: The Enemy Within," for the *Marine Corps Gazette*. He publicly acknowledged his emotional problems. He wrote that he was irritable, sometimes enraged, paranoid for no reason, unable to sleep. He hallucinated and suffered flashbacks, he wrote; he turned to alcohol. He was hospitalized and put on twelve different medications. Travis successfully completed his treatment at the hospital; his medication was adjusted and he did well for a time. He was in a better mood, trying to help other soldiers until, inexplicably, he started to exhibit the symptoms of PTSD all over again.

In Fort Carson, Colorado, Private Tyler Jennings, a machine gunner, spoke out about PTSD on NPR's *All Things Considered* in 2006. After returning from Iraq, Jennings, who received a Purple Heart after his first tour, wouldn't follow orders from his superiors; he had nightmares; he used drugs; he beat his wife in his sleep. Following his appearance on the radio, he was court-martialed for misbehavior. Jennings's experience, as the reporter Daniel Zwerdling put it, "symbolizes a dilemma that's facing the whole army—should officials discipline soldiers who have illnesses like PTSD and then misbehave? Or should officers forgive those soldiers and do everything possible to help them? Studies show that soldiers who have PTSD commonly misbehave. It's a side effect of their illness."

The easiest solution for the armed forces, of course, would be if no one talked about PTSD at all.

"Don't ask, don't tell" didn't apply only to gay people, you know. Silencing as a weapon has been around forever, used against those who would challenge the power structure. Salem "witches." Rape and incest survivors. Children beaten by their parents. McCarthy-era writers. Blacks. Women. Soldiers with PTSD. Jews. Employees. What's the story you aren't telling?

On the subway, I hope I can somehow control the whole car I am in, make everyone behave, stay in their own personal spaces. Be aware of themselves. Don't hog. Then it will all be OK. I will make it wherever I am going unscathed. I have hope every time. I try my hardest. When I step from the platform into the metal car, my hackles go up. I am on alert. Ready. My skin feels porous, penetrable. I am too short, too weak, too female. I need people to move back, make a bigger space for me. Don't touch me, bump me, stare at me. I need to sit down. I need the boundaries of the seat. I am ignited into rage oh so easily. A man sitting with his legs spread in a V encroaches on my portion of the seat. I silently push back to gain equal ground for my legs to go out straight, not uncomfortably to the side. What's mine is mine. If he doesn't respond, I ask nicely, "Could you close your legs a little, please?"

His refusal is where things start to go south. A heat rises within me and covers my body in a cold sweat. The back of my head tingles, and I salivate like you do just before throwing up. My eyes become hard; things start to close down, narrow in. My mind has exploded inside my skull and I have no access to thought. I am somehow being run by another part of my being, watching with horror as well as acting out. The watching me is powerless to intervene in any way; she is helpless all over again. My face is flushed. My ears are buzzing. It's the V legs now, but it could be a big backpack pressing into my back or, worst of all, a tall man whose dick is eye-level as I'm sitting down, who keeps leaning toward me to let people pass behind him or lurching toward me as the train takes a bend. I am wearing a straitjacket. I am suffocating.

Here's what I've done: I have thrown hot coffee at a man who wouldn't stop staring even after I asked him "What the fuck are you looking at?" I have pushed my elbow, hard and constant, into the body of a man sitting next to me who refused to move over a few inches. I have spat at a man on my way out of the subway car. I have stepped on a foot hard, feeling it crunch under me as I exited. I had to prove my point: Don't fuck with me. My heart pounded and I could barely control my legs to get out the door. I had wooden legs, full of leaded adrenaline.

I got out of the Vietnam of my childhood taking place on the subway. Disoriented, I fell onto the city street, looking for refuge, which is found in walking, walking, always in movement.

Kellee Twigg told the *New Yorker* a story about sitting in a PTSD support group for spouses of soldiers at Marine Corps Base Quantico in Virginia:

[A] 22-year-old girl gets up and says, "He's got guns all

over the house, including a 9-mm. he puts between the mattress and the box spring. And one night I woke up and he had the gun up to my head, calling me an Iraqi. So I had to talk him all through that and get him to put the gun down."

He went berserk.

Berserkers were elite Norse warriors who fought in a nearly uncontrollable, trancelike fury, which may have been aided by the use of hallucinogenics. I have another article: "On Going Berserk: A Neurochemical Inquiry," from the *American Journal of Psychiatry* in 1956. The author, Howard D. Fabing, writes:

> This fury, which was called *berserkergang*, occurred not only in the heat of battle, but also during laborious work. Men who were thus seized performed things which otherwise seemed impossible for human power. This condition is said to have begun with shivering, chattering of the teeth, a chill in the body, and then the face swelled and changed its color. With this was connected a great hotheadedness, which at last gave over into a great rage, under which they howled as wild animals, bit the edge of their shields and cut down everything they met without discriminating between friend or foe. When this condition ceased, a great dulling of the mind and feebleness followed, which could last for one or several days.

It's common knowledge that amphetamines, among other drugs, were used during the Vietnam War to hype up the soldiers for combat as well as to keep them awake and hyper-alert for long periods of time. How much evidence, both ancient and modern, do we need to understand not only the cost of war, but the reluctance that must be overcome—the deep perversion and corruption that must take place—in order for human beings to fight in battles?

Jonathan Shay, M.D., makes an explicit connection between the berserker rage of soldiers and the hyper-arousal of PTSD. In "Achilles in Vietnam: Combat Trauma and the Undoing of Character," he writes:

If a soldier survives the berserk state, it imparts emotional deadness and vulnerability to explosive rage to his psychology and permanent hyper-arousal to his physiology—hallmarks of post-traumatic stress disorder in combat veterans. My clinical experience with Vietnam combat veterans prompts me to place the berserk state at the heart of their most severe psychological and psychophysiological injuries.

Fort Bragg, North Carolina, covers more than 251 square miles in four counties and is home to almost 10 percent of active US Army forces. By population, it is the largest U.S. Army facility anywhere in the world. The elite Green Berets and the secretive special mission unit Delta Force, among other divisions, are based here. The Green Berets use "unconventional warfare," also called "guerilla warfare."

Since 9/11, the typical soldier based at Fort Bragg has been deployed between three and six times on tours lasting from a few months to a year, to combat zones in Iraq and Afghanistan.

According to the Army, there were 832 victims of domestic violence at Fort Bragg between 2002 and 2004. In 2007 alone, Fort Bragg investigated nearly 550 domestic-violence incidents, a 38 percent increase from the year before.

Fort Bragg, June 11, 2002

Sergeant First Class Class Rigoberto Nieves, a Green Beret, had been back from Afghanistan for two days. On his third day at home, Sergeant Nieves shot his wife and then himself in their bedroom.

Fort Bragg, June 29, 2002

Master Sergeant William Wright, also a Green Beret, had been back from Afghanistan for about a month. He strangled his wife, Jennifer, age thirty-two, whom he met in high school and had been married to for twelve years. The night of her murder, their sons—Ben, thirteen; Jacob, nine; and John, six—heard their mother crying. In the weeks prior to the murder, Sergeant Wright had asked for psychological help. According to Jennifer's father, Archie Watson, Wright told his superiors he "was upset and didn't know what to do." On July

19, he led investigators to his wife's body in Hoke County and was charged with murder. In photos of his arraignment, he stands in handcuffs and shackles, his eyes cast slightly down and fixed on a middle distance in front of him. His shoulders slump forward. His eyes are red around the rims, and he looks as if he needs a shave and something warm to drink.

Fort Bragg, July 9, 2002

Sergeant Cedric Ramon Griffin, twenty-eight, stabbed his estranged wife, Marilyn, thirty-two, who was asleep in the master bedroom, at least fifty times in the chest, neck, back, and abdomen before setting the house on fire. As she was dying, she told her daughters, ages six and two, to run to the neighbor's house. Marilyn died in the fire, but the girls escaped.

Fort Bragg, July 19, 2002

Sergeant First Class Brandon Floyd, a member of the elite Delta Forces, home from Afghanistan for five months, had been fighting so vehemently with his wife, Andrea, a retired soldier, that she took their three children—Harlee, eight; B.J., five; and Garrett, four—to Ohio to stay with her mother. A few days after she returned, neighbors heard Andrea and Brandon screaming and fighting. Two shots rang out, and then it was quiet. Sgt. Floyd had shot his wife and then himself inside their home. Andrea's mother is now raising the children. "I told them the truth," she says. "I told them Daddy wasn't himself for one brief moment in time."

CNN, July 26, 2002

"Army sources at Fort Bragg say there's no common thread among the cases and suggest it may simply be an 'anomaly' that so many incidents have occurred together."

Common: Ordinary, of ordinary qualities.

Thread: A long, thin strand.

Anomaly: A deviation from the standard of what's expected.

Fort Bragg, Summer 2008

Three killings of women by soldiers. More than one involved stabbings.

I can't go on. I can't tell you any more. Do you understand yet what is happening?

Fort Bragg, August 17, 2009

Specialist Jacob Gregory Swanson, twenty-six, was a paratrooper who served five yearlong tours in Iraq and Afghanistan between 2001 and 2005. Born and raised in Fort Bragg, he had enlisted in the Army right out of high school. By 2005, he had been discharged and was receiving disability payments for his diagnosis of post-traumatic stress disorder. Swanson was working at a paving and rock company, driving a truck. On August 19, on his lunch hour, he had an argument with his girlfriend. He did not return to work that afternoon. Authorities found Amy Salo, his girlfriend, in the bathroom of his house with a gunshot wound to her face, and Swanson on the floor of the living room with a gunshot wound to his head. The gun was lying close to his body. It is unclear where Salo's three children, ages three, ten, and twelve, were at the time of the shootings. In lieu of flowers, Swanson's mother asked that donations be made to the Wounded Warrior Project, which helps spread the word about the treatment and prevention of PTSD.

If I stop here, who will write about the five murders committed in 2008 by members of Fort Carson's Fourth Brigade Combat Team, who had returned from serving in Iraq? Or about how the suicide rate among veterans is twice that among nonveteran civilians?

Dr. Ira Katz, head of mental health services for the US Department of Veterans Affairs, testifying before a congressional committee, denied a suicide epidemic. He told CBS News there had been 790 reported suicide attempts among veterans in the VA's care in all of 2007.

But then an email came to light that Dr. Katz wrote to a colleague in February 2008: "Shh! Our suicide prevention coordinators are identifying about 1,000 suicide attempts per month among the veterans we see in our medical facilities. Is this something we should (carefully) address ourselves in some sort of release before someone stumbles on it?"

Shh!: Used to call for silence. Variant of HUSH.

Liar: Someone who makes an intentionally false statement.

Cover-up: An attempt to prevent people from discovering the truth about a serious mistake or crime.

Hippocratic Oath: An oath taken by doctors swearing to practice medicine ethically.

I'm choking her. I have my two hands around her neck and I am squeezing hard. I am inches from her face, screaming the most obscene profanities I can think of. But I don't have to think hard at all. The disgusting words come easily. Her face is turning deep red and blue. I can feel the hard lump of her windpipe under my thumbs. She is pulling at my forearms, but I am locked in. Nothing can break my grasp. I am leaning in toward her with the power of my hips and thighs. My feet are cemented to the floor. She doesn't have a chance against the force of my past. She has done nothing to merit this. She is my lover. Whom I love. I let go of her neck and push her down to the floor in secret fear of what I could actually do, and as she sobs, I go into the bathroom, slam the door, and take out the razor blades. Sitting on the edge of the tub, I make long cuts down the underside of each arm until the burning, stinging blood rises to the surface. If I were braver, I would cut to my bone.

I'm house-sitting in a mansion in San Francisco. I have driven as far west as I could get from my family home in Connecticut. I am house-sitting because I am homeless and it's either my car or this empty house to sleep in. There are large, curved glass windows without any panes—just giant sheets of smooth glass—along the front of the house.

At dusk, I am hunted. The ghosts come out at dusk, and in the middle of the night I hear voices. My mother's. My father's. The group-home leader, the nurse on the psych ward, the neighbor, the social worker from child services, the minister. They blur into a cacophony of terror and confusion. I will not be afraid. I will not show weakness. The doorbell rings. A friend. I let her in, but I am irritated by her every move. I scream at her. She leaves in terror, and it's too late. I am uncorked again. I throw every shoe I can find through the glass windows, one by one. I throw the shoes hard. I have a good arm. The combination of athleticism and anger makes for swift, deft movement. Shattered glass lies in the lawn, sprinkled on the hedges, glistening on the pathway. I am covered in sweat. I don't know how this could have happened. I go to the garage and take a hammer off the workbench. I lie down on the living room couch and don't move. The light fades to black, but I don't get up to turn on the lights. I have to pee, but I hold it. I am paralyzed. Frozen. I spend the night on the couch in my clothes and shoes, with the hammer across my chest in case anyone comes into the house. The wind screams through the house all night.

Remember how I told you I am the wrong kind of Wonder Woman? Instead of magic bracelets, I have decided I want a gun. I am standing in a gun shop, turning over different handguns at the glass counter. I have weighed the outcome and decided that prison won't be so bad. I am planning on killing my parents. I am shaking so much that I feel embarrassed, so I leave the shop and walk around the city until happy hour. At happy hour, I drink just enough alcohol to pump myself up. I go to a gay bar and antagonize other women until I am in a fistfight, my childhood comfort.

My stomach is a tight, sickening knot. I'm bleeding, bruised, terrified, totally alone. I turn around and spit on my way out of the bar. Fuck you. I can't say it hard enough. Nothing seems to soothe me. I wipe snot and blood from my nose, across my cheek, with the back of my hand, and then wipe my hand on my jeans, glaring at the world. The roots of my hair hurt from being pulled.

One more. I have to tell you this one. It's so thick and snarled and fated that you might feel overwhelmed. But don't do it. Stay with me. Try. This is not fiction. The pieces fit into a puzzle that spells *atrocity*.

Connection: A relationship in which a person, thing, or idea is linked or associated with something else.

Linked: Connected; joined physically.

Relationship: The way in which two or more concepts, objects or people are connected; the state of being connected by blood or marriage; the way in which two or more people or organizations regard and behave toward each other; an emotional and sexual association between two people.

Association: A connection.

Atrocity: An extremely cruel act, typically involving physical violence or injury.

Ronald A. Gray. Have you guessed his residence? Yup. Fort Bragg.

Gray was born in Cochran, Georgia, in 1966. But he didn't grow up there. He grew up in Liberty Square, a 753-unit public-housing project in Miami, Florida. The complex is also called the "Pork 'n' Beans," for the inexpensive meal that is said to be the staple diet of the tenants. It was built in the 1930s, and the attraction for African-Americans at the time was the concrete structures and indoor plumbing. A four-foot concrete wall along the edges of Liberty Square separated the black and white communities.

Outrage: An extremely strong reaction of anger, shock or indignation.

Ronald A. Gray grew up with his mother, his sister, and a stepfather who was in and out of the picture. At eighteen, Ronald enlisted in the Army. By the time he was twenty-two years old, he had pleaded guilty in state court to two counts of murder, five counts of rape, and other offenses and been court-martialed for two murders and an attempted murder. All of his crimes were committed in a two-year span while he was in the US Army, stationed at Fort Bragg.

At trial, Ronald's mother and sister testified he had been extensively abused by his stepfather physically and sexually.

Colonel David Armitage, a military forensic psychiatrist, testified that in Ronald's early life, he had experienced

> fairly substantial socioeconomic deprivation, multiple male figures in the home, multiple physical moves, living in substandard poverty conditions, circumstances in which the electric lights were turned out by the electric company because bills were not paid. . . . He had a [stepfather] at one time who was extremely abusive to his mother and abusive to himself, using belts on him to the point of inflicting injury, drawing blood.

Ronald raped, sodomized, repeatedly shot, repeatedly stabbed, beat with blunt objects, gagged with cloth belts, and hog-tied several women. Two of them died, but one survived multiple stab wounds to her neck and identified him.

I'm deep, way deep, in this microfiche. I barely know how to work the machine but am too ashamed that I might be truly stupid, so I don't ask for help. Hour after hour, I gaze at this machine, which is hard to operate and seems encoded with left-brain activity. My left brain didn't develop properly, I'm sure of it. I'm forty-five years old and I still don't know my multiplication tables by memory. I can't do division or fractions. I can't add or subtract without using my fingers.

There was no logic to my childhood. Things that should have been definitive weren't. I created an alternate reality to survive. Imagination delivered me. The left side of my brain might have shorted out, the neurons not fusing properly. A series of imperceptible strokes with each trauma that prevented synapses from forming. It's a jumble of floating cells in the left hemisphere, still trying to connect. Illogic trying to become logic.

A few cells made it. The ones needed for writing. Writing comes from the left, so here I am.

Hooray for me.

People zoom around me with stacks of books; other people doing research at these machines look straight ahead, reading and taking notes. Everyone looks very important. I should sit up straighter in my chair. I swivel my head back and forth, looking for any sign that someone else is panicking, as I am. But I'm not giving up. I want this information. It's in here somewhere. I'll fight this inner war again, with its endless mutations that try to stop me, thwart me, imprison me, silence me.

Finally. After lunch and a few minutes in the bathroom trying to keep it together, to reabsorb the rage and sublimate it with breathing, after self-talk and a call to my girlfriend, I see something. It's a 2005 article by criminal defense lawyer and Georgetown University law professor Abbe Smith: "The 'Monster' in All of Us: When Victims Become Perpetrators." I read the following, and my heart beats hard and fast:

> Although victims do not always become perpetrators, a truism repeated by prosecutors at sentencing, as if it were a profound revelation never before put into words, it is the rare serious perpetrator who was not also a victim. . . . It is the rare death row inmate whose life does not read like a case study of extreme deprivation and abuse. It is the rare juvenile incarcerated in an adult prison for rape or murder who has had anything other than the cruelest of childhoods.

Gray's childhood and combat training were a lethal combination. Whatever level of damage Gray brought into the military, his repressed rage commingled with the training in aggression he received at Fort Bragg to unleash a torrent in his nervous system and brain functioning, with devastating results. Eighteen years of hurt, humiliation, and pain would leave two women dead and one severely injured.

Gray would pay with his life for what happened to him and what he acted out on others. After pleading guilty to twenty-two felonies in Superior Court, he was sentenced to three consecutive and five concurrent terms of life imprisonment. He was also tried by a military court composed of commissioned and enlisted soldiers at Fort Bragg and convicted of fourteen charges that included premeditated murder, forcible sodomy, rape, and robbery.

He was unanimously sentenced to death on April 12, 1988.

As if that weren't enough, he was additionally sentenced to dishonorable discharge, total forfeiture of all pay and allowances, and reduction in rank to private.

Ronald was twenty-two years old at the time of his sentencing.

As a member of the US Armed Forces, he could not be executed unless the president approved the death sentence. On July 28, 2008, President George W. Bush approved Gray's execution.

If the US District Court for the District of Kansas had not issued a stay of execution, Ronald A. Gray would have been put to death by lethal injection in Terre Haute, Indiana. Army personnel would have conducted the execution. They may yet.

Terre Haute: French for "high ground."

High Ground: A position of superiority in a debate.

Early spring. Hyacinths on my desk. Intoxicating, sweet, fresh, alive—the sticky, cloying scent of a novice's hope. Hope for light, for warmth, for thawing soil.

I cannot change the past. I cannot mend the brokenness. I cannot stop the endless cycle. But I can be a different kind of carrier. Sometimes I beg. On my knees, even though I don't believe in God. I call out to anyone who can hear: *Please.*

Regret is my compass. I am an alchemist, trained in the transmutation of my nervous system. I have installed trained guides beside me. I am saving at least one life.

Incantation, chant, spell, charm, recitation, mantra. *Please. Please. Please.* That's what I whisper most of the time. I ride a commuter train home, and one guy pulls a gun on another guy during a name-calling fight. I am in the seat right beside them.

Frozen. Terrified. *Please, please,* I am whispering under my breath. *No, don't do this. Please, sir.*

I have constricting pains behind my left breast. My grandparents died of heart attacks.

We are barely alive in the violence. We collectively hold our breath. Is peace just a bumper sticker, a charm on a necklace, a hip idea? Killings, rapes, and beatings are passed from one generation to the next like heirlooms. I dreamt last night of a training camp for inner disarmament and extended healing. We wore all-white linen, and simply refused to participate any longer. Basic-training camps were empty and it was possible to heal children. A silly, embarrassing, sentimental dream, I know.

> *Practice:* To carry out, perform, observe, repeat, go over, polish.

> *Nonviolence:* The use of peaceful means, not force, to bring about political or social change.

> *Peace:* Freedom from disturbance; quiet and tranquility, mental calm, serenity; freedom from civil dispute or dissension between individuals and groups.

> *At peace:* Free from anxiety or distress, in a state of friendliness.

> *Make peace:* Reestablish friendly relations; become reconciled.

I keep writing. I must. Over and over and over. The same story a million ways.

This essay is dedicated to victims of violence everywhere who didn't make it through.

Beth Wiles, *received her M.F.A. from Sarah Lawrence. She is currently an M.Div. candidate at Union Theological Seminary in New York City.*

Thief of Souls

Jessamine Price

Twenty years ago, I didn't know my experience was called psychosis. I did know I was afraid as I spent a long afternoon pressed to a dorm-room mattress, unable to move under a weight of dread, trying to distract myself with the bulky RCA television in the corner. The only channel I could get was showing Tom Hanks and Kevin Bacon in *Apollo 13*. They struggled slowly in the absence of gravity to make it back to Earth.

My heart was about to stop, I thought. My next breath would be my last. But the next heartbeat came; the next breath swam from my lungs.

I didn't care whether the Hollywood astronauts survived or asphyxiated. Their plight bored me. But I forced myself to watch. Hanks and Bacon blathered on about their problems to ground control. I wished they would be quiet, but I didn't turn off the TV. Hearing my own thoughts would be worse.

I was sure I was pregnant, and I didn't know what to do.

I had no physical signs of pregnancy. My weight was unchanged, my appetite good, my periods regular. Furthermore, I had never had much interest in the young men at my college, who appeared to come in one of three models: the one with gelled hair, the one in the baseball hat, and the one who came out of the closet during freshman year. It would be another year before I graduated and discovered the world of interesting men beyond New Jersey.

That September, I was a virgin.

No earthly way existed for me to be pregnant and, given that I was an atheist, I thought unearthly ways seemed unlikely. Yet I was completely sure that I was pregnant.

The delusion had started a couple of weeks earlier, with the beginning of the school year at my small liberal arts college in the far outskirts of New York. I'd spent the spring semester in London, where the rain and darkness sent me deeper and deeper into a gray depression. Back in America, my summer of data-entry work was equally uninspiring. I was excited to get back to college and start my senior year. But Septembers rarely lived up to my high hopes.

Soon after I moved into the dorm, anxiety followed. My stomach hurt with the weight of it. My muscles ached with the strain of not screaming, of holding still and acting normal despite the constant flow of adrenaline telling me to run. And then somehow—I don't remember where or how I first had the thought—a realization grew in me: The aches and pains meant I was pregnant. That feeling of heaviness and terror came from something living inside me, growing and seeking to be born.

Though I knew the thought was irrational, I went through the same panicked thoughts as any college student. When was the baby due? Was it too late for an abortion? Would I have to leave college?

I tried to reason with the delusion. *I've never had sex,* I told it. *I think I'd remember.*

Are you sure? it replied. *You got pretty drunk at those parties last spring. You know you blacked out a few times. Jeez, you don't even know who the father is.*

This right-hook had Rational Thinking staggering on the mat. I did carouse a lot that spring when I was studying in the UK. Was I sure I remembered everything? I calculated. I was in the second trimester, and it would be noticeable soon. The baby was coming in January. I wouldn't be able to finish college. But where would I go then? I couldn't, or wouldn't, turn to my parents for help. My dad had always been quick to criticize any kind of irresponsibility. He would disown me, I thought. My mother was in the ninth or tenth year of a deep, intractable depression, and I hadn't asked her for help with anything important for years.

If the pregnancy had been real, perhaps I could have come clean and moved forward one way or another. But the terror was made worse by its complete irrationality. Despite the firm grip of the delusion, I was just rational enough to suspect that something in my brain was wrong. Unfortunately, this small rational voice didn't help much. Rational Thinking told me to just forget about it, to get my head straight. *Don't tell anyone,* Rational Thinking said, *because you're not really pregnant, so there's no point confessing you're pregnant, right?* Rational Thinking said, *They'll think you're crazy.*

The struggle wore out my body as well as my mind. It was easier to stay in my dorm room alone.

I skipped dinner that evening. I didn't care if Tom Hanks and Kevin Bacon made it back from the moon, but I dreaded the dining hall. I couldn't let my friends suspect anything was wrong.

As I lay there, my heart seemed to beat too quickly and too loudly. I took my pulse with a couple fingers at my throat. I had heard of panic attacks, heard they made your heart beat faster, but my pulse was normal. I felt slightly disappointed. A panic attack would have been a physical thing that I could take to a doctor. But if it wasn't a panic attack, I concluded, I really must be crazy.

Watch the damn movie, I told myself. Thinking made me feel worse. I forced my attention to the screen. I pretended to root for the heroes because that would be the normal thing to do, but I hated them. I felt numbness, not relief, when they landed back on Earth.

Throughout that week the fear kept me lying awake at night, tense and still, afraid to roll over in bed, afraid even to shift position slightly. I developed the fear that my loft bed, homemade from two-by-fours, would suddenly collapse and send me plummeting to the floor, causing me some horrifying injury. I would be paralyzed, I was sure.

For several nights, the fear of paralysis settled into my mind as firmly as the pregnancy delusion. I spent the nights in a fevered wakefulness, convinced that if I moved, the bed would collapse. I had to stay awake and keep still. Compounding my fears, I was sure that if my roommate ten feet away realized I was awake, she would somehow know everything happening to me. She was a good friend and not a judgmental person; besides, she had her own concerns that autumn and probably hadn't noticed a thing. But I was terrified. I had to pretend I was asleep in order to fool her.

I'm losing my mind, I thought.

Almost two decades would pass before I realized I had been suffering that September from a form of psychosis. The term *psychosis* carries so much baggage: images of nineteenth-century lunatic asylums or the homeless people who roamed Fifth Avenue and Washington Square Park in the years after deinstitutionalization and before Giuliani. As a medical term, however, *psychosis* refers to one of the brain's most startling dysfunctions: the impaired perception of reality. Hallucinations—misleading or unclear sensory impressions—are the best-known form of psychosis, but psychosis can also occur as fixed delusions, mistaken beliefs about reality that vary from the mundane to the outlandish.

Psychosis is one of the most troubling symptoms of schizophrenia and bipolar disorder, but it can result from other conditions as well: sleep deprivation, drug use, head injury, temporal lobe epilepsy, certain diseases—even certain medications—and half a dozen assorted mental illnesses, from anorexia to post-traumatic stress disorder (PTSD) to postpartum depression. Psychiatrists know that major depression can lead to psychosis if it goes too long untreated. In "New Approaches to Managing Psychotic Depression" from the *Journal of Clinical Psychiatry*, Alan F. Schatzberg estimates that 25 percent of people hospitalized for severe depression also suffer from psychosis, but such patients don't appear in statistics because they hide their delusions from doctors. Even in the psych ward, we don't want to sound crazy.

Researchers struggle to describe and explain what happens to the brain during psychosis. The central mystery of psychosis is its ability to convincingly mimic reality. The hallucinatory voices in a brain with schizophrenia can sound louder and more real, more present, than the actual voices of doctors and friends. Psychotic delusions are so resistant to logical argument that psychiatrists refer to them as "fixed delusions" to distinguish a clinical brain dysfunction from a mere "false belief," which can change in response to changing evidence. I knew rationally that my roommate couldn't read my mind as I lay awake at night, but the evidence didn't matter. I was living in a warped version of reality where my roommate could read minds and virgins could be pregnant.

Reading about fixed delusions today, at the age of thirty-eight, I find it obvious that I was suffering from a kind of mental illness when I was twenty. Yet, curiously, it wasn't obvious to me at the time. I had taken freshman psych. I knew that thoughts and emotions come from our brains, and I knew that brains can fail. But the worries running through my mind didn't feel like brain pathologies. They felt like my own thoughts; they spoke in the familiar voice of my own mind, like every other thought that formed the scaffolding of my identity. If some hostile force could impersonate me and go undetected by my own mind, how could I know that any of my thoughts were truly mine?

The word *psychosis* comes from *psyche*, the Greek word for "soul," and means "a disease of the soul." The soul: the very thing that allows us to use words like "me" and "mine." The "I" in my mind that narrated my life as it happened—the "I" that narrates this story now—was broken. Even with my rational mind still occasionally on board, I was unable to perceive that the scared, pregnant part of my mind was wrong, because it spoke with the same voice as the rational "I." My own voice. When psychosis stole my reason, it used my own mind to jimmy the locks. This thief of souls can slip past our defenses no matter how tough we think we are, because it comes disguised as the soul itself.

I also had the misconception that mental illness is always incapacitating. When I was ten, not long after the birth of my little sister, my mother developed a nasty case of depression that she was unable or unwilling to acknowledge for years. I thought mental illness looked like my mother's spontaneous weeping fits or her fear of placing telephone calls.

By thinking of mental illness merely as a set of behaviors, I overlooked for years the emotions and thoughts that accompany it. I thought I could prove to myself I wasn't crazy that September by acting like I usually did. In the mornings, I forced myself out of bed in time for my first seminar at eleven. I went to classes, stayed up late doing homework, and hung out with friends watching The *X-Files* on Thursday nights. The charade took all my strength, though, and gave me little comfort.

In the moments when my fear subsided, I tried rational means to clear up the delusion. Surely a negative pregnancy test would reassure me, I thought. I drove to a drugstore in the next town over—I was terrified of running into someone I knew—to buy an at-home pregnancy test, which I hid deep in the bottom of my backpack as if it might try to leap out and embarrass me in public.

Driving back to the dorm, I debated intensely which restroom to use. It would be dangerous to use the bathroom closer to my room. There was the risk of my roommate coming in, recognizing my shoes under a stall door and somehow immediately knowing that I was there to take a pregnancy test. She would know everything, although I wasn't even sure what "everything" was anymore. But the danger of humiliation scared me so much that it was hard to breathe.

So I walked a hundred more feet to the bathroom further down the hallway. Unzipping my backpack, I felt sure that the stranger in the stall next to me knew exactly what I was doing. In my nervousness, I had to read the instructions several times. I waited for the results in dread, knowing the answer would be "yes." When the inevitable "no" appeared, my delusion didn't skip a beat.

The instructions say that it's only accurate 97 percent of the time. Seventy-five percent, if you take account of user error. My delusion reviewed every potential complication described in the fine-print warnings. Then it made stuff up. *Doctors don't know everything. They only know what average female hormones do. What if you have freaky, abnormal hormones?* It sounded convincing. I went back to my room weary and confused.

How do delusions evade objective evidence? The only explanation I could come up with at the time, in that mental state, was that the delusion persisted for the simple, obvious reason that it was true. I was pregnant. The test was wrong. The evidence of my body and memories was wrong. Why else would I be so sure of something?

I did realize the fear was making me ill. In clearer moments,

I wondered what to do. Researching medical topics wasn't as easy in 1995 as it is now. I looked up "false pregnancy"—pseudocyesis—somewhere, but it didn't describe my problem. I wasn't having any of the hormone changes, weight gain, and morning sickness of pseudocyesis. I was only vaguely familiar with the words *psychosis* and *delusion*. As long as I continued to go to class and get good grades, I was convinced my mental health was okay.

Looking back, my worst agonies only lasted two or three weeks, maybe four, but it's hard to be precise because it felt like months. Occasionally, I became optimistic and resolved to master my fears. In one such mood, I took the bold step of giving up caffeine. I stopped drinking coffee cold turkey and vowed not to touch the Diet Dr. Pepper in the mini-fridge. Caffeine contributed to anxiety, I heard, so quitting would cure me, right?

In early October, I also did something that, to my knowledge, no one in my family had ever done, except perhaps my aunts who moved to Manhattan in the seventies. I made an appointment at the campus counseling center, a couple of rooms hidden away in a gloomy Victorian. When I rattled the heavy front door and went inside, the front parlor smelled like dust and old wood. I was terrified I would run into someone I knew.

I was relieved when the receptionist in the dim parlor arranged an appointment without asking questions. When I met with the counselor a few days later—in a small brown attic room where the ceiling sloped deliberately and the other walls sloped accidentally—she turned out to be a quiet, approachable woman only a few years older than me. Still, it took an effort of will to open my mouth and say something, anything, aloud.

I can't remember how I explained why I was there. Did she understand what I was saying? Did she appreciate the strength and weirdness of the delusion? I suspect I lied. I suspect I told her I was afraid, very afraid, but that I didn't tell her about the mysterious force that had hijacked my thoughts and sense of reason. I just said I was afraid of getting pregnant, making it sound like a normal twenty-year-old's anxiety. She asked a quintessential therapist's question: Who was I afraid of letting down?

So we talked about my dysfunctional family and the stresses

of the past summer. As I talked, I did feel a slight lessening of the pressure in my chest. The therapist didn't tell me I was crazy. I was fascinated when she said I had a lot of stressful things in my life. I didn't think of my life as stressful, except right before a research paper was due. It reassured me that she thought I had actual reasons to be anxious. My brain was anxious exactly as it should be. Nothing was wrong with me.

Thanks to the talking—and perhaps to cutting back on caffeine—my anxiety subsided to bearable levels. By the end of October, I realized something inside me was different. I felt lighter. I couldn't remember why I had worried I was pregnant. As the anxiety faded, so did my delusion, and eventually I packed the experience into the back storerooms of my memory. I only visited the therapist three times. I cancelled my fourth appointment to work on a history paper.

Six years passed before I visited a counselor again, six years punctuated by long stretches of fear, guilt, despair, and crushing physical weakness—symptoms of chronic depression that I refused to acknowledge, or perhaps couldn't see clearly enough to recognize. But I'm lucky that my first delusion was my last. I suppose I had what psychiatry's *Diagnostic and Statistical Manual* calls "major depression with psychotic features." It's an awkward phrase, but accurate.

According to the National Institutes of Health, three people out of every hundred will experience psychosis during their lifetimes. In the United States, that means nine million people. Out of those nine million, around six million will have bipolar disorder or schizophrenia, but roughly one million will have what I had, depression accompanied by delusions or hallucinations. Few are aware that clinical depression can cause psychosis if the depression is severe or goes untreated for too long. Even though the complaint sounds petulant, I can't help wondering when common mental illnesses will get the same public attention and research funding as common cancers or heart disease.

I also avoided talking about mental illness for years. My phantom pregnancy was so confusing and shameful that I forgot about it almost entirely. I never thought of telling anyone, even when, years later, I consulted therapists and psychiatrists for relief from depression. Then, just last year, I was reading something about psychosis and I discovered that fixed delusions sounded oddly familiar. I already knew where the author was going as he explained that a person can be completely convinced of a belief that is obviously wrong. To me, this made perfect sense.

I suspect one reason I forgot the episode is that I had no vocabulary for describing what happened. I couldn't frame a sentence to express the suspicion that my thoughts were not my own, that something had moved into my brain and squatted there malevolently. The personal pronouns "I" and "me" utterly failed to capture the multiplicity of voices in my head. My experience went against everything I believed about the brain, the mind, and the self.

The delusion that haunted me at twenty should have made me suspicious of my convictions, particularly those beliefs about my excellent mental health. But another eight years passed before I understood that I had chronic, major depression, combined with occasional anxiety. Ironically, perhaps the most powerful delusion I've ever had was the belief that my spells of suffering were simply bad moods.

Here we come to the strangest question psychosis raises: Can we actually understand ourselves through simple self-examination? I'm relatively smart, an assumption supported by some real-world evidence. I got a tough master's degree at Oxford, and I was once a three-day champion on Jeopardy! But when I go up against the illusions, delusions, and denials of my own mind, do I stand a chance? Or do I become a snake trying to devour her own tail?

I'm not alone in finding insight elusive. Psychosis—even a relatively simple, short-lived delusion like mine—is confusing enough that few seek help for it during the first or second episode. Those with schizophrenia, with its complex and distressing psychoses, take an average of nine years to begin medical treatment. That's how hard it is to doubt the reality behind our own thoughts. Nearly twenty years later, I still feel rattled when I consider how easily I once lost my sense of reality.

One possible conclusion is that all mental illnesses interfere with our ability to know ourselves, though not necessarily as dramatically as psychosis. For years, my depression convinced me that sadness and despair are the average emotion and that anyone who goes around happy most of the time is lying. But now I think I was wrong. Was my acute skepticism about happiness that different from the pregnancy delusion? I see both now as a form of what neuroscientists call *anosognosia*—the inability to perceive one's own mental illness.

Perhaps our ability to perceive reality—and to know ourselves—is itself on a spectrum. On one end are people with recurring psychosis. On the other end are those rare holy people who have experienced enlightenment. The rest of us are somewhere in the middle, getting muddled up most of the time and only occasionally relaxing enough to see ourselves clearly.

I don't believe suffering will make me stronger—I can't stand that cliché of illness literature. Perhaps, however, it has made me more compassionate.

Not long ago, when I was answering phones for the information helpline at the National Alliance on Mental Illness, I spoke to a man whose wife of twenty years had developed paranoid schizophrenia. Her delusions of acute danger had led her to flee her husband and five children for a life of homelessness on the city streets. He knew that the laws on mental illness gave him no way to force her into treatment, but he was grieving and worried for his wife's safety. People living on the streets with a mental illness often become the victims of crime. He said he'd do whatever it took to help her, if she'd accept it. So how, he wondered, could he convince her that she was ill?

Just that morning, he told me, he had been sitting by the window in the little diner he opened downtown, close to the shelter where his wife often stayed. Suddenly, he saw her face pressed to the glass. She was staring, searching—"as if hoping to glimpse me or the kids," he said. He bolted out the door before she could run away.

"I love you, honey," he said. "Please come home."

She just looked down, he said. She mumbled something, turned, and walked away.

"Why?" he asked me. "Why doesn't she make sense?"

Hearing how much he still loved her, I wanted to give him a satisfying answer. I wanted to tell him that love would conquer all—but I couldn't. Paranoid schizophrenia can cause intensely convincing delusions. His wife might never doubt her own mind long enough to seek treatment.

All I could give him was a story. I'd never told anyone of my experience, but I found myself telling this stranger a thousand miles away. I knew my delusion didn't make sense, I told him, but I couldn't make it go away.

His wife, I knew, was in there somewhere. She wasn't choosing to hurt him, but psychosis is strong. It wouldn't let her love her own family.

"She did hear you," I said, as convincingly as I could. "She knows you love her."

I had no way of knowing what this faraway woman believed, but I wasn't lying. I have spent years cultivating the hope that, just as anyone can experience insanity, so can anyone find themselves sane at times. I still believe in the human brain. If its failures are bizarre, its successes are nevertheless spectacular. I remember that even when I was most confused, some part of myself was somehow still "me"—at least "me" enough that I can tell this story now. If the mind is a mystery, it is surely a holy mystery, one that leaves room for grace.

Note on Sources: Unless otherwise indicated, all information and research is from the National Alliance on Mental Illness at www.nami.org/psychosis.

Jessamine Price *is a teacher and writer with an M.Phil. in history from Oxford and an MFA in creative writing from American University. She is currently working on a book investigating the global popularity of Korean television.*

Acknowledgments

Any book is the work of many people. *Show Me All Your Scars* was made possible by generous support from the Jewish Healthcare Foundation, which has an ongoing commitment to removing the stigma surrounding mental illness, and restoring hope. We would like to thank Karen Wolk Feinstein, in particular, for her singular vision and enduring friendship and encouragement.

The Creative Nonfiction Foundation and In Fact Books also would like to thank the almost 600 courageous writers who submitted their stories for consideration for this project; Matt Spindler for managing our dedicated readers; Hattie Fletcher, Landon Houle, Sarah Gray and Chad Vogler for their editorial efforts; Ellen Ayoob for managing the production process; and Victoria Blake for her ongoing partnership.